The City is Me

The City is Me

by Rosane Araujo

intellect Bristol, UK / Chicago, USA

First published in the UK in 2013 by
Intellect, The Mill, Parnall Road, Fishponds, Bristol, BS16 3JG, UK

First published in the USA in 2013 by
Intellect, The University of Chicago Press, 1427 E. 60th Street,
Chicago, IL 60637, USA

A catalogue record for this book is available from the
British Library.

Cover designer: Holly Rose
Cover: image, conception and creation by Rosane Araujo
Copy-editor: Heather Owen
Typesetting: John Teehan
Production Manager: Melanie Marshall
Translator: Lucio Paulo de S.Ferreira

ISBN 978-1-84150-639-5

Printed and bound by Hobbs the Printers Ltd, UK.

Because Freedom is not being any and other Person, but being this unique and absolute city, this absoluticity which nobody else is as only I am, even though I am imprisoned in it: citadel of singularity, UniCity.

(MD Magno, 2006)

Temple of Poseidon – Athens – Greece
Photo: Manoela Dantas, 2011

Contents

Acknowledgements

The City is Me is the result of an Urbanism doctorate dissertation, at PROURB (Post-graduate Urbanism Program) in the College of Architecture and Urbanism at Federal University of Rio de Janeiro (UFRJ) / Brazil. For this reason I thank Professor Denise Pinheiro Machado, for accepting my urban issues; Professor Lucia Maria S. A. Costa for her fundamental support and very important tips for the structuring of the dissertation; Professor Rachel Coutinho and each professor, colleague, contributor and employee at PROURB/UFRJ, a place where one strives for excellence in research in the field of Urbanism.

I thank Professor Ana Clara Torres Ribeiro (IPPUR/ UFRJ) for reading and for presenting precise analysis of the thesis, which were very useful for future reflection.

This research was awarded a national prize as the best Brazilian dissertation in the area of Architecture and Urbanism: "Prêmio Capes de Teses 2008". For this reason I thank CAPES: Coordination for the Improvement of Higher Level Personnel, Secretary of Education - through its representatives among which I highlight its president, Professor Jorge Almeida Guimarães as well as Professors Emídio Cantídio de Oliveira Filho and Sandoval Carneiro Junior - as much for this outstanding award which brings recognition to researchers and research in Brazil, as for the encouragement of my Post- Doctorate internship, very fruitful for the settling of issues raised by the dissertation.

I thank Professor Clara Irazabal for her kind and generous reception at Columbia University that was decisive for me to return there often; I thank very much Columbia University in New York, through Professors Robert Beauregard and Prof. Mark Wigley, for designating me as a Visiting Scholar (2010-2012) by the Graduate School of Architecture, Planning and Preservation, which allowed me access as a member of their community.

I thank Prof. Nuno Portas for a memorable meeting at the Sacred Heart Church, in Lisbon, and the lesson in Architecture that this meeting provided.

A very special thanks to MD Magno, for the tool that enables to articulate the transformations of the contemporary world and some possible solutions.

I also thank each member of the group NovaMente, a Brazilian center for advance research and innovation in Psychoanalysis.

I thank Gilles Grelet who published in French, by L'Harmattan publishers, a small chapter I wrote on this subject at an early phase of its articulation.

I would like to thank ECIA, an architecture and engineering company, for their support.

I cannot thank enough Octavio Araujo and Rudicéia as well as a great number of relatives and dear friends here represented by Isadora Dantas, Manoela Dantas, José Dantas, Otavio Azevedo, Fernando Azevedo, Carlos Azevedo, Carlos Fernandes, Aristides Alonso, Potiguara Mendes da Silveira Jr., Mariza Weber, Teresa Rosolem, Antonio Boente. Finally, I am very grateful and would like to thank colleagues, editors, and all the kind people involved in this project.

Preface

Part One: This is what I wrote before I read the book:

At this point, Rosane Araujo had just sent me a pdf and I hadn't yet read the book. But let's imagine that I was in a bookstore and I saw that title, "The City is Me". Because I happen to know the author, my attention, already drawn by the title would now become more focused. What would I do? Like you might, I would check the blurbs on the back cover and the table of contents. And then I would make a decision as to whether I wanted to buy the book or not. So here is what the title and the table of contents suggested to me:

"The city is me". First reaction: Yeah, right! So is the world, so is the universe. The world is what I know of it. Even what other people know about it that I do not or did not know, feel, or understand, once I were given a chance to find these things out, they could only come to my attention alone, hence to be known and equated by me only. The rest, that is everything that I neither know nor suspect, simply does not exist for me. So I can easily imagine that this book will eventually tell me that the world, in fine, is me. Of course, it is different for each one of us and contains only what we see and what we are exposed to. But for the city to be selected above so many other belonging and defining environments we live in, that must mean something. So I go to the table of contents to see why: it is full of intriguing and suggestive chapter headings. I can see that the book will attempt a careful and duly-referenced demonstration that the concepts of the city and the philosophical and psychological knowledge about the self are connected. But there is one word that springs to my eyes: "orbanism". Instantly I get a kind of intuitive confirmation that the slip from city to world I mentioned above is actually implicit in the contraction of urb and orb. That does it. I am buying the book!

Part Two:

Well guess what? I went straight to the definition of "orbanism" in chapter 3 and, to my complete surprise, I found myself quoted just about that concept:

...the 21ˢᵗ century urbanism would transmute into orbanism, where, given that we would no longer have borders or limitations as reference, we would treat as city not only the world, but also the known and yet to be known universe.

Some authors, in different fields of knowledge, already point to this direction. For instance, Derrick de Kerckhove, (former) director of the McLuhan Program in Culture and Technology and professor at the University of Toronto, affirms that in the informational context in which we live, architecture and urban planning will start to be thought in terms of communication accessibility, not only in terms of road and water infrastructure. To give sense to what he means, he produces a new terminology and affirms that the work of the cybertect is to create trustworthy routes and useful environments in cyberspace and between cyberspace and the real space. We can then add that we are talking about cybertecture, which is the conception of an architecture in which the tools and questions at stake are immersed in the new technological and digital environment that we are starting to inhabit. It is not the world that is globalizing, it is us. Cyberculture implies "seeing through" matter, space and time with our informational techniques. Technology enables us to have physical access and displacement to distant regions, creating a situation where we are contained in the global sphere. When we think globally, communicate and trade from the place which we occupy, we include the global sphere internally: "we contain the earth in our minds and in our networks".

Curiously, it is the only place where I am quoted, but it proposes the central issue of the book and underlines an uncanny community of mind between Rosane's and my own thinking.

Aside from the fact that *The City is Me* proposes excellent surveys of current concepts of the city and of the self, bringing them together in a persuasive way, the book is making it possible for the reader to redefine space for him or herself. The book hence is both theoretical and experiential. It is a modifier of sensibility.

It worked for me. For example, as I was reading *The City is Me*, even though I was completing the editing of a book on a related theme (*The Point of Being*, Cambridge Scholars Publishing, 2011) I realized that the idea of the city that I carried in my head was still a separate, abstract, but defined entity, squarely installed in Euclidian space. In fact, in spite of years of working with Marshall McLuhan and with his radical observations about space and time, I had been unable to rid my mind of unquestioned assumptions about the city or myself for that matter. Here then is a simple story I was told in McLuhan's class by one of his friends that will help the reader to find a way to a revolution in spatial sensibility: Michael Smart, a toponymist based in Toronto, whose job at the time was to find the first-nation names of lakes and hills in the vast expanses of bush far north of the city, told a stunned audience at one of our Monday Night Culture and Technology Seminars that when, as night was rapidly falling, he asked his Indian guide if they were "lost", the answer that came was: "No, we are not lost, the village is lost". This response implied a radical revision of a human's relationship to space, one that we can associate with very early experience of space by non-urban dwellers. In other words, for the guide, space was not something that can be traversed, as it is implied in Shakepeare's most famous quote : "All the world's a stage…". It was, as can sometime be surmised from the Iliad and the Odyssey, something that traverses or occupies the person. This story, indeed, provides a clue to what Rosane Araujo is trying to do, namely to invite us to radically change our perception of the city, and of ourselves.

The exciting – and visionary – argument that Rosane Araujo offers to our imagination is that *places can move along with people.* Indeed, the places we occupy online are nowhere in particular, and, within our cellular phones we carry the world in our pockets: Araujo explains: *We use everyday a non-Euclidian space: the space for several activities shared by citizens is now, also, in electronics.*

Like my own, her investigations have sought much help in McLuhan's work, concentrating here on the theme of the human scale, which is not so much lost as augmented considerably and in need of attentive revision:

Metropolitan space is equally irrelevant for the telephone, the telegraph, the radio, and television. What the town planners call "the human scale" in discussing ideal urban spaces is equally unrelated to these electric forms. Our electric extensions of ourselves simply by-pass space and time, and create problems of human involvement and organization for which there is no precedent. (McLuhan, 2007: 125)

The city is me signifies utterly this change of scale that has made us at once global and local. What is helpful in the book is that it gives substance to our globality, as well as indicating our new hybrid condition.

Elsewhere she specifies:

… once connected to the exterior world, these devices extend our nervous system to the endless connections of the network. And once we break the limits of our skin we are also connected to the architecture, which means that some of these electronic organs can be built in our surrounding environment.

This may seem to be pushing the idea, that she credits to McLuhan, of electricity as the extension of our central nervous system as far as architecture can take it, but it is also a way of giving organicity to technological environments and tools. It also helps to understand why the city should be privileged as the defining field, the starting point of an ubiquitous consciousness (also understood as the awareness of ubiquity).

Another key issue raised by this book is the continuity between body and environment.

If we define individual as being that contained inside the skin that confers a corporeal image, we have to acknowledge that this does not exist without the most basic worldly exchanges, like air, atmosphere, gravity, etc. The environment is part of the individual, and the individual composes the environment, without the possibility of separating them and assuring their existence

Perhaps McLuhan's most beautiful thought is relevant here: *"In the age of instant information, we wear all mankind as our skin."*

Likewise, I call "global art" various works, installations, events that reflect our change of scale. Maurice Benayoun uses a world media scanning software to create maps of the Earth in tag clouds of emotions culled from media outlets in 3200 cities in his symbolic piece "Emotional traffic" (http://www.benayoun.com/e-mechanics/PART10.HTM). The number of artists who take the whole world in consideration in their thought and work is growing. Global emotions are also frequently aroused by YouTube. One in particular created a short-lived but intense worldwide phenomenon of street-based emotional behavior. Free Hugs (http://en.wikipedia.org/wiki/Free_Hugs_Campaign) invited people to exchange a benevolent embrace in the street. The Youtube viral video carried practically the example of this practice in Sidney to thousands of cities around the world. This kind of emotion is only beginning, but it should catch on to reveal more of the depth of the themes covered by *The City is Me.*

The most powerful example for me is a artwork site called Wi-Fi SM (http://www.unbehagen.com/wifism/) that expresses strongly the extension of self into the world. It is not presented as an art piece but as a commercial product. It is so tongue-in-cheeky satirical that I suspected immediately it was an art piece. In fact it is a website created by French artist Christophe Bruno. The piece is based on interactive software that allows one to search the web for the frequency with which given keywords appear in various news and current affairs databases. In this case the user is invited to select a few among dozens of keywords indicating pain and suffering. The ad for the site says that, once a certain number of these words is reached, the site radios an tiny electric shock. I called the author and asked if it really worked. He answered that he got it going once or twice, but that in reality the apparatus could be costly at the beginning, but once prototyped could indeed do well on the market. Why am I taking this potentially completely inoperable installation seriously and what has it got to do with *The City is Me*?

What the piece, whether it works or not, is showing is a latent need for a connection to the multitude. With its indeterminate, but infinitely present invisible society, suddenly a specific kind of relationship becomes possible and, for some, even desirable. Is it new? Yes for the current times, but no because it is really a fresh retrieval of what, during the Middle Ages, was common practice: self-flagellation to help Christ to expiate the sins of the world. This kind of sensibility, an indeterminate and outer-projected collective guilt feeling, is still very much underground, for the moment is bound to grow as we face more threats from the global environment. *The City is Me* carries new responsibilities which have not yet matured into a describable ethic. In fact the author invites further reflection on the matter in the very last paragraph:

How to elaborate the political and administrative management as from this understanding of city? How to think everyday practice in this totally inclusive city? How to administrate the conflicts and consensus as from the understanding of this concept of city? How to create mechanisms of an ad hoc administration? What are the skills necessary to the performance of the orbanist? This subject is of utmost importance and we will continue it in the future.

So we are now eager to read the next book by Rosane Araujo.

Derrick de Kerckhove

d.dekerckhove@utoronto.ca

Wicklow, August 2, 2011

Introduction

Chicago - EUA
Photo: Isadora Dantas, 2011

If there is to be a "new urbanism" it will not be based on the twin fantasies of order and omnipotence; it will be the staging of uncertainty; …the reinvention of psychological space … Since it is out of control, the urban is about to become a major vector of the imagination. Redefined, urbanism will not only, or mostly, be a profession, but a way of thinking, an ideology: to accept what exists. (Koolhaas, 2002: 6)

Here is a subject that matters: understanding what City in the twenty-first century is, from the point of view of a person. Cities have already been examined under the most varied of parameters: geography, geometry, economics, medicine, nodes and networks, global markets, religion, psychology, demographic density, information flows, censuses, senses and poetry. Indeed, there have been a virtually endless number of studies on the idea of city.

This study takes into consideration that each person is unique and his or her particular history, DNA, connections, life experiences, passions, repulsions, epoch, geographic city of residence, fantasies and all else that composes him/her constitute a particular vision of the world and the city that each person is. It also considers the general transformation we are all passing through and that is affecting all areas of knowledge and human endeavor. It is an attempt to give a new definition of city and person today. This applies to anyone, whether due to professional interest – because of the need to formulate urban projects – or out of personal interest – from a desire to understand the current epoch.

For this purpose, you need to trust and accompany me in the construction of the idea that will be revealed as the text progresses. Although the terms *city* and *person* are immediately identifiable, we know that various names can express the same concept, that various concepts can be expressed by the same name, that a new word can be created to specify more clearly the reasoning one seeks to convey, or that a term banally used can gain a completely new definition, illuminating an area of understanding and supplying the sense and comprehension of a new moment of thought.

This book – the result of an award-winning doctoral dissertation[1] in the area of architecture and urbanism – aims to present a new concept of city. When taking on as theme the hypothesis *the city is me*, we start from the polysemy of the concept of city which is highlighted by several authors today. Thus we do nothing but associate to the several theoretical positions which decided to face the challenge of rethinking Urbanism in a way that is coherent with the risk, the uncertainty, but also to the potentialities that distinguish our times.

For this purpose we will apply a psychoanalytical theory to Urbanism in order to define this new concept of city. As we know, the fields of knowledge are no longer conceived within borders[2], and moreover, the practice of passing from the method of a particular discipline to another is old and represents a success story in intellectual production. What interests us is that nowadays, given the permeability of knowledge, it is possible to have Psychoanalysis explain Urbanism and to have Urbanism explain our times.

We have included in our work the results of researches done by several thinkers in the field of Urbanism (or that have indirectly contributed thereto) in order to show the conceptual shifting suffered by the city as well as in order to point out that we share the inquisitive status that configures these present days. When we included thinkers from the fields of Philosophy, Biology, Computer Science, Psychoanalysis, Physics, etc., we had the intention of showing the shifting also suffered by the concept of *I*, and presenting more complex forms of reasoning, as well as the intention of making it clear that we share the characteristic perplexity of a reflexive posture, which, in our opinion, seems to resume the general status of contemporary thinking.

What is ultimately common to such investigations, ours included, is the fact that they are heirs to the same change of thought that had taken place in the twentieth century, which enabled communication technologies on a micro-electronic base.[3] Whoever agrees with the trinomial city/society/technology formulates Urbanism from the notions and references – information, communication, network, complexity, digitalization and its technological substitutes in large and small scales – which were only possible thanks to the accomplishments of generations of researchers and thinkers who, starting in the 1930s, expanded the matter of knowledge based on the idea that to know is to build, which is, however, henceforth understood and practiced from indetermination, undecidability, and complexity. This is a line of thought fully acknowledged by Manuel Castells, who says:

> At the core of the technological change that unleashed the power of networks was the transformation of information and communication technologies, based on the microelectronics revolution that took place in the 1940s and 1950s. It constituted the foundation of a new technological paradigm, consolidated in the 1970s, mainly in the United States, and rapidly diffused throughout the world, ushering in what I have characterized, descriptively, as the information age. (Castells, 2004: 6)

We understand that the concept of city, just like any other concept, is a historically-built product. It is a conceptual tool that suffers reformulation pressures whenever great transformations structure new times. We also understand that a "new Urbanism" should take into consideration complexity and indetermination. Following this line of thought, we wish to consider the inflections which, from Geometry as an artificial construct to the computer as a material thought, allow one to understand that the twenty five centuries that have qualified Architecture as a knowledge and a technique of permanence are giving way to a materially-liquid Architecture (Solá-Morales, 2002: 126), compatible with the proposition: *the city is me.*

The world went through a transformation in the twentieth century which has demonstrated not only the inefficacy of any willingness of truth or foundation, but also, and above all, the communicational, non-linear, "fluid", "liquid", artificial aspects of knowledge and of the world transformed by it. The effects in the field of Urbanism are palpable. The notion of urban project, for instance, marked a rupture of the urban planning practices that were common in the post-war period (Vivianne, 1998: 62). The redefinition of an inhabiting population was sought, giving it back the role of agent and giving space to the cultural component that could not be eliminated and that molds the spaces and their social representations (Christelle, 1998: 109,111).

The theoretical and political posture is no longer the *planning* from objectives that include demands (functions, density, template) and the previous means to fulfill them, thus moving on to *how to deal with* the situations here and now for which there are no trustworthy parameters besides their permanent reformulation. In that sense, the formulation of the 'urban project' idea from the end of the 1970s onwards, and the debates it brought up, coincide with a cultural moment of the West when there started to be awareness of the interdependent bonds that linked natural events, human interventions, the psychological and cultural motivations, based on the contribution of knowledge coming from the fields of Biology, Ecology, Cybernetics, Anthropology, Physics (Vivianne, 1998: 98). At the end of the 1990s and beginning of the new century, the consequences of such understanding started to be felt.

It is symptomatic that authors such as François Ascher assimilate to Urbanism the references brought by the sciences of complexity, along with their notions of indetermination and unpredictability, and by Cybernetics with the idea of *feedback* (Ascher, 2001). It is symptomatic that authors such as William Mitchell, Manuel Castells or Saskia Sassen approach the city issue from the angle of digital technologies, space of flows, electronic markets and transterritorial "centers" formed by means of telematics. It is, finally, symptomatic that these and other contemporary conceptions of city are unanimous in establishing the relativity of the notions of centrality (political, administrative, financial, territorial) and their geographic fixation; of organization (political, administrative, financial, territorial) and its vertical functionality; of planning and its causal implementation *a priori*. In their stead they choose analyses that take into consideration the uncertainty, the risk, the unpredictability, the indetermination and the multiplicity in a globalized world. Posture becomes reflexive in the sense that it includes the constant reviewing of social practices in the light of the information that concerns the practices themselves, in a permanent examination of the possible choices, reexamining them in regard to what starts to be produced.[4]

At the heart of the studies that cross the city, architecture, environment, society and technology lies the question of what is artificiality as construction and nature as a given thing; of society and culture as human production and the physical world which man integrates and transforms. Several contemporary authors have already diagnosed that there is not, in fact, a difference in nature between that which is given and which is built, the spontaneous and the industrial, the natural and the cultural.[5] It is interesting to highlight the articulating aspect that constitutes any artifact in the world, be it set as physical, biological, cultural or technological data. We deal with *formations*[6], that is, information systems (universe, life, society, ecosystems, etc.) that express themselves in their own language, but which may be transcribed into another as long as we have the adequate cognitive tools. *Formations* vary widely in terms of constitution, structure, behavior and function, and demand different approach- and handling protocols; *formations* resist more or less transformation and coupling with others, but maintain a basic connectivity and translatability which, ultimately, depend exclusively on the existence of compatible knowledge in order to perform the connection of a given informational arrangement into another.

The current state of discussions in the field of Urbanism, into which we insert the hypothesis: *the city is me*, aligns therefore to the words of Gaston Bachelard:

> We now have less need to discover things than we have to discover ideas. Experience divides itself. Simplicity changes turf. Simple is that which is solid, uniform. What is composed is the element. The elementary form reveals itself to be polymorph and changing at the very time that the massive form tends to be amorphous. And all of a sudden the unit shines.
>
> What needs to be sacrificed? Our rude pragmatic certainties, or otherwise the random and useless new knowledge? No hesitation: it is necessary to move to the side where one thinks more, where one experiences in the most artificial manner, where the ideas are the least viscous and where reason likes to be in danger. If, in an experience, we do not jeopardize our reason, such experience is not worth being tried. (Bachelard, 1972: 8)

Urbanism is formed from several fields of knowledge that are applied to considering the city. Their developments and applications are always, or almost always, original from fields such as Philosophy, Sociology, Anthropology, etc. For instance, we can quote Joseph Rykwert, for whom Urbanists are divided into two groups: "the narrators of great historical movements" – those who follow Hegel's ideas – from Karl Marx to Joseph Alois Schumpeter, up to Francis Fukuyama and Jean Baudrillard; and the "paladins of the free market" (Rykwert, 2004: 10–11). In each author we can, ultimately, locate the source of inspiration and doctrine. Even those "paladins of the free market" know very well their doctrinal sources.

In several contemporary authors we observe the concern about rethinking the cities into the new context of the world. Rem Koolhaas, in his paper "What ever happened to Urbanism?" (2002), says that the notion of city has suffered an unprecedented distortion and that generalized urbanization has changed the urban condition and left it unrecognizable. Solà-Morales (2002) takes the notion of city beyond its buildings and architectures and states that nowadays we deal with cities that have changed radically in comparison to pre-industrial times and to the big city based on rationalization projects as a production unit. Today the megalopolis about which Jean Gottman was worried in the 1960s, and the global cities Saskia Sassen talked about in the 1990s have such different characteristics that the contribution made by Architecture in these such non-concentrated and highly connected aggregates is being rethought in completely new terms, regarding the parameters by which classic Architecture understood architectonic activity, as well as regarding the principles and methods with which modern Architecture has tried to rethink the relations between a new Architecture and a new city.

The city no longer allows itself to be reduced to the great modernist utopia. The ideals of Fordist and Taylorist thoughts applied to the city, resulting in economy of scale, long-term programs, common and collective interest projects, repetition and segregation of urban functions, rigid divisions into zones and mass solutions, etc., have already been properly criticized. Ascher[7], moreover, insisted on opposing to each of these concepts something more in accordance with our times, announcing a neo-urbanism with reflexive characteristics and performance characteristics, flexibility, multifunctionality, with solutions in equipment and individualized services and an economy of variety.

Time is no longer measurable solely from a historical, cumulative point of view. We live in an imbricate time configuration. Add to that idea the fact that the contraction of space and time depends on speed, which is not equally accessible to everyone, so that time is not equal to everyone. Likewise, the concept of space has changed. We use everyday a non-Euclidian space; the space for several activities shared by citizens is now, also, in electronics.

Space is a concept that, as such, is produced according to the symptoms of an era. Throughout man's history this concept changes and changes the vision of world.[8] The conception of Architecture and Urbanism is closely linked to the concept of space. Space as material support for social activities has acquired the characteristic of being able to continuously transform itself through the flexibility of its use, the simultaneity of its usage and meanings, the overlapping of information. Such malleability of transformation, frailty and transitoriness confers a fluid, moving, non-distinguishing character to the contemporary urban space.

If we also consider, as data for the understanding of the matter, the full use of the virtual space which is, at the same time, public and private, local and global, a non-place and a place with another geometry, we can say that the city – as a place of exchange, communication, interaction, dwelling, work – is, potentially, anywhere. The spaces and their functionalities are scattered everywhere. This subversion of space usages and this multiplication of connection possibilities constitute a new reality. Not to mention the already trivial concept of *virtual city* which has been the theme of a magazine[9] and book[10] and that designates *Netropolis* – the world's largest metropolis: the network that unites computers all over the globe, as well as cities based on the World Wide Web and which work as a political tool for different urban objectives: global urban marketing, incentive to tourism and business, communication between citizens and local government, commerce, etc.[11]

Some of these articulations have been worked on for some time. In the 1960s McLuhan stated that

> metropolitan space is equally irrelevant for the telephone, the telegraph, the radio, and television. What the town planners call "the human scale" in discussing ideal urban spaces is equally unrelated to these electric forms. Our electric extensions of ourselves simply by-pass space and time, and create problems of human involvement and organization for which there is no precedent. (McLuhan, 2007: 125)

He goes further when he posits that men have become nomads and informed and involved in a total social process as never before and that, with electricity, we "extend our central nervous system, instantly interrelating every human experience" (ibid: 401).

It is a fact that we live in a time of dwellers in electronic surroundings. Our actions in the physical space are associated with our actions on cyberspace. Buildings incorporate artificial nervous systems, sensors, screens and computer-controlled equipment. Several electronic systems have an increasingly important role in responding to the needs of their inhabitants. Geostationary communications satellites and the global systems of the LEO satellites (Low Earth Orbit – a system that covers Earth in a uniform manner) cover a great extent of land and sea, turning the planet's surface into an intelligent, fully-covered place. This proliferation of intelligent spaces will produce a new type of urban tissue and will radically reform our cities (Mitchell, 2001: 74).

Our assumption is that for a broad understanding, capable of considering the different contributions of the new concepts of city and its architectonics, a radical displacement is necessary towards basic concepts that are closer to a *topology* than to an Euclidian geometry (with the ideality and rigidity of forms and the oppositions of the system – inside/outside, left/right, etc.). When we plan and build a building or an avenue, we must necessarily be subject to Euclidian logic so that the structure may continue to stand and to function. On the other hand, when we wish to understand how the network society, the digital city or the informational city work we necessarily have to be subject to the logic of topology in order for that structure to make sense and continue to function.

Topological[12] space suspends the rigid dualistic and idealistic logic of Euclidian space because it concretely studies the qualitative aspects of spatial forms or their laws of connection. This new mentality, in Mathematics and elsewhere, opened, in the twentieth century, a rich field for investigation, application and metaphorization when developing increasingly abstract ideas (in a broad, refined and inclusive sense) of unilateralism[13], inclusion and transformation. This observation has already been very clearly made by Virilio when he referred to a new vision of world, of time, of immediateness, of ubiquity and of instantaneity and that is expressed in Architecture through the end of orthogonality and through the "topologization" of life (Virilio, 2001: 7). Thus we can use the topological reasoning as our conceptual reference of space and base for the increasingly complex comprehension of the concepts of city[14] which, henceforth, should no longer be restricted to Geography or to Euclidian Geometry.

Topology is adequate to the development of this study because it follows a logical reasoning in which unilateralism replaces bilateralism, dissolves the Euclidian opposition and thus includes the flexibility and the change without the ruptures that take place in everyday life. Thus, this is a start for the understanding of the relativization of usages and functions which are so evident in the contemporary city. It therefore enables comprehension of the permeability between concepts which were once antagonistic or different and today are relativized due to the use of space, use of technologies, the inclusion of speed as a determining factor for distance, hypermobility of goods, people and information, the ubiquity generated by telecommunication in real-time, or not. Among several other concepts we can stress public and private space; inside and outside; near and far; global and local; dwelling and work; real and virtual; person and city. There is, therefore, multifunctionality, polymorphism, passage and reversibility in urban forms. It is also a path for demonstrating that there is no "outside" according to this reasoning and that "me" and "city" are parts of the same concept.

The contemporary reformulation of the concept of city acknowledges the heuristic value of working with conceptual constructions within a perspective in which there is *no hierarchy between the object of study as real and its approach as "representation"*. In other words, between the facts and their descriptions, the distance is no greater than between what is known and what is built. To set the matter strictly in terms of Urbanism: the real of the city one tries to reach is a practice of such a reality, a practice of the city, or yet "representation is active: it does not only 'say' the city, it 'makes' the city".[15]

It is indisputable that, in order to express our reality, we can no longer appeal to the concept of city as it is historically understood. We just need to see the enormous quantity of neologisms used by contemporary authors – Ecstacity, nodal city, informational city, city of bits, e-topia, metapolis, etc. – as an attempt to situate the city within the current changes. But it is evident that the process of semantic and conceptual splintering of the idea of city is related to the process of decentralization and fragmentation of the notion of "I", of urban "being". Likewise, it is enough to see the number of new terms used by contemporary authors – post-organic, post-human, post-biological, cyborg, etc. – to situate the notion of man.

Given the huge transformations, in all fields, associated to the facilitations generated by the techniques in a planetary networked environment, in order to define the city we must define the Person. From a topological perspective, as we will see throughout this work, constituted places mix with people. When thought of by their quality of interaction networks, places are displaced according to the displacement of people. For instance, where are the headquarters of the American government? If we think exclusively about the "White House" we will certainly be making a mistake, given that the headquarters are wherever the President of the United States, along with his political network, is.

When he (person and institution) moves, the center of power moves along with him; all connections of power move along. This applies, on different levels, to any person. Another good example of this situation, given by Manuel Castells, is mobile telework as a model of work that is being consolidated. This model considers the worker to be a nomad who performs his tasks through contact with his office via cell phone, internet, fax, while on a trip, visiting his clients or on his regular way, thus establishing the concept of "office on the run" (Castells, 2003: 192). It is the office (considered a place, physical space geographically locatable) that moves along with the worker. This opens the perspective where we can think that, nowadays, *places can move along with people.*

According to this logic there are no exclusions, everyone is included. In the case of a citizen with very precarious living conditions, we can say that the city he is lacks all sorts of resources. The inhabitant of the slum district of Rocinha, geographically located in the neighborhood of São Conrado, city of Rio de Janeiro, certainly does not participate in the same city as the inhabitants of the noble neighborhood of São Conrado. He is geographically there, however he does not have the same urban reach of his "neighbors". We therefore believe we can affirm, and that goes for anyone, that when it comes to different levels, anyone is excluded from the city that is defined by the other person.

Starting from the idea that the concept of city, of urban, has left geometric and geographic places and that it is necessary to define person in order to define the city one is, and vice-versa, we will try, in order to clarify the "Me" in question and the concept of "Person", and also to make explicit the constituent elements of our hypothesis, to understand them according to the psychoanalysis-based theory called New Psychoanalysis.

In short, there is a correlation between the understanding of "city" and that of "citizen", so it is necessary to define person in order to define the city. There is an inseparability between the human being and the world, inseparability, therefore, between me and the city. It is a dynamic where it is not possible to understand these elements separately: we build the world that builds us at a common time. Our life story makes us build our knowledge of the world. What we intend to develop throughout this research is the idea that *any* citizen, *any* Person can say *the city is me.*

We then start from the double objective of deepening the study of Urbanism and developing the innovative potential of reflection, aiming at the analysis of a *new concept of city*, which currently gains an increasingly more distinct configuration. Our Project will be developed according to the following structure:

Chapter 1. Given that our work aims at elaborating a new concept of city, this chapter intends to define what is a concept; to show how the concept of city came to be and consolidated itself; and to do the epistemological defense of the right to propose a concept because we assume there is no separation between reality and symbolic representation;

Chapter 2. We will expatiate about the different neologisms brought by contemporary authors and their definitions, trying to show that the concept of city is in question and undergoing a process of relativization and dematerialization;

Chapter 3. There will be a brief explanation about the conceptual changes of city and about the moment when its comprehension experiences great relativization. It will look at transference and analogy of the term "fluid Architecture", proposed to Urbanism by Solà-Morales, using the reasoning of the Moebius Band. We present elements that indicate the passage from the solid state of Urbanism to the fluid state and this argument is used to introduce the theme: *the city is me*. In this chapter we develop a concise history of topology in order to introduce the subject. We restate the proposition of dealing no longer with Urbanism, but instead with a twenty-first century *Orbanism*;

Chapter 4. We succinctly expose the thought of a few authors from the fields of Philosophy, Biology, Psychoanalysis, Computer Science, and Physics with the objective of showing the different approaches and the shifting of the concept of Me, subject or individual. The systemic thinking, networked thinking and rhizomatic thinking are presented to point out organized forms of decentralized, inaccurate and random articulations in order to analyze the situations of world.

Chapter 5. Here we introduce some concepts of the New Psychoanalysis theory that supports this research in order to explain the concept Me = Person, which sustains the hypothesis: *the city is me*. Subsequently, the equivalence Me = Person will be used as heuristic tool for reading the city and the definition of Me;

Chapter 6. We formulate the hypothesis "The City is Me" through articulations of the concepts of *me* and *city*. We also use the concepts of pole, focus and fringe for the understanding of urban.

Conclusion. A synthesis of the main ideas and final considerations.

Bibliography used to build this study.

Authors Index – List of cited authors

General Structure of this book

The general structure of this book is as follows:

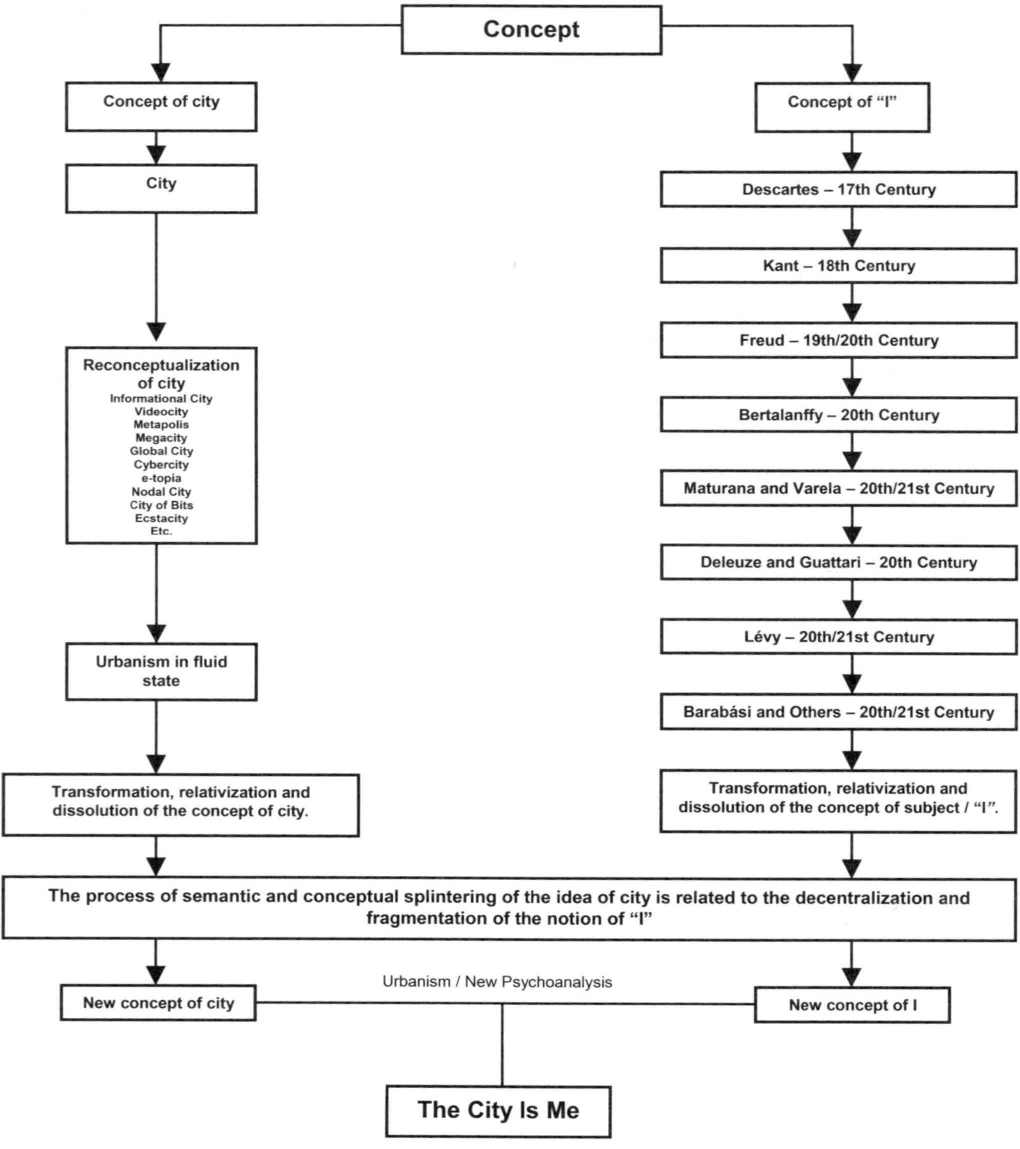

Chapter 1

About Concept

Pyramid of Kukulcan – Chichén Itzá – México
Photo: Isadora Dantas, 2009

We must think with concepts because, most of the time, we think that we think with things, but it is false. (Magno, 2005: 195)

Conceptualizing is an activity which is inherent to every task of describing, classifying and making previsions about cognoscible objects. That is undoubtedly a very general definition, liable to include any sign or semantic procedure referring to any object, concrete or abstract, particular or universal (Abbagnano, 2003).

There are as many concepts as there are cognitive situations that involve some kind of naming – mainly when facing the syntactic and semantic apparatus of a language – which abstracts, formalizes, discerns, distinguishes, separates and sometimes opposes, significations for comprehensive and explanatory purposes. Automobile, comet, G/god(s), State, man, red, sadness, Universe, entropy, square of the hypotenuse, mammals, square root of 2, pi, infinite, unicorn, speed, social class, city, territory, space, time (space-time), identity, value, desire, reason, excluded middle, renaissance – these are but a few of the countless concepts we use as basic cognitive activity of being in the world and proceeding to its description, classification, comprehension, explanation, ordering, transformation, conservation, projection, modeling or simulation.

A concept is usually indicated by an available name in a language's lexicon. Thus, when I say "house" this word encompasses a more-or-less defined set of images and recognizable scenarios in a given list of meanings. The concept, however, is not limited to the lexicon because several names may express a similar concept just as several concepts may be expressed by the same name, or yet a new word may be created to show more clearly the idea one tries to make explicit.

From that perspective, "habitation", "dwelling", "residence", "home" may all be taken as equivalents to "house", just as the name "house" may, anthropologically and historically, mean the domestic space in traditional societies[16], the *oikos,* understood as a social-economic unit in the Sumerian city (Bouzon, 1998: 21); or a space of morally-imposed social representation, characteristic of the Brazilian society as heritage of the colonial period and built on opposing tension in relation to the "street" (Da Matta, 2003); or even the "house" transformed into "street" through the social diversity that inhabits and transforms social urban space, relativizing the difference between public (street) and private (house) (Santos, 1985).

But the concept is not only an abstract entity identifiable by the presence of a word, be it new or rearranged.[17] As an object of the thought that operates thanks to the language and to other signs, the concept possesses a mediating function that organizes the internal order of the speech, being, therefore, a fact of broader comprehensibility, subject to suffering progressive restrictions regarding its epistemic definition. A concept is not identifiable with things either, even if it maintains a relation of co-pertinence with reality. I do not trip over the concept of "house", which is different from the house that I can see being demolished. One could say that concepts have a particular property of being abstract entities produced by human understanding and that move farther from products of the imagination, perceptions or affections, all of them mental states which can evoke the conceptual work, but which are not directly correspondent to it.

There is also the matter of validity of concepts; that is, the discussion about their true or false character as, upon coherently and systematically building explanations about the world, a conceptually-organized speech operates through exclusion of the statements or principles that are in opposition to it. The true values – statement or included principle – and false values – statement or excluded principle – are thus distributed. Ever since the Greeks, we work with the rule known as "law of the excluded middle": given a statement A and its negation B, they both cannot be simultaneously true.

But something happens when we face the infinite array of coherent and systematic explanations that mankind has been capable of forging. For instance, let us consider the matter of origin and functioning of the cosmos. It may be explained by the parthenogenesis of the Goddess-Mother Nammu who, according to the Sumerian myth, generated An (Sky) and Ki (Earth) (Eliade, 1978: 80); or by the pre-Socratic principle of the Unlimited which originates all things; the fountain whence all beings extract their provenience and where they perform their dissolution[18]; or by the initiative of Olorum who, according to the Yoruba, initiated the creation of the world, entrusting its finishing and ruling to a lesser god (Eliade, 1978: 75); or by the creating act of Yahweh, supreme deity of the Hebrews, who manifests his power to men through thunder, lightning, smoke, storm, fire or rainbow (Eliade, 1978: 127–128); or by the principle of mutation which takes place in the alternate game of *yin* and *yang* understood as being the constitutive factors of all reality (Jullien, 1997: 30), or even by Newton's gravitational theory, broadened and overtaken by Einstein's theory of general relativity.

What does this variety of testimonies show us from the conceptual work point of view? The insufficiency of the *law of the excluded middle* and the related need for it being suspended as methodological posture and exercise. "Mythical", "scientific", "religious", "rational", "philosophical", "sapiential" explanations, despite their different specificities, have worked for centuries or millennia in the most diverse cultures demonstrating that, from the point of view of value they are all equivalent, leaving to discussion, if and when it is the case, their force of authority and power of performance as far as the problems that may be presented by them are concerned, and for which there may or may not be possible solutions.

Once, the possibility of suspending the validation judgements as a previous methodological posture is in place, we can then choose a conceptual set to the detriment of another. This means operating conceptually: I lend validity – in a broad sense, the value of truth, belief, ideology, effectiveness, adequacy, opportunity – to a given set and circumstancially exclude others. I proceed to the fixation, relation and hierarchy of sense units, whence result universes more or less autonomous in meaning. In short, the concept is not a simple entity, but a functional complex in which each "doctrine" or "knowledge" places the elements as they find most adequate, true or effective. This universe cannot stop producing some kind of enclosure given that it follows rules of internal coherence, which ensure the necessary link between notions, differentiating itself from other knowledge procedures.

However the game of comparison, choice and exclusion between concepts is dynamic. The very plasticity of human language and cognitive competence takes over the task of creating points for passage and translation between concepts, facilitating their presentation, explanation and transmission. Besides, there are conceptual fields that are dedicated to exploring the convertibility of knowledge and the transitivity of fields of knowledge, creating a universe of conceptual problematization that facilitates exactly the production of epistemic-value conceptual equivalencies.[19] For instance, there is the book compiled by Lepetit, where, in order to present the transference of self-organization models (originally from Physics, Chemistry, Biology and Artificial Intelligence) to urban studies, it counts on the contribution of demographers, archeologists, economists, geographers, historians, etc. In the same book, the compiler establishes the following difference between the immediate past and the present: "In contrast with the monotonous time of classical mechanics and of the functionalist urbanism, the time of self-organization theories is characterized by the unexpected course of some of its evolutions as well as by complexity" (Lepetit, 2001: 137).

In the field of social research and, more specifically, in Urbanism, we encounter an active process of conceptual questioning. Traditional definitions become troubled – medieval city, renaissance city, pre-industrial city, industrial city – committed to a comfortable diachrony and, very often, indifferent to the plurality of social representations that come across in the construction and experience of the city. We assume that "the representation is active", and "does not only 'say' the city, but 'makes' the city" (Lepetit, 2001: 268), and turns the latter into a kind of mediating and mobilizing space of the mental equipment of a time, its beliefs, techniques, institutions, social orders, etc. One seeks, therefore, scenarios that enable highlighting of the polysemy and 'polyphony' of the city, betting on the epistemological gain of the study of such notions as clarifying the very considerations on the contemporary conditions of urban modification.

In that sense it is important to stress the current state of questioning about the possibilities of comprehension of the contemporary urban space, given the relativization of the parameters of its definition, parameters that were accumulated throughout millennia of construction and representation of the city. Along with that, we will link to that question the fact that any understanding results from the network that informs and forms a given comprehension of reality. Thus we intend to develop inclusive arguments that consider the multiplicity of possibilities that any reality offers. That being said, how does one understand the city today? How does one apprehend the plurality of its representations? What has changed?

1.1 The concept of City

> Like Magritte, we will have to say, before our *corpus* of definitions, *this is not a city*, but its apprehension. (Lepetit, 2001: 246)

Let us think a little about the idea of city. It is almost impossible to imagine the history of human occupation of the planet disentangled from the urbanization process, already traditionally considered as equivalent to civilization. We grew used to conceiving urban space from its most immediately visible and traditionally established marks, which, with a little historical imagination we see in the Neolithic period: the furrowed soil, the agglomerate of inhabitations creating bonds of physical proximity, the palisade, social time regulated by the cyclical rhythm of agricultural work, regulated, in turn, by environmental regularities difficult to relativize … and, at last, the human groups, scattered around the planet, generating and raising children in face of the most varied social strategies which domesticate the sexual polymorphism, polytropism and polyvalence that make the human species so oddly creative.

Men and women socially turned into "ventriloquist machines"[20] of the kinship rules, those countless regulating principles of sexual/social reproduction of the species, that articulate social and cosmic order and disorder, uniting, separating, punishing, condemning, restraining, terrorizing, seducing, and creating myths for people in their more-or-less compulsory social insertions, even though far from definitely having the last word on the human experience: social, physical and geographic settings where protection, defense and nourishment activities took place for a long time.

Following historians such as Lewis Mumford, we can, according to classical parameters, synthetically establish a route where the concept of city has its origin in the references inherited form the Neolithic village, associated to birth and place, blood and soil. The village's components were rebuilt in a more complex way and were incorporated by the new urban unit. Around the year 5000 BC, some villages turned into cities; then food producers started to produce surplus in order to provide for the population of specialists: craftsmen, merchants, fishermen, warriors, priests.

With the rise of the city, many activities which used to be scattered and disorganized were gathered within a limited area, contributing to a considerable technological expansion (mathematical calculation, writing, astronomical observation, the calendar, are just a few examples). The city becomes a structure equipped to store and transmit the goods of civilization with a maximum amount of ease within a minimum space. Such concentration expanded human capabilities in all directions. The city mobilized the human potential, achieved domain over transportation, and communication over long distances in space and time enabled enormous inventiveness and accelerated development in engineering, besides promoting a substantial increase in agricultural productivity.

From there, references were established that organize the traditional way of conceiving the city and are present in several historical experiences: physical and geographical conception of space that confirm ideas of settlement, delimitation, belonging and exclusion; preponderance of the physical form of the city converted into the materiality of the streets, houses, religious space, administrative space, space of workshops, market; city as a meeting place, place of protection, place of exchange, place of cultural interaction, place of creativity and technical evolution, a "special receptacle destined to store and transmit messages" (Mumford, 1991: 114), place of transmission of cultural heritage.

The main characteristics of the city as aesthetic symbol were already configured, even if primitively, in the citadel, around 2500 BC (Mumford, 1991: 104). Its form varied in time and space, but the lastingness of some solutions is surprising. The street, the house block, the market, the religious and administrative space, the space of workshops are visible symbols we are still used to thinking of as a possibility when conceiving the city.

1.2 The city

What is the city? How did it come into existence? What processes does it further: what functions does it perform: what purposes does it fulfill? No single definition will apply to all its manifestations and no single description will cover all its transformations from the embryonic social nucleus to the complex forms of its maturity and the corporeal disintegration of its old age. (Mumford, 1991: 9)

Well, considering the city is considering the *concept of city*, in the sense of a historically-built conceptual tool, whose successive elaborations suffer the impact of the transformations that history itself imposes on the social agents of a given space-time which, in turn, experience the demand of conceptually elaborating a consentaneous consideration with the problems of their time. The city, in turn, that transforms itself today thanks to the flow of capital and information, accelerated by the new technologies, may be considered as e-topia, metapolis or cybercity: forged words that involve the issue of relativization of traditional parameters that identify the urban, such as physical and geographic space and chronological time. Given the contingency of ours being the age of the "network society", of the "global city", of the "metapolis", of the city of "bits", of the "e-topia", of the "digital" or "instant" city, it is in our interest to contribute to the debate, broadening its analysis conditions with the proposition: *the city is me.*

Thinking the contemporary city implies the elaboration of a problem and its conceptual formulation. We work with conceptual constructions within the perspective that there is no hierarchy between the object of study as real and its approach as 'representation'. In other words, between the facts and their descriptions, there is no more distance than between what is known and what is built. In order to place the issue in strict terms of Urbanism, we once again quote Lepetit: the real of the city one tries to reach is a practice of such reality, a practice of the city (a way of dealing with the city) (Lepetit, 2001: 266–67). Or yet, we may remember the statement by Castells that "there is no separation between 'reality' and symbolic representation".[21] Our hypothesis, *the city is me,* is the conceptual formulation that there is no distance/difference between reality and symbolic representation. If we wish to cross into these terms, "the city that a person is" are their symbolic representations. A *person-city* is a set of symbolic representations.

So, for instance, with the concept of *territory,* Solà-Morales examines not only the matter of the "system of inhabited spaces, with its topographic, historical and social determination; but also [territory] as a starting point, meeting place of the formative activity which is at the same time the architecture and the city in any sense we may give to these terms" (Solà-Morales, 2002: 25–27). Starting from the issue conceptually elaborated as *territory,* the author also seeks what Social Sciences, Geography, Economics, Anthropology and Urban Sociology have to offer as "propositions" about contemporary city and Architecture (Solà-Morales, 2002: 25–27).

Likewise, *the city is me* takes, as conceptual construction, a field of articulation and analysis. In order to do so, it will establish a grid of conceptual relations whose intelligibility depends on the very space it creates. However, if it consisted only of this, a meaningless monologue would be all that was left; an impossible exercise, by the way, because, if we articulate, we do so already within a context with the objective of having a dialogue with it. The context from which we start is necessarily co-participant of the formulation of the very problem presented. The proposition, *the city is me,* gains its whole sense within the studies of Urbanism, which is its privileged interlocutor, because we start from the current state of perquisition about the contemporary city. Just like other authors, we seek efficient tools to take care of the matter which, if not new, configures itself, however, as highly undetermined and without immediately visible parameters, because these parameters were properly deconstructed by the very process (of relativization of the city concept), which now demands new consideration in order to establish new conceptual tools.

Chapter 2

Reconceptualizing the City

Shanghai – China
Photo: Isadora Dantas, 2010

Megalopolis, metropolis, postmetropolis, cyburbia, exopolis, global city and an enormous et cetera of neologisms formed from the classic Greco-Latin terms of polis, urbs and civitas seem to have opened the way for the permanent proposition of new words that allow denominating a reality that is understood as being no longer equal to that of the historical city. (Solà-Morales, 2002: 24)

The notion of limit has disappeared along with the almost unlimited urbanization: we can no longer see a city, nor enter or leave it. It has become "non-optical". That is due, on one hand, to the material presence of an infinitely extensible city, and, on the other hand, to the concomitant disappearance of the identification marks which rest on the opposition city/non-city (Cauquelin, 1996: 34).

The place, from the perspective of full use of technologies, has dissolved itself as casing. Communication takes place in a space of abstract characteristics that no longer demand physical presence. Telephone communications are responsible for a link and have built a kind of virtual enclosure (Cauquelin, 1996: 34), in which all forms of communications over distance now take part.

Any human being, from anywhere on the planet, can potentially participate, as an active member, of the world city. Urban also defines itself by the fact that the individual is articulated to a network of electronic inter-relationships.

The city is no longer reduced to its *geo*-metric and quantitative supports, nor to the cognitive competences developed on the verbalization capabilities of the human species. The reach of the accomplishments, conjectures, technological implementations, research programs, etc. has eliminated any possibility of indexing the notion of city to a random border criterion (physical, mental, cultural, ethnic, linguistic, financial, technological). More than that, the shifting of the notion of city accompanies and is accompanied by the shifting over what is perhaps its fundamental support: the idea that there would be a carbon-based[22] human reality, destined to perpetuate the heterosexual-family-reproductive-cultural-urban-geographic-couple design.

In other words, if during the Neolithic period we saw the implementation of a concept of city using, as reference, the sedentarism, the geography, the soil, the chronological time, the domestication of man, the recognition of consanguinity and, consequently, the family bonds, the heterosexual reproducing-couple bonds, we currently watch the establishment of concepts of city in which this initial base is quite non-configured and relativized, as well as of other concepts which even disregard these initial data. So, the city is then defined from different parameters such as finances, informational and planetary connection capability, nodes and networks, demographic density, virtualization, sensorial experience, etc. On the other hand, we can, contemporarily, oppose to each of the base references listed in the beginning of this paragraph, a different way of life: the exacerbated mobility of contemporary life gives back to man a certain nomadism, add to that the possibility of procreating without the need for sexual relations, communication over distances, relativization of chronological time and of geography due to the use of technologies, the new parameters of family relations with partners of the same sex, etc. The fact is that the concept of city as was historically understood no longer expresses our reality. Just see the large number of neologisms used by contemporary authors in the attempt to situate the cities according to present modifications.

The field of Urbanism and the conceptualization of city are therefore in question. The definition of city was broadly relativized, several concepts were introduced trying, each of them, not only to better apprehend the specificities occasioned by the inseparable interaction between space, technology and society but also to more adequately incorporate the new players, the new types of social relations and the new usages and functions that have arisen for the city.

We will now highlight some contemporary concepts of city, with the double objective of presenting, in a simplified manner, the understanding of each author regarding the contemporary city and the general definitions they elaborated about them. Evidently some concepts overlap, others are exclusive, others are inclusive, and others are even more particularized. The choice was random, but not naïve, given the fact that there is interest in identifying cities classified in ways different from those which we are used to thinking. The second objective is to make explicit the huge concern and mobilization present in our field of Urbanism in order to propose concepts in accordance with the ongoing changes. It is to this trend that we intend to align ourselves with this work. Within this perspective we can highlight some definitions for the contemporary city, through the following reviews made about books by important authors.

2.1 The informational city

In his book *The informational city: Information technology, economic restructuring and urban development* (1995), the sociologist Manuel Castells presents the thesis that there is a general process of transformation of the space taking place in all societies as they, increasingly, articulate themselves in a global system. The *space of flows*, a form of spatial articulation of the power and wealth of today's world, occupies the center of this transformation. It is in this context that he conceives the arrival of the *informational city*, our society's social and spatial form of city, just as the industrial city constituted the urban form of the type of society that is in crisis today. It is a city made of the productivity potential as well as of the destruction capacity; of the technological feats as well as of the social miseries of our times.

For Castells the spatial dynamics of the information activities expresses a new and complex organizational and technological model, simultaneously characterized by the persistent centralization of high-level activities in financial centers of larger metropolitan areas and by the decentralization of data-processing offices towards smaller areas and, especially, out of the main metropolitan areas.

This complex territorial development is not ruled by centralization or by decentralization. In it, what is crucial is the relation between both processes – exactly these binary processes of simultaneous centralization and decentralization associated, both of them, to the same socioeconomic dynamics – which explains the complexity of the new social and spatial form that is the informational city. The essential in all these spaces is their level of inter-relation through communicational flows, in which the connections of the intra-organizational network constitute the defining connections of the new spatial logics. Therefore the space of the organizations in the informational economy is increasingly a space of flows.

The *space of flows* implies an *organizational logic* which is non-spatial. Even if the organizations are located at specific places and their components are dependent on geographic space, the organizational logic derives, essentially, from the space of flows that characterizes the information networks. The flows are structured to constitute the fundamental spatial dimension of large-scale information-processing complexes.

This characteristic directly influences the configuration that cities take on today, given that the interests of a local entrepreneurial elite, as well as those of a working class local resident, or even those of a local market, are constantly subordinated to the necessity of the organization being simultaneously connected to financial markets, professional groups, strategic alliances in the economic world and to the potential to install and update the necessary technology, all dependent on the interactions in the space of flows.

The restructuration of capitalism constituted a key force on the remodeling of cities and regions in the end of the 1970s and beginning of the 1980s, when production and the use of the then New Technologies of Information and Communication (NTIC) joined to forge the relations between these technologies and the new forms and spatial processes. This combination deeply changed the emerging socioeconomic system, giving place to the complex generation of a new urban-regional process as socio-spatial effect of both fundamental macro-processes in all advanced capitalist societies – the restructuration and the informational development. For Castells, the interaction between technology, society and space is responsible for generating a new urban-regional process that serves as material base to our lives in this age of information primacy.

The specific spatial model of the then emergent information technology industries resulted in two fundamental characteristics: the distinctive character of its raw material – the information – and the uniqueness of its product – process-oriented equipment with application in every aspect of human activity. Other factors – the search for profit, for instance – also determined its spatial behavior, but what was evident was the technological means by which profit can be obtained. These technological means become the appeal of the new industries, which move increasingly farther from the activities in which the old industries were involved. Technology starts to work as mediator in the relation between economic rationality and the spatial structure thence resulting.

The production of information technologies becomes then, in fact, a spear-point for the formation of a new hierarchic production space that extends itself all over the world, divides countries and differentiates locations with the connections necessary to the economic and functional logic of the process maintained by the new forms of communication. This new space is represented by a variable geometry that depends solely on the ups-and-downs of companies, regions and countries in the technological echelon.

The relation between technology and work is decisive upon the form taken by urban dynamics. This new relation, established between these two topics and located at the base of the transformation of the urban social structure, was called "dual". In the new socio-spatial configuration of this dual city, new technologies, even though they do not constitute the causal factor, are extremely important due to their instrumental role in the process of work restructuration. Two cities are typical for the understanding of this structure: New York and Los Angeles.

These two American cities had, at the end of the 1980s, the largest part of the growth of highly paid jobs and, at the same time, were inhabited, for the most part, by ethnic minorities incapable of obtaining these jobs. Therefore, the duality manifested itself in the spatial coexistence of a large professional and executive middle class sector with a growing urban subclass. The dual city exemplifies well the emerging and contradictory development of the new informational economy and the conflictive appropriation of the central city by social groups that, even though they constitute different worlds in terms of lifestyle and structural position in society, share the same space.

The dual city has always been a classic theme in urban Sociology. The contrast between opulence and poverty in a shared space has always interested scholars. However what was already seen at the end of the 1980s was a new form of urban dualism specifically connected to the restructuration and expansion process of the informal economy. What was in question was, above all, the dismantlement of capital-work relations institutionalized during the long formation process of the industrial society. And more, the transition of industrial production processes to the informational coincided with the rising of flexible production that, under the historical conditions of that moment, seemed to tend to equating itself to the deinstitutionalized capital-work relations. There were, therefore, simultaneous processes of growth and decline of industries and companies that took place more intensely at the nodal points of economic geography, especially in large metropolitan areas where the greatest part of the knowledge-intensive activities were based.

According to Castells, an important social trend then stood out: the historical appearance of the space of flows overcoming the meaning of space and places. Its harmful effect is the production of a negative geometry that denies the specific productive sense of any place outside its position on a network whose shape constantly changes in response to messages of invisible signs and unknown codes. This is the result of the separation between functional flows and historically-determined spaces as two different spheres of the human experience. People live in places and power establishes its dominance through flows. Between non-historical flows and irreducible identities of local communities, the cities and the regions disappear as places with social meaning.

The emergence of the space of flows questions the meaning of the cities and of the well-being in our societies, but, who knows, is it possible that from there will appear a new socio-spatial structure formed by local communities that control and give shape to a network of productive spaces? That way, as is Castells' wish, our historical time and our social space will be able to converge towards the integration of knowledge and meaning in a new city no longer dual or global, but informational.

2.2 The videocity

In his book *O espaço crítico e a perspectiva do tempo real* (1993), urbanist Paul Virilio develops the concept of videocity, or city with no doors, which is that where urban space loses its geopolitical reality in sole favor of instant systems of transmission whose technological intensity continuously deranges the social structures and promotes a "post-urban" and transnational concentration. Our times would be that of the development of retinal persistence techniques (audiovisual) where we pass from the aesthetics of the progressive appearance of a stable image (analogical) to the *aesthetics of the disappearance* of an unstable image (digital).

From the emergence of forms and volumes destined to persist in the duration of its material support (stone, wood, terracotta, screen, papers, etc.) ensues images whose persistence is solely retinal and whose duration is that of the "time of sensitization" that escapes our immediate conscience. Hence, at the screen interface, everything shows itself with the immediacy of an instantaneous broadcast. Therefore, after the distances of space and time, it is the *distance-speed* that comes to abolish the notion of physical dimension.

The representation of the contemporary city is no longer determined by the ceremony of opening the doors, the ritual of processions, of parades, the succession of streets and avenues. Urban architecture should, from now on, relate to the opening of a *technological space-time*. Place unit without time unit, the city disappears in the heterogeneity of the temporality regime of advanced technologies. Urban form is no longer expressed by a random delimitation, a dividing line between here and there, but by the programming of a "schedule" on which the entrance indicates only an audiovisual protocol where the audience and the audience rates renew the welcoming and the reception of the public.

2.3 The metapolis

François Ascher develops the concept of metapolis in the book *Métapolis ou l'avenir des villes* (1995). For the professor of the French Institute of Urbanism, metapolis is a set of spaces in which the total, or part, of the inhabitants, of the economic activities or of the territories is integrated in the daily functioning of a metropolis or of a set of large cities. With a common bowl of employment, of residence and activities, the metapolis is formed by heterogeneous and not necessarily contiguous spaces and comprises some hundreds of thousands of inhabitants. Presenting itself in quite varied ways, metapolis constitutes itself from pre-existing very different metropolis and integrates a heterogeneous set of new and diverse spaces.

Metapolis encompasses the metropolitan zones in a strict sense and, besides that, the new spaces arisen from metropolization. They are the vast urban regions that agglomerate cities of all sizes in which the urban zones and the rural zones intertwine. In other words, metropolization and metapolis form the scenario in which economic, social, political and cultural forces act and will act in a lasting way. It is certain that these forces influence metropolitan dynamics and the evolution of the metapolis, but it is the very unfolding of urbanization that configures a context from which they cannot escape and, for that, represents a kind of limit to the influence of these economic forces.

Metapolis is a space of mobility in which relations of proximity in great part dissolve because it is connected to multiple national and international networks and, sometimes, maintains with distant territories more intense relations than with its close surrounding zone that no longer performs a role of territorial rearguard.

2.4 The megacities

Manuel Castells approaches the megacities in his book *The network society [in The Information Age: Economy, Society and Culture – vol. I]*(1999a). According to him, megacities may be defined as agglomerations of great dimensions that concentrate the essentials of economic, technological, social and cultural dynamism of countries. Connected to each other on a global scale, they spread in space and form true urban nebulas, in which field, city, creativity and social problems integrate at the same time. They are centers of economic, technological and social dynamism in their countries and on a global scale.

Spatial form present in different geographic and social contexts of the new global economy and of the emerging informational society, megacities are defined not only by their size – agglomerations with over ten million people – but also by composing the nodes of the global economy and concentrating higher directive, productive and administrative functions of the entire planet. They also enclose the control of the media, the true politics of power and the symbolic capacity of creating and diffusing messages.

Not all megacities are influential centers of the global economy, even though they equally connect huge segments of the human population to this global system. They also work as magnets for their hinterlands – in other words, the entire country or region where they are located – and should be seen as a function of their gravitational power towards the main regions of the world. They articulate the global economy, connect the informational networks and concentrate world power. The fact that they are physically and socially connected to the global and disconnected from the local is what makes them a new urban form. In other words, they are externally connected to the global networks and to given segments of their countries, but act internally as if they were disconnected from local populations.

2.5 The global city

Sociologist Saskia Sassen elaborates her concept of the global city in her book *As cidades na economia mundial* [*Cities in a World Economy*] (1998[1994]). From the assumption that, in the current economic age, there are two different characteristics – the integration of systems and the geographic dispersion of economic activities – the author states that this situation has contributed significantly to the strategic role performed by large cities. The cities have not become obsolete. On the contrary, besides continuing to concentrate command functions, they have gained two other roles: (1) they are places of post-industrial production for the main industries, for the financial sector and for specialized services; and (2) they are multinational markets in which companies and governments can acquire financial instruments and specialized services.

Therefore global cities function as a network; they are centers of world commerce and bank activities and command posts, global markets and places of production for the information economy. Key places for advanced services and for the telecommunications necessary for the implementation and the management of global economic operations, they constitute nodes of circulation of resources and tend to concentrate the headquarters of companies, especially those who operate in more than one country.

2.6 The cybercity[23]

The concept of cybercity was developed by the philosopher of contemporary virtual culture Pierre Lévy in his book *Cibercultura* [Cyberculture] (1999). The relation between the city and cyberspace takes place through the articulations between urban functioning and the forms of collective intelligence that develop in cyberspace. They are two qualitatively different spaces – territory and collective intelligence, the latter having cyberspace as support – that articulate in such a way that there is no elimination or replacement of the territorial forms by a cyberspatial functioning, but rather a compensation of the inertia and rigidity of the first by the articulation performed in real time on the second. This allows urban matters to be elaborated through interactive and collective communication, enabling the simultaneous placement of competences, resources and ideas.

The project of cyberspace related to collective intelligence focuses on enabling, in a broader sense, the conscience of what human groups do together and giving them support for the solution of problems according to an inclusive logic. The perspective is that all have access to the processes of collective intelligence, to cyberspace, on a network capable of accommodating individual and social manifestations of elaboration of the city's problems, of participation by directly-affected citizens in the several deliberations, of free access to knowledge, etc. In short, this articulation enables the use of the virtual in order to better inhabit the territory, establishing an electronic democracy.

It is important to see that, with these differentiated concepts of city, we start having, simultaneously, the reconceptualization of what is a citizen, person or inhabitant of this space. In Lévy's case, cybercity characterizes cyberspace, which is the space of those who *inhabit all the media with which* they interact. Thus we see that the inhabitant of the cybercity has, among other characteristics, the possibility of ubiquity, and the finding that his body is not restricted to its corporeal configuration.

2.7 The e-topia

This concept was elaborated in 1991 by William Mitchell. E-topias are economical and ecological cities that function more intelligently than the familiar urban models and that, contemporarily, are replacing them. Their design principles would follow five basic points:

1. The dematerialization that consists of replacing a physical service for a virtual one (for instance, the home banking electronic system). There is an analogous benefit when information is separated from its traditional material substratum, because an email message that is read on the screen does not use paper. If we do not produce a material object and if, instead, we use a dematerialized equivalent, it will never turn into a residue that will need to be treated.

2. The demobilization, whose idea relates to the immeasurably greater efficiency of moving bits instead of people and goods. The liberation is obvious by the reduction of consumption percentages of fuel, by the smaller contamination, by the smaller need for space and for transportation infrastructures, by decrease in manufacturing and vehicle maintenance expenses and by the decrease of traveling time.

3. The mass customization that has to do with the fact that if the machines of the industrial age brought standardization, repetition and mass production savings, the intelligent machines of the computer age can guarantee very different savings

of intelligent adaptation and automated customization. Silicon and computers can be used on a large scale to enable automatic customized supply of what is strictly necessary in a particular context. For instance, a customized electronic newspaper system, printed at home, could have the profile of the user's interests and be used to select and print only the articles and advertisements more likely to be read.

4. The intelligent functioning that refers to the attribution of a greater intelligence to mechanisms and systems that need this resource, thus allowing waste reduction. For instance, an elementary system allows turning a house's lights and devices on and off. A slightly more sophisticated system exchanges some switches for timers, but if one intends an even greater effectiveness, it is necessary to have a system that knows the user's way of living, that finds out the dynamic variations of electricity prices and that optimizes the employment of lights, heating, air conditioning and home appliances according to a prevision model permanently maintained and updated.

5. The soft transformation that relates to the possibility of creating completely new neighborhoods and cities, organized with the intention of taking advantage of the new dematerialization, demobilization, mass customization and intelligent functioning opportunities. In the most developed regions the primary task will be adapting existing buildings and public spaces in order to satisfy needs very different from those that oriented their original construction. The new infrastructure will be more moderate and less harmful in its physical effects. In many cases integration may take place almost invisibly. Electronically-served spaces for the purpose of information work will not have to be concentrated in large contiguous areas, as in industrial and commercial areas of current cities, and, unlike industrial facilities, will not negatively affect the quality of the surrounding areas.

According to Mitchell (2001), these would be the characteristics of the new smart cities. In the twenty-first century the condition of civilized urbanity may be based less on the accumulation of objects and more on the flow of information; less on geographic centrality and more on electronic connectivity; less on the consumption increase of scarce resources and more on their intelligent management. We will be able to adapt existing places to the new necessities without the need of demolishing the physical structures and building new ones. Physical and virtual places will work interdependently and, in general, will mutually complement each other within a changing urban life model, instead of replacing those for others according to the existing models.

It is evident that this transformation encompasses the concept of the citizen who starts to participate in multiple dispersed, overlapping communities through different electronic means – browsing on virtual public spaces, participating in electronically-prepared meetings at remote places. Mitchell affirms that, nowadays, we are inhabitants of electronic surroundings instead of mere users of informational artifacts.

2.8 The nodal city

The concept of the nodal city – as conceived by Kok-Meng Tan (in Solà-Morales & Xavier Costa, 2005: 172–87), professor at the National University of Singapore – is based on the urban transformation over the last 30 years in Singapore, but may also serve as development model for many Asian, American and European cities.

Kok-Meng Tan considers the human condition as a node where a fast, mass-transportation network and a network of global economic flows intersect. This node is often integrated to metro stations and monitored by an electronic security system. This nodal city is formed through the high concentration of urban functions in a limited space, and could also be considered as a city within a city because the occupants can work, live and entertain themselves there around the clock without leaving it.

This model has been used in host cities that wish to attract global capital and to stand as global cities, for these nodes relate to the globalization process in at least three ways: by representing an icon of global flows – this agglomerate of urban functions configures an emblematic symbol of the global cities; by exercising a support structure to the global flows, as the nodal city counts on an informational infrastructure and accommodates the services and functions that global players and companies need for the maintenance of their activities; by acting as support for the global flows in the city they occupy.

Nodal cities can also be classified according to their consolidation time. Therefore, in an instant nodal city the functioning and usage are marked by an inauguration of its configuring physical space, while in the gradual nodal city, maturation takes place over a long period of time, during which the city expands and consolidates itself.

The nodal city presents, among others, the following characteristics:

- constitution of a transportation node: physical space constituted over a fast mass transportation node;
- implementation of high buildings whose floors are distributed above and below ground level;
- establishment of great densities through vertical overlapping;
- simulation of urbanity within the space, bringing into this node urban diversity and the organization of transitory events that take place in a common space;
- total use of the surfaces through the occupation of spaces with their commercial culture of electronic and visual information that seduce the eye;
- creation of a horizontal extension by contiguity and continuity between non-contiguous spaces through the establishment of physical connections, *macro connectors*, that extend communication horizontally, and *micro connectors* and *hybrid connectors* that enlace the surroundings, beneath and above the streets, allowing communication between contiguous and non-contiguous spaces;

- elaboration of responses for the urban surrounding – creation of urban windows through outdoor platforms, a type of public space that has, among other purposes, that of incorporating the urban surrounding view to inside the node;
- constitution of a network understood as interconnected system of nodes without center and without periphery, composed by material and non-material things, and comprising people, merchandise, services, information, etc.

The nodal city is a global object at a local space, and its culture is focused on general consumption. In order to maintain itself as a node, its performance includes a self-regulating organism capable of quickly absorbing changes and speculations of the moment. It must be tuned to any cultural or political trend and follow *ad hoc* social movements. Its permanence depends directly on its capability to adapt and adjust to the changing forces of the contemporary city. In short, Kok-Meng Tan considers it as the city that can sustain the aspects of a new urbanity.

2.9 The city of bits

William Mitchell, in the conceptualization work of the City of Bits (1995), assumes that the development of a global infrastructure capable of connecting the entire world reconfigures, once and for all, the ancient relations between space and time, definitively revolutionizing our lives. Furthermore, he identifies a new dimension in contemporary cities, invisible and immaterial, related to the informational networks of the new communication technologies (Mitchell, 1995: 5). Even if we can point out the beginning of this process in the nineteenth century, as with the appearance of the telegraph in 1837 and of the telephone in 1876, it was in the twentieth century, notably from the 1960s onward, that we saw the introduction of the so-called digital technologies[24] and, along with them, the worldwide computer network. Ever since then, revolution and technology have been keywords in the comprehension of contemporaneity, and it would not be different in the context of the cities.

The reality of the geographic dispersion and virtual mobility in which we live is boosted, on one hand, by the appearance of communications networks and, on the other, by the miniaturization of electronic components and by the effective production of mobile technologies. Remote access and telepresence become basic phenomena in a world that decentralizes production, once confined to the assembly-line structure of the typically Fordist factory. Consumption and entertainment possibilities multiply, detaching from the need for physical displacement, and work, currently associated with the emblematic figure of the *laptop*, is perpetuated. In this context of changes Mitchell imagines architecture and urbanism associated to the commoditization of bits and to the dominance of *software* over the material dimension of the shape. New needs emerge in these hybrid spaces, setting the challenge of imagining and creating digitally-mediated environments, adequate to the lifestyles and communities, simultaneously demanded, enabled and engendered by contemporaneity.

Presenting the arguments of this work by Mitchell, we observe that the worldwide computer network, associated with some sort of electronic agora, today plays a role as fundamental as the Greek prototype of public space, with its centrally-delimited location, played in the life and in the urban diagrams of the Greek polis. That happens because our actions on the network are organized by other principles, clearly different from those that are at stake in the spaces of the traditional cities. (Mitchell, 1995: 8)

In fact traditional cities propose geographic displacement as a condition to interact with other people: going out is always an act inserted in a vast network of relationships through which we play a role, be it through the place where we go (different places are, in general, attended by characteristic players always having their implicit scripts and habits) or how we behave (the clothes and language we use, etc.). The worldwide computer network, in turn, subverts and displaces many of these presuppositions, redefining our notions of community, urban life and shared spaces.

Mitchell approaches these differences in seven pairs of oppositions. The first three – spatial/antispatial, corporeal/incorporeal and focused/fragmented – theme the possible redefinitions of the notions of space, subjectivity and identity on the network. After all, in this environment – no specific place and all places at once – identity mingles with electronic addresses and aliases we take on, while geographic location becomes indistinguishable and imprecise. Therefore what matters is not where you are, but rather your access code that can be used on any computer anywhere on the planet.

A break of geographic codes then takes place, according to which the places we attend determine who we are, which, in turn, determines the places we can attend. In this sense, our corporeity and our action power, once biologically limited, scatter through fragmented, fluid identities, formed by associations created and adopted by us through aliases, profiles or through software known as agents.[25]

The last four pairs – synchronous/asynchronous, narrowband/broadband, voyeurism/ engagement, contiguous/connected – outline new types of interaction between real and virtual spaces. First of all there is the rupture of the space-time unit on the network, configuring a situation different from the synchronicity experimented in the face-to-face model. Such a situation raises a series of implications from the point of view of cities, whose style traditionally considers a determined space and time for any event, be it for lunch, work, public transportation, a theatre play or even a television show. That makes each city, given its spatial configuration, have its own daily, weekly or seasonal rhythm. However, on the network, people communicate in a continuous and asynchronous manner, because each one personally chooses the best moment to log in. Therefore, if the value of a property in urban space was set due to its location, the value of a connection is set by its bandwidth, which, inevitably, raises discussions about access and other forms of exclusion.

The increase in the power of processing and data transmission, combined with new *input* and *output* devices (prosthesis, smart gloves, etc.), allows – and promises – to broaden the telepresence experience, forging immersive and multimodal realities that involve physical engagement, extrapolating the limits of the computer screen and the mere visual and voyeuristic stimulus. The promise that we will stop being spectators and will become participants and inhabitants of these new worlds implies the possibility of dissolving the distinction between real and virtual (Mitchell, 1995: 20). This happens because places in cyberspace constitute parts of codes being performed by some server and that acquire their own architecture when they go from the plane dimension of the text to the two-dimensional or three-dimensional. In this sense cyberspace – just as the urban space, marked by delimited borders and by access control (be it to countries or properties) – has public (like the streets) and private (mediated by info-technical passwords) places. It proposes the logical clicking connections (linkage) instead of the spatial contiguity of physically-set paths.

Therefore the network is, above all, an invitation to the planning and construction of "the City of Bits (capital of the twenty-first century)" (Mitchell, 1995: 24). And, for Mitchell, the establishment of this new city places itself as a challenge that promises to revolutionize notions that have already been canonized and to rebuild the speech used by architects ever since the classic age. According to him:

> This will be a city unrooted to any definite spot on the surface of the earth, shaped by connectivity and bandwidth constraints rather than by accessibility and land values, largely asynchronous in its operation and inhabited by disembodied and fragmented subjects who exist as collections of aliases and agents. Its places will be constructed virtually by software instead of physically from stones and timbers, and they will be connected by logical linkages rather than by doors, passageways, and streets. (Mitchell, 1995: 24)

This new city is marked by a new degree of connection with its inhabitants. Once the human body becomes obsolete, constantly requiring upgrade devices, it also becomes projectable and programmable, as well as the environments it attends. In this context the humanist subject – embodied in the figure of Leonardo da Vinci's Vitruvian Man, for whom the cities of the Renaissance were built – seems to give place to a new sort of inhabitant, proper for the cities in the digital, electronic age. And the role suggested by the author for these new hybrid environments is that of hosting cyborg citizens, people who became places of intersection between concrete spaces and cyber space.[26] Considering the several levels of interaction between machine and human forms – from telepresence to sophisticated electrosomatic constructions –, the author affirms we are all cyborgs[27], and suggests the retheorization of the body in space as a good starting point for the work of the architects and urbanists who will plan these new cities (Mitchell, 1995: 28).

Mitchell themes the cyborg from six fundamental relations: nervous system/bodynet, eyes/television, ears/telephony, muscles/actuators, hands/telemanipulators and brains/ artificial intelligence. The first considers the conversion of the body into a construction that comprises several domains of the existence. One of the situations proposed by the author is the connection of several electronic products we use or carry (portable cameras, mobile phones, pagers, palmtops, walkman, pacemakers and other medical devices) into a single body, mobile and connected by a network (*wireless bodynet*) that allows it to function as system integrated by exonerves and connected to the worldwide digital communications network (Mitchell, 1995: 29).

These small organisms began to appear in the 1990s and became increasingly small: from portable they turned into wearable, taking the shape of our bodies. Mitchell's forecast is that this process will deepen: gloves, contact lenses, clothes that contain circuits, implanted chips, etc. So the interface of these small electronic organs with our muscles and our sensory system would enable the traffic of bits through the gap that once separated silicon and carbon.

It is in this perspective that cyborgs become modular and reconfigurable beings for whom the borders between interiority and exteriority, between self and other are destabilized (Mitchell, 1995: 31). That destabilization takes place because, once connected to the exterior world, these devices extend our nervous system to the endless connections of the network. And once we break the limits of our skin we are also connected to the architecture, which means that some of these electronic organs can be built in our surrounding environment. Therefore the act of residing at a place gains a new meaning which, according to Mitchell,

> has less to do with parking your bones in architecturally defined space and more with connecting your nervous system to nearby electronic organs. Your room and your home will become part of you, and you will become part of them. (Mitchell, 1995: 30)

He also foresees that, in the future, the connection of these electronic organs to the network will eliminate even the need of being close to or owning them. Therefore, with the dissolutions of the body's borders, perhaps metaphysics will be forced to reformulate the body/mind division into a possible mind/network articulation (Mitchell, 1995: 31).

Following the mutation of our bodies, spaces that shelter us transform themselves. With the substitution of circulation systems by telecommunications systems, the traditional sorts of construction dissipate into the solvent of digital information and from the residue of these recombining fragments mutant spaces originate.

Buildings differentiated from each other by their different usages and the inventory of these usages represented the social structure and its divisions. Under that condition, the internal organization of a building – its parts, the relations established between them by the circulation system and the evident hierarchies of power and control – reflected the structure of an institution and physically diagrammatized its characteristic activities. Currently, institutions do not sustain themselves only through their physical dimension. They depend equally on their telecommunication systems and computer programs. This digital and virtual dimension has superseded physicality and reduced demands for concrete space: the stock of bits replaces the storage in libraries and linkage replaces accessibility, dissolving the imperative of circulation in architectural projects. Therefore screens take the place of doors and interfaces replace the façades and the public faces of institutions.

Another example of privileged place for the identification of ongoing transformations regards information-related businesses. If the production of paper documents (books, newspapers, magazines, etc.) is traditionally done in a centralized, large-scale manner, the distribution chain presents itself as a problem for the circulation of the information inserted there. It demands specific places for each of the stages involved in this process – the editors' office, printing locations, storage, sale and, at last, reading. Located, in general, at appropriate parts of the city, they perform important roles in the distinction of spaces of the urban tissue. However, when we separate information from its characteristic material supports, storage and transportation become unnecessary[28], we can turn bookstores and video and CD stores into bitstores of immaterial products.

Similarly this process of dissolution and digitalization promises to transform the shelves of libraries into database servers, in a procedure that is an expanded version, even if a very slow one, of a process that computer science knows as a database server: requests are sent and, in response, stored items are sent back. In theory the interfaces of personal computers also work in a similar way: icons on the screen work as doors to the streets, making access points visible. Clicking on an icon (action compared to knocking on a door) places the user in a space where files can be requested. In response, software return data stored on disc, showing them on the screen for handling.

As for galleries and museums, Mitchell's forecast is that these will transform, becoming virtual museums. However, if the old museums were projected to present immutable collections in orderly and fixed sequences, the modern are characterized, rather, by offering flexible spaces for installing temporary shows. At virtual museums images replace concrete objects and the temporal sequence shown on a screen plays the role of a spatial sequence distributed in a circulation space (Mitchell, 1995:59). That way, extensive galleries become unnecessary and dealing with the audience, even a large one, becomes easy, given that what is important is not the size of the gallery, but rather the bandwidth.

Mitchell considers that, as the expansion of the networks would reach sufficient bandwidth and became a technology available at home, the expansion of this consumer market would justify investments that would make interactive products not an exception, but rather the newest rule. Live performances could be broadcast in a sort of "virtual auditorium" with buttons capable of sending applause or other coded responses. Sport events transmitted in 3D could offer the viewer the opportunity to select a particular angle, while matches – which traditionally gather athletes in delimited physical spaces separated from the viewers, such as in football or on tennis courts – would then involve countless network participants. The same thinking is extensive to several other sectors.

In education and medicine, networks rapidly create new practices and new ways of sharing knowledge, forcing changes in spaces and enabling the appearance of virtual teaching structures, and specialized medical care for geographically-dispersed populations, because the doctor will no longer need to be in the same room, or even on the same continent as the patient. In the prison system, changes are seen in the emergence of electronic monitoring devices so that many functions of the traditional prisons may be performed without physical confinement, without walls or cells. An example is the *Electronic Supervision Program* that enables home confinement of American criminals, placing them under the monitoring of anklets equipped with transponders connected to telephone modems. When they move farther than a pre-established distance from the surroundings of this device, a central control is automatically alerted.

In banking, money also turns into information circulating infinitely in cyberspace, thus allowing banks to have their branches in this virtual space. Given that the process of data transference from automated teller machines to the banks does not depend on the physical or spatial, but rather on electronic connection, they quickly scatter to the places where people truly need money: supermarkets, shopping centers, airports, etc. This results in the disintegration of traditional banking centers for it is no longer necessary to go to a given place in order to perform transactions.[29]

Another sector directly affected by this set of innovations is the financial market which saw the development of the organized trading of shares, futures contracts and options at the same time as the spaces that became increasingly more elaborated and specialized in order to do business. Transactions are made from computer to computer and no longer between co-present people at the same physical space. Buy and sell orders are inserted in electronic systems that discriminate the bids, notify the traders and transfer values between bank accounts in a few seconds. Therefore markets go global, brokers have their jobs replaced by computer algorithms and computer networks become the new spaces for these virtual transactions.

The development of the virtual shopping center dissolves the need to travel to the places where the sellers and the stock of products were traditionally concentrated. Therefore street showcases are replaced by computer screens and, in this context, what matters is the electronic contact between the players involved on the negotiation. That way, physical spaces are bypassed by computer networks associated with warehouses strategically located to facilitate the distribution of the products. Besides that, even where traditional physical structures resist, they become more and more technological: electronic payment terminals, bar codes, satellite communication systems to connect dispersed stores and trucks transporting products, besides sophisticated electronic real-time stock control and price-adjustment mechanisms capable of inserting a product's correct price on the displays of several stores in just a few seconds.

Working spaces transform as well. Offices can be displaced from commercial centers towards cheaper locations in the cities' suburbs, from where workers would maintain electronic contact with the small – but still visible – central offices. Satellite offices could be transferred to locations where labor costs were lower. That way the location of services and the standards of mobility toward work alter: workers could go by bicycle to one of these satellite offices in the suburbs of the cities or to telecommuting centers (which allow working from a distance on a communication infrastructure) instead of commuting by car or public transportation to the central offices.

Insurance companies and other businesses that deal immaterial products and receive orders to be executed afterwards could be easily replaced by network communication. A significant part of this informational work could be transferred to the home of the workers, in suburbs or even distant rural areas.

Residences transform, too. The living room becomes the place where digital activities establish themselves in the physical world: work, news, entertainment, education, bank transactions and shopping become available at home through electronic devices. In general, these devices act as mediators of the information flow to the inside and outside of the houses. Therefore, progressively, houses will become places with electronic addresses besides their traditional addresses. And the functions of several spaces inside a house will be largely established through the installation of these different types of devices, and as networks and electronic information devices supply a more extensive array of services there will be less occasions to leave the house.

This kind of analysis, however, reveals only a part of the story. The consequences of such transformations on urban spaces also affect – deeply – our ways of life. And once again Mitchell states:

> Efficient delivery of bits to domestic space will, in addition, collapse many of the spatial and temporal separations of activities that we have long taken for granted. Many of our everyday tasks and pastimes will cease to attach themselves to particular spots and slots set aside for their performance – workplaces and working hours, theaters and performance times, home and your own time – and will henceforth be multiplexed and overlaid; we will find ourselves able to switch rapidly from one activity to the other while remaining in the same place, so we will end up using that same place in many different ways. It will no longer be straightforward to distinguish between work time and "free" time or between the space of production and the space of consumption. Ambiguous and contested zones will surely emerge. (Mitchell, 1995: 100-101)

Instabilities and ambiguities in the use of spaces equally defy the forms of ongoing social representation and distinction. In many societies there are separate spaces for different genders and age groups (architecturally defined for children, teenagers, adults and retirees). On the urban scale, social differences are made clear by the presence of several, easily-identified, domains: low-income housing projects, prisons, convents, orphanages, hospitals, official residences for politicians and religious leaders. However such categories lose their clarity when spaces depend on software and flow of bits. That is why Mitchell believes there will be a profound ideological significance in architectural recombinations that follow from electronic dissolution of traditional constructed spaces and their spatial and temporal patterns (Mitchell, 1995: 103).

Consequently, communication networks require and engender these new spaces. Buildings and their compartments now no longer relate only to the urban space, but to cyberspace. They should progressively work as the interfaces, enabling the traffic of bits. Equipped with sensors and with a given processing power, besides sophisticated internal communication capabilities, they should be reconfigurable and programmable for different usages. Mitchell suggests that, instead of the living room, we should have only "residential spaces" that can be programmed for work, education or entertainment. Instead of centralized schools and hospitals we can have specific systems that may be installed in different places – be it on an airplane seat or in distant rural communities. Theme parks, for instance, will turn into available and reprogrammable simulation networks. Therefore,

> rooms and buildings will henceforth be seen as sites where bits meet the body – where digital information is translated into visual, auditory, tactile, or otherwise perceptible form, and, conversely, where bodily actions are sensed and converted into digital information. (Mitchell, 1995: 105)

The task of building these reprogrammable places will not just involve the placement of wires on the walls. With the development of technologies, miniature computer devices will disappear into the structure of buildings and sensors will be present everywhere. "In the end, buildings will become computer interfaces and computer interfaces will become buildings" (Mitchell, 1995: 105).

The race to claim and inhabit this new space is open. For Mitchell we are entering an era where electronically-enhanced bodies live in intersections between the physical and the virtual worlds. This new condition is marked by the occupation and interaction provided by telepresence, by the mutant forms of architecture that emerge from the fragmentation and recombination, induced by telecommunications, of the traditional types, and by the emergence of virtual cities that correspond, complement and, in some cases, compete against concrete urban spaces. The task set for the twenty-first century is that of projecting the "*bitsphere*" – a worldwide, electronically-mediated environment, where networks are anywhere and where most available tools, from the global to the nanometric scale, have some degree of intelligence and some embodied communication capability. And this new environment "will overlay and eventually succeed the agricultural and industrial landscapes that humankind has inhabited for so long" (Mitchell, 1995: 167).

2.10 The ecstacity

Architect Nigel Coates, professor at the Royal College of Art in London, postulates a new manner of seeing architecture, in which architecture and city are relative to an experience. His book *Ecstacity* (Coates, 2003) proposes the resizing of the terms 'architecture' and 'city', where, more than presenting a project of city, he intends to have us experience it – experience would come before formal stylistics or functional qualities of buildings. In it, architecture – or its own broad version of it – is the vehicle for a looser and more open framework that stimulates the space in each of us.

Originality starts in the elaboration of the book, with its fragmented texts, horizontally and vertically formatted, and in different languages that blend with graphs, sketches, unusual photographs over drafts, drawings and glossaries in decrescent order. The lack of content hierarchy enables the reader himself to decide where to start the reading and, since this book is a guide to Ecstacity, there is the feeling that we are wandering around different spaces, so what follows is a review with fragments of the book.

The appreciation of the relation between experience (unusual, daily, historical, current, future and unpredictable) and architecture (planned, projected, functional) stands out in Nigel Coates' conception on the Ecstacity. What is intended is that architecture be open and may promote the experience in a relation where it produces and is affected by what happens. From this conception comes the challenge of thinking how location, identity, freedom, diversity and safety can live together.

In this context, the city is no longer thought of as simply the accumulation of buildings and services; it is thought of as a complex universe of interlocking worlds, from road markings to phone cells, from the Internet to surveillance networks. It is a cultural microcosm that "exports and imports data, moves money, exchanges cultures and ideas" (Coates, 2003: 147).

With the objective of placing the sensual side of all cities in the foreground, the six chapters of *Ecstacity* serve as a guide to experiencing a city, and through the involvement of the reader with the text, he (the reader) becomes the guide of this book explored as if it were a city.

Ecstacity is an imaginary place that uses fragments of seven cities around the world (Coates, 2003: 17) – London, Bombay, Tokyo, New York, Rio de Janeiro, Rome and Cairo. This concept of city is essentially global, multicultural and multidimensional. The resulting street plan of this fusion shows the mixture and the contiguity of streets of geographically very distant cities, as well as the unusual vicinity of architectural symbols, the same way that Copacabana beach washes unexpected places. The seven cities unite and reunite in a constant process of competition and synthesis, where the central point is its E-lasticity. The informational and the physical spaces are constantly materializing into one another.

For Coates, Ecstacity, far from being science fiction, is "a reading of the world we're in now" (Coates, 2003: 25). Through some questions – such as "Where is Ecstacity?" "What does it feel like to be there?", "Where does the city start and stop?", "How do you map desire?", "Does space equal money?", "Is there a body beneath the city?" – he starts his guide with a definition:

ECSTACITY: half-real and half-imaginary, Ecstacity builds on the increasingly global outlook of existing cities … it partners a fluid architecture of hybrids with the information world we already inhabit … it invests the everyday with conflations of scale, of story, of emotion, replacing institutional power with shared grounds of identity and desire … here, each of six[30] sections frame an experiential interface with the city … they coincide to ask the question 'what next for the city in the 21st century?' (Coates, 2003: 3)

Ecstacity relates to an experience where people are the starting point. Their activities interpenetrate and intertwine in the general tissue of the city. It is its inhabitants, not its buildings that grant meaning to it. Man-made environments allegedly allow people to project their own fantasies on them. Its context is not in local historical traditions, but in a wider global context that includes cinema, fiction and entertainment architecture. "The dark and glittering world of night clubs, a place where you can be anybody and anything seemingly can happen," (Coates, 2003: 25) is one of Coates' favorite references which translates the contemporary city as chaotic and dangerous, but also beautiful and exciting.

In Ecstacity, the spaces where we live, work and unfold over each other, hitting each other, performing a slow type of spatial copulation that ensure that no space is supreme or self-sufficient.

"Far from the need for the city to pacify us with a vocabulary of order and permanence," one "should push for visceral qualities in the environment. This is why, ebbing and flowing, Ecstacity's constructs switch between those of the physical city and the proto-architectural experiences it contains. It responds to a common need for contrasts, realities, stories and emotions," says Coates (2003: 42).

This mixture of structures of existing cities is a reference to the global merging of cities. Three essential elements are interrelated: "the geography (as map, infrastructure, matrix), the events (from roaming, drifting aimlessly in the city, to surviving) and the body (or bodies)." The instruments are the senses and their "cyborgian amplifiers" (Coates 2003: 271). Besides uniting the material of world cities, it uses vanguard ideas among urbanists, seeking to set off projects for differentiated, unpredictable lifestyles in particular spacing and timing (Coates, 2003: 33).

When considering the interrelation between experience and the city's physical infrastructure, the author suggests that the city can take on certain human characteristics and, conversely, humans can take on certain urban characteristics. The key to that is in the idea that the body is at the root of Ecstacity's feel for space – "not some idealized body, but yours and mine … invisibly, you carry your own initial architecture with you … challenging and matching the world you are part of … it's your most intimate space …" (Coates, 2003: 185). So, in a way, "there can no longer be the traditional difference between the world of objects and the spaces they populate;" the Italian difference between *mobile* (mobile) and *immobile* (buildings), that which moves and that which is still. One can call them, all of them, *ammobil* (Coates 2003: 237).

The urban medium in Ecstacity is neurological, interactive and responsive and, more than any other city, it maintains "a biological interface with its inhabitants" (Coates, 2003: 187). In order to experience that, it is necessary to undress, says Coates. Stripping back the protective layers one finds out how to confront the city in order to open the mind and the body, making it possible to live "the city as a psycho-sensual field." "A city is immersive" and the first space is the body, then the street, the car, someone else's arms (Coates, 2003:187, 191).

Discovering this architecture requires a leap from the rational reading of the city in order to explore it intuitively, allowing oneself to wander in it and experiencing its sensual condition, its scent, its sensations and aberrations, that is what can enable someone to explore its visceral condition. It is necessary to allow the city to affect us, to capture us. The buildings work as if they were inside our own body. They know the body's mechanisms and, in turn, the body's mechanisms know theirs. Just like the body, buildings have an alternation between desire and action and are aware, with the same intensity, of the looks of the outer world and those of the interiority. The lifestyle of Ecstacity's residents constantly plays with relations that connect the real and the imagined, the abject and the artificial. Hence a building is not only an idea, a metamorphosis captured at a moment. It really transforms itself (Coates, 2003: 245, 247, 335).

The functional identity of the inhabitants is taken so far as to the point that they turn into the very cities they serve. Within these pleasant and repetitive territories some places turn into specialized and sufficiently powerful conditions to irradiate their identities into the infinity of their surrounding world. Their risky collection of terminals, ramps, passageways, shops, chapels, temples, entertainment halls and movie theatres constitute a fractal simulation of Ecstacity. The limits of identities are being drastically widened, adding who one was to whom one is and will be. His entire past, his history, is being added to his present day. Desires and necessities in general are not all that is carried by the individual, but rather the wholeness of what he is.

While buildings and advertisements conspire in order to irradiate idealized messages of lifestyles, in the city people do things on their own. They are the advertisements. Nowadays you do not just choose your lifestyle, you create it. The odds of you making your own advertisements and regularly starring in them are high. "Now, sex, or at least euphemistic allusion to it, seems to play a part in everything," from advertisement to architecture. Looking at a city up close – its movement, imagery and voluptuous spirit included – we see that it wishes "to project an ethic of civility and humanity, profit and accessibility." The city is constantly trying to affect its inhabitants to the point that, in Ecstacity, flirting is celebrated as a quality that makes the city go round (Coates, 2003: 193).

Ecstacity often makes its inhabitants feel as if they had crossed from one territory to another, from one event to inside the other one. Being in two situations at once is all that best characterizes this relation. When one hybridizes the dynamic events of a building, the building becomes more subjective than objective, maybe leaving the impression of being in two places or two conditions at once, and that the stability of one single center was disturbed. Spaces conflate divided territories in order to lead them beyond their façades and to discover chaotic multilayered systems, causing a breakdown of conventional thresholds (Coates, 2003: 261, 159).

Due to the lack of institutional restraint, an event may slide to the other (Coates 2003, 349). You are always in two situations at once, or at least each of them contains the way to the other. Work and entertainment are no longer different things; Ecstacitizens work and have fun at the same time, even when asleep. Different forms of occupation are arranged through different sorts of space that are mixed together, hybridized, into a single form. Once together there are no reasons why they should not merge in order to create a coherent spatial organism that contains these dynamics. These are spaces merging and, more than that, copulating, discharging an erotic relation with people in and around them. Beyond the reach of institutional forces there is a strong possibility of intimate spatial mutations occurring. Throughout the entire city buildings and events are changing – the city does not work like a clock. There is a frenzy resulting from the overlapping cultures that are in perpetual state of amplification of their identities and in constant negotiation (Coates, 2003: 133).

As Einstein demonstrated, matter and energy are interchangeable, but the greatest part of architects seems to not have yet taken that into consideration. Buildings need to transform and reach a mode of dimension that performs the passage from matter to energy, from data to sensations (Coates, 2003: 367).

Coates reasons that we are coming to the point where architecture can go a step further. As part of a campaign for intimate dynamics we are learning to exaggerate the pleasure factor. "Architecture can expand its ontology in order to encompass the entire field of perception, not in the 2-D blueprint nor in the formal qualities of architecture as object, but as a field itself." (Coates, 2003: 421) It is time to orchestrate spaces in a way that they reflect the multiplicity of life itself, in which the two primary means are the body and the city.

Although restrained by being mapped out in print, Ecstacity offers itself as a dynamical paradigm capable of embracing each of its multi-various inhabitants, each one able to act as both stimulator and respondent (Coates, 2003:43). A chameleon-like city where transformation, movements, sensorial experience and elasticity mix together, not differentiating Ecstacitizen and city.

2.11 Other concepts of city

Besides the above-mentioned concepts, several others could still be presented. That of city of control, for instance, conceived by Michael Hardt and Antonio Negri (Hardt and Negri, 2001: 318) as the city that concentrates specialized production services, financial services and the centralization of administration, planning and production control.

Digital city is that inhabited by tele-workers and by tele-communities who use information and technological communication to work and communicate over distance. This city is provided with fiber optic cables that enable enormous speed on the Internet. Since it is formed by a system of virtual spaces interconnected by the expansion of the information superhighway, it cannot be defined by conventional administrative or geographic parameters often employed to identify the physical limits of the city. As examples of the composition of the digital city we can mention non-spatial communities of immaterial nature: virtual interactive discussion groups, 24-hour bank network, digital network of work and information supply over distance, etc.

The 24/7/365 city indicates world cities such as London where social, cultural and economic activities take place 24 hours per day, 7 days per week, 365 days per year. In a city like that there is no time off, no certain day to rest and no seasonal shifts or use cycles.

Instant city, in turn, is the one that is formed by the temporary gathering of people at a particular place, at a determined moment and for an event of common interest. Examples of instant cities include thousands of delegates who perform at the World Economic Forum in Davos, Switzerland, every year, or the gathering of thousands of people at *Rock In Rio*, the "City of Rock". If we consider a technological space, non-geographic, but rather a broadcasting time, this city exists for the length of time of the gathering correspondent to the electronic transmission of a great event. There is an instant city, for example, when one billion people are gathered around the final broadcast of the World Cup. Instant cities have a limited time and specific space to happen; these are established in several ways. Therefore they may vary considerably; some may be exclusive and insular, others may be inclusive and open;

Sustainable city is that considered to be economically vibrant, socially just and ecologically viable. The term often includes the notions of justice and equality and requires that the present demands be fulfilled without compromising the fulfillment of the needs of future generations. In opposition to that, Dystopia city refers to the uncontrollable agglomeration of urban poverty, social chaos, crime, pollution, homeless population, mendicancy and other forms of deprivation. It would be the equivalent to the underworld of the global city, where under-education, under-location and the precarious living and working conditions aggravate the marginal condition in contrast to the growing fortune of a few.

In short, there are as many concepts as there are understandings and visions of the contemporary world. Each of them tries to deal with the specificities generated by the change of paradigm of a concept that is, certainly, not restricted to geography, geometry or to chronological time and that is definitely in question. An appropriate moment to present our proposal.

Chapter 3

Urbanism In Fluid State

Photo montage: Isadora Dantas

Even before speaking about architecture, let us think about building a vision of the
world, of time, of immediateness, of ubiquity, of instantaneousness … It is necessary to
give dynamism to architecture, fluids and non-solids. It is necessary to understand that
the solid, as *state*, is over just like the mass, we are now in the age of fluids dynamics…
(Virilio, 2001: 7)

The title of this chapter references Solà-Morales' concept of contemporary
architecture and has as its guiding principle the model text where we find the
statement "a liquid architecture … will be that which replaces firmness by
fluidity and the primacy of space by the primacy of time" (Solà-Morales, 2002: 127),
which may be applied to urbanism. Moreover the "need for place design to address the
unprecedented *spatial fluidity* we now have to perform day-to-day activities anywhere
and at anytime" (Horan in Castells, 2003: 195, our italics) is already acknowledged. This
fluidity, as opposed to the Vitruvian principle of permanence, indicates the necessity of
the huge malleability that space planners need to consider for the inclusion of the new
articulations that maybe universal mobility demands.

Due to the nature of modern communication techniques, displacements multiply,
elongate, representing a relative form of autonomy for inhabitants regarding their actions
in urban space. This allows them to organize their existence according to more personal
temporalities and spatialities. Comparatively, we can say that, just as in the Neolithic
agricultural revolution new relations between people and places of production were
established, and in the Industrial Revolution between people and machines, in the global
digital world we will reconstitute "relations of people and information". This will certainly
be the "enabler of new social constructions and urban patterns" (Mitchell, 2001: 19).

The references that sustain the concept of city are being questioned, without it being
possible to create a definition of city regarding the hegemony of any one of its constituent
elements. Organization of production, consumption, reproduction, transmission,
experience and power – in other words, in all areas where human activities are
concerned – is subverted by the codes forged by the New Technologies of Information
and Communication. In the 1960s, McLuhan had already announced the change of
paradigm when he said that man "in the electric age returned physically and socially to
the nomad state … But it is global, and it ignores and replaces the form of the city which
has, therefore, tended to become obsolete" (McLuhan, 2006[1964]: 385–86).

The spatial geographic location (cities, companies, governments, dwellings) is relativized by the space of flows that imposes a logic that suspends the priority of physical contiguity in the dynamics of exchanges. Global cities, for instance, perform an active role of centrality in world economy. However there is no longer an immediate relation between this "centrality" and geographic entities such as the financial "center" or "district" because electronic connectivity allows the network of transactions to circulate regardless of the physical location of companies and business centers. That is why the city as *metapolis* is fundamentally a "space of mobility" where hierarchies of exchanges are dynamic. What matters is its capability of generating knowledge and processing information, and these being shared on networks.[31]

The same technological act that relativizes spatial proximities and establishes new, more intangible, bonds also subverts the temporality regime, which generates the disappearance of the uniformity and homogeneity allegedly existent between physical displacement and chronological time. The level of technological accessibility dilutes temporal succession, undoing the proportion relation between "traveled" space and the chronometry of "before" and "after". That way, after understanding the concepts of "timeless time"[32] and "local time"[33], we could think that time is "casuistic", where it could only be defined one case at a time according to a thorough examination of the accessibility level of the person concerned. One space accommodates different temporal overlays, at the same moment different spaces become present; the several temporalities of urban life are no longer clearly separated because many activities may develop at the same time, all in a similar imbricated reality: behold the contemporary city.

3.1 Brief introduction to topology

The 'topologization' of life. (Virilio, 2001: 7)

In the eighteenth century, Swiss mathematician Leonhard Euler (1707–1783), while dedicating himself to the study of polyhedrons, made a decisive contribution to the constitution of the mathematical field that would be known as topology (it was named so in 1836, but this denomination was only fully used in the twentieth century) (Pont, 1974: 2). Euler inserts himself in a mathematical tradition that, dating back to Leibniz, speculated about the demand and possibility of a geometry that would directly express relations of place in the same way that algebra expressed magnitudes. These are, by the way, the terms in which Leibniz, in a letter to Huygens written in 1679, made the following comment:

After all the progress I have made on these matters, I am not yet satisfied with algebra, due to the fact that it offers neither the shortest ways nor the most beautiful constructions in geometry. This is the reason why I believe it to be necessary to use yet another properly geometric or linear analysis that expresses to us the *situm* directly, as algebra expresses *magnitudinem* (Pont, 1974: 2).

Searching for this new algebra or new geometry, Leibniz uses the expression *analysis situs* – which would last until the twentieth century – even if, probably, he had never knew of the science known by that name (Pont, 1974: 2).

From Euler onwards the properly topological problem of reciprocal situations of places starts to be outlined more clearly and the persistence regarding the nature of the problem is visible in the work of the mathematicians who, in sequence, dealt with it. For Euler,

besides this part of geometry that deals with the magnitudes and which was, for a long time, cultivated with great zeal, there is another, unknown until this day, to which Leibniz made the first reference and called geometry of position. According to him, this part of geometry devotes itself to determining the position and to searching the properties that result from this position. In this work magnitudes are not necessary, nor calculating them[34] (Pont, 1974: 14–15).

Almost one century later, the then young German mathematician Johann Benedikt Listing (1808–1882), writing to a friend, speaks for the first time of "topology", to indicate a field of mathematical investigation that no longer fell under the laws of composition of known geometry. Listing says:

Leibniz defined this science as the study of connection and of the reciprocal situation of bodies in space, regardless of the relations of magnitude, that depend on geometry; he named it *analysis situs*. However, since the term geometry cannot decently characterize a science from which the notions of measure and extent are excluded; since, besides that, the denomination geometry of position has already been given to another discipline and, given that ultimately our science does not yet exist, I will use a name that seems convenient to me, topology. (Quoted in Pont, 1974: 42).

Farther on he says: "A definition of topology could be: study of the qualitative laws of the relations of place, susceptible science, of this I have a deep certainty, of an exact research method" (in Pont, 1974: 42).

However, who conceived, in a consequent manner, the notion of topological space and gave it an autonomous theory was Bernhard Riemann (1826–1866) (Bourbaki, 1984: 175). Thinking about the foundations of geometry, Riemann indicates that

under this name [*analysis situs*], which was used by Leibniz, although perhaps with a somewhat different meaning, it is in order to include that part of the theory of continuous quantities which studies these quantities not as independent of their position and measurable one by means of the other, but in abstracting every idea of measurement and studying solely their relationships of position and inclusion (Bourbaki, 1984: 176).

We can then say, in a simplified manner, that the topological transformation of a figure is a transformation made without rupture: filling a chamber with air is deforming it topologically (at least for the time that precedes the burst); stretching a rubber band, regardless of its final shape, is to produce a topological deformation. It is humorously said "that a topologist is a mathematician who cannot differentiate a lifebuoy from a cup of coffee" (Pont, 1974: 1).

The joke is not without reason because, with topology, we move away from the model supplied by Euclidian space and move on to working within the perspective of positions and properties thence resulting, without considering the Euclidian demand for determination of magnitudes and calculation of quantities, for the ideality and rigidity of the forms and of the system's bipolarities (inside/outside, left/right, etc.) that remain insurmountable, except if we attack it in its laws of composition (Magno, 2004: 55–80).[35]

Thus, topological space suspends the rigid dualist and idealist logic of Euclidian space because it concretely studies the qualitative aspects of spatial forms or of its laws of connection, attentive to the mutual position of forms, the order of their parts, their correlation and composition. This new mentality, in mathematics and elsewhere, opened, in the twentieth century, a rich field of investigation, application and metaphorization, when making available increasingly more abstract reasonings – in the sense of being broad, refined and inclusive, and not in the retrogressive sense of Euclidian ideality – of unilaterality, affinity, inclusion, transformation and passage.[36]

3.2 A form that creates its permanent mutation

> Frederick Kiesler understood quite well – for him, somewhere, the Moebius Band and the Klein Bottle were the model of the architecture of the future – ... Wright was inspired by it for the Guggenheim museum. Wright also dedicated himself to dissolving ruled surfaces. (Virilio: 2001, 7)

Out of the three classical defining concepts of architecture[37] – usefulness, firmness and beauty – firmness is the one that most clearly expresses the material characteristics of this field of production and study (Solà-Morales, 2002: 125). It concerns physical consistency, stability and permanence that defy time and build concrete and tangible spaces.

The laws that govern this tangible space and its tectonics are in accordance with the gravitational force and with the plane and three-dimensional Euclidian logics. For a long time, stability and permanence were key specifying notions of the field of architecture, signaling its "physically consistent, constructively solid and space-delimiting material condition", that made architecture, for 25 years, "a knowledge and a technique connected to permanence" (Solà-Morales, 2002: 126).

The reversion of these principles is the foundation of the contemporary thinking about the city, its definitions and functions – thus the importance, to our work, of Ignasi Solà-Morales' proposition of a liquid or fluid architecture, compatible with the functionality of the Moebius band. Let us see of what this proposition consists and how, from then on, we can articulate the idea of "urbanism in fluid state".

Change and transformation are fundamental characteristics of contemporary culture. Therefore a "materially liquid architecture" is concerned about granting configuration not to stability, but rather to the moving fluidity of reality. Its main focus turns towards the

> fluid, changing forms, capable of incorporating, of physically being present, not with the stable, but rather with the mutable, not seeking a fix and permanent definition of space, but giving physical form to time, to an experience of durability in change that is completely different from the challenge of time that characterized the classical mode of operation (Solà-Morales, 2002: 126).

A *liquid architecture* represents a system that is not limited to a configuration, but where "space and time are simultaneously present as open, multiple, non-reducible categories, organizers of this openness and multiplicity" (Solà-Morales, 2002: 130). So, transposing this reasoning to urbanism, "urban" is constituted today through the multiplicity of the experience of spaces and time, establishing itself on the continuity and on communication between things. Stationary spaces dilate due to the cohabitation of multiple functionalities; measurable time turn into flows, with their different and shared rhythms. Thus the demand for inclusive categories of analysis that include change, continuity and diversity in their dynamism.

In short, we understand fluid and changing forms in urbanism in the sense of space which, as material support for social practices, may continuously change through the flexibility of its use, the simultaneousness of its usages and meanings, the overlaying of information. This malleability of transformation, frailty and transience, grant contemporary urban space its fluid, moving and undistinguishing character.

Thus, the metaphor of the Moebius band interests us exactly because it allows the construction of logical reasoning compatible with this demand. When we compare this mathematical object and its properties to those built by the logic of Euclidian geometry, the characteristics of mutation, mobility and flow, typical of the contemporary city, become evident by analogy.

A band, or Moebius band, is a mathematical object conceived by conceptual tools of topology. Its characteristics escape the determinations of Euclidian geometric space. In the latter we are rigidly located in a system of bilateralism and opposition (external vs internal; right side vs left side), without communication or passage between spots locatable on opposite sides of a surface thus constructed. By correctly manipulating a cylinder[38], for instance, we see that it is a bilateral surface where there is no continuity or passage between the sides (internal vs external), except if, for example, we were to attack this surface by puncturing a hole, which would immediately disfigure the mathematical object.

A topological object such as the Moebius band follows another logical principle, where unilateralism replaces bilateralism, dissolving the Euclidian opposition between sides. How does this happen? We can concretely build a Moebius band (see drawing below) by taking a strip which, instead of being encircled so as to obtain an Euclidian cylinder, suffers a torsion of 180 degrees. We obtain an object that has only *one* surface or side on which we can travel *continuously*. On this unilateral surface we can randomly mark a spot and, running the length of the strip we will observe that, before reaching the starting point, it turns "inside out". The reasoning that interests us is that we have a *unilateral* surface that bears the inscription of positions that reciprocally turn into one another, in continuity, in such a way that the oppositions disappear.

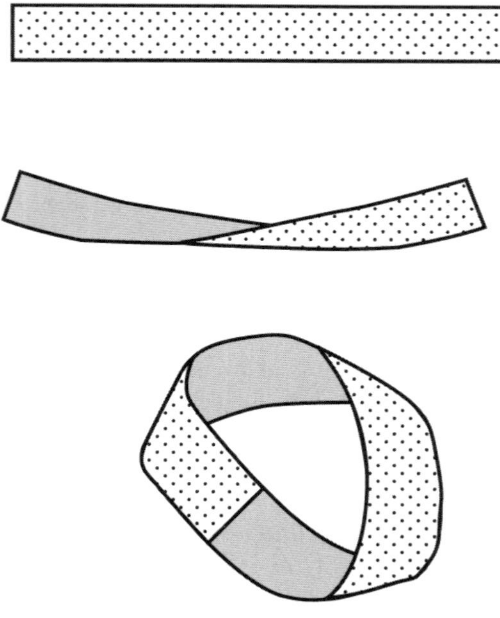

Moebius Band[39]

The proposition of "urbanism in fluid state" considers, in analogy with the Moebius band, the equivocation of usages and functions which are so evident in the contemporary city. Therefore it may include the flexibility or change without ruptures that takes place in everyday events, made evident by the concepts we developed in the previous chapter and at the beginning of this one. It therefore enables the comprehension of permeability between concepts that were once considered antagonistic or different and that are, currently, relativized due to the use of space, employment of technologies, inclusion of speed as determining factor of distance, hypermobility of goods, people and information, ubiquity generated by communication over distance, be it in real time or not. Among many others, we may stress the following concepts: public and private space, inside and outside, near and far, global and local, residence and work, real and virtual, person and city. Consequently, urban forms enclose multifunctionality, polymorphism, passage and reversibility.

The notion of the "network society" is a good example of this. The contemporary city may be considered the topological space, electronically built, which reconfigures itself as technology introduces, assimilates and changes forms and functions (new and old) in a virtually infinite reach. The nodes that form the network that the city is have their performance assessed according to their capacity, larger or smaller, of absorbing relevant information and processing it efficiently. Once redundant and useless, those nodes may be deleted or absorbed into new nodes. What is important is the network's power of performance, which tends to reconfigure itself as the function of the dynamics of its constituent nodes, which only exist and work as its components. Thus, "the network is the unit, not the node" (Castells, 2004: 3).

We know that the notion of "network" is not restricted to the twenty-first century world. Human organizations depend on and design themselves through networks of exchange and communication which they are capable of creating. For François Ascher, for instance, the growth of the cities was the historical correspondent to the development of means and techniques of transportation and storage of goods necessary to supplying increasingly numerous populations, of information necessary to the organization and division of work and trading, and of people, busy with techniques of construction, urban governance of flows and wages, protection and control (Ascher, 2001; Castells, 2003: 7). Considering the technologies available at each time and place, the connectivity each group was capable of creating brought a larger or smaller displacement capability, access to material resources and knowledge that transcended the limits of each delimited location.

The qualitative leap that takes place in the second half of the twentieth century freed connectivity from material limits thanks to technologies with sufficient liquefaction capability in order to install a highly flexible, adaptable and self-reconfigurable communication regime (Castells, 2003: 5). The topological nature of electronic communication is fully exhibited by the contemporary capacity of continuous flow of interactive information, and in several directions. Today we constitute a network society whose specificity is the extension "and augmentation of the body and mind of human subjects in networks of interaction powered by microelectronics-based, software-operated, communication technologies" (Castells, 2004: 7), to which, added the genetic engineering technologies, make available a complex system of decoding and recoding of the living matter.

Likewise, wireless connections and portable access devices create "continuous fields of presence that may extend throughout buildings, outdoors, and into public space as well as private" (Mitchell in Castells, 2004: 11). This also denotes the asynchronous character of communication because it is not necessary to coincide time or space in order for it to take place. An example of such a situation is mobile telework as a work model that is settling in. This model considers the worker to be a nomad who performs his tasks through contact with his office, via cell phone, internet, fax, while on the move, visiting his clients or on his regular way, thus establishing the concept of "office on the run" (Castells, 2003, 192). This example is particularly interesting because it shows the qualitative character of transformations, where we clearly have a situation in which the displacement of locations, of functions, takes place simultaneously to the displacement of people. This takes us to a more detailed reflection of this contemporary phenomenon in which people and places merge, where there is no distance between habitat and inhabitant – this is an important reasoning for the comprehension of our work – where each one will define himself, one case at a time, according to connections and articulations in question at every moment.

3.3 The twenty-first century *Orbanism*

In the contemporary world, being urban is being connected (Araujo, 2001: 113), not only in the informational sense, but in the broad sense of all possibilities and uses of available connections. In this context, instead of citizen or townsman, the most appropriate is to retrieve the old concept of *cosmopolitan*, "citizen of the world" (Araujo, 2001: 113). The events of material, personal, mental and financial exchanges, of the establishment of social connections, of social, political and economic insertion will take place through the interface generated by mental, social, personal availability and also through the equipment available. As the city is the place of these events we can say it will be wherever the cosmopolitan will be. Therefore the twenty-first century urbanism would transmute into *orbanism*[40], where, given that we would no longer have borders or limitations as reference, we would treat as city not only the world but also the known and yet to be known universe (Araujo, 2001: 114).

Some authors, in different fields of knowledge, already point to this direction. For instance, Derrick de Kerckhove, director of the McLuhan Institute of Technology and professor at the University of Toronto, affirms that in the informational context in which we live, architecture and urban planning will start to be thought in terms of communication accessibility and not just in terms of road and water infrastructure (Kerckhove, 1997). To give sense to what he means, he produces a new terminology and affirms that the work of the *cybertect*[41] is to create trustworthy routes and useful environments in cyberspace and between cyberspace and the real space (Kerckhove, 2000: 70). We can then add that we are talking about *cybertecture*, which is the conception of an architecture in which the tools and questions at stake are immersed in the new technological and digital environment that we are starting to inhabit. It is not the world that is globalizing, it is us. Cyberculture implies "seeing through" matter, space and time with our informational techniques. Technology enables us to have physical access and displacement to distant regions, creating a situation where we are contained in the global sphere. When we think globally, communicate and trade from the place which we occupy, we include the global sphere internally: "we contain the earth in our minds and in our networks" (Kerckhove, 1997: 193).

Ignasi de Solà-Morales supports the thesis that our civilization has abandoned the stability of the past and taken on the dynamism of energies that configure our surroundings. Therefore, our culture prioritizes the exchange, the transformation and the processes established through time, which changes the way of being of things and makes us consider fluid forms. As we have already mentioned, this means that the replacement of firmness by fluidity and the primacy of space by the primacy of time will constitute a *fluid architecture* as a system of events where space and time are simultaneously present as open and multiple categories. This *liquid, fluid architecture* "is the result of a fold over itself, a chance from the inside of a Moebius band where it is not possible to escape the form that creates its own permanent flotation" (Solà-Morales, 2002: 134).

These and other concepts used in contemporary urbanism seek to take care of questions presently arising. Whether we like it or not, the point of view and the references are changing. It is therefore necessary to situate what is city within the new perspective that has settled on the world.

According to Manuel Castells, we are at a stage where culture – after we have superseded nature to the point where we force ourselves to artificially preserve it as a cultural form – referring, above all, to culture itself. In this sense, when we have reached a level of wisdom and social organization that leads us to live in a predominantly social world, history would be starting and not ending, as some authors at the end of the twentieth century would have us believe. We are, rather, at the beginning of a new age, whose "central technology of our time, communication technology … relates to the heart of the specificity of the human species: conscious, meaningful communication" (Castells, 2004: 6).

We can therefore speculate that we are immersed in a comparatively new context of existence. A new mankind is about to be built and it will represent, consequently, a new society and a new conception of the city. A new mapping, no longer geographic, is constituting cities and the ongoing relationship and exchange bases. Therefore, using Rem Koolhaas' indications that the new urbanism should place "uncertainty" in the scene and be capable of reinventing the "psychological space", our research proposes an intentional displacement, where the approach moves from the geometrical, geographic and infrastructural urban issues towards a broader, more generalizing approach on one hand, and more particularized one on the other, towards the concept of city.

Our understanding is that a Person's connections define the world and the city the Person is. Therefore the equivalence City = Me is suitable. However, in order to establish this equivalence, it is necessary to present a concept of Me compatible with this statement. This will be the objective of chapter 5. However, before we move directly to the concept of "I" that interests this study, we will try to show, in chapter 4, the understanding of "I", referring to Descartes, Kant and Freud, as well as Bertallanfy's General Systems Theory, Maturana and Varela's autopoietic system, the rhizomatic thinking of Deleuze and Gattari, Lévy's cognitive ecology and the complex networks of Barabási and others.

Chapter 4

Reconceptualizing *I*

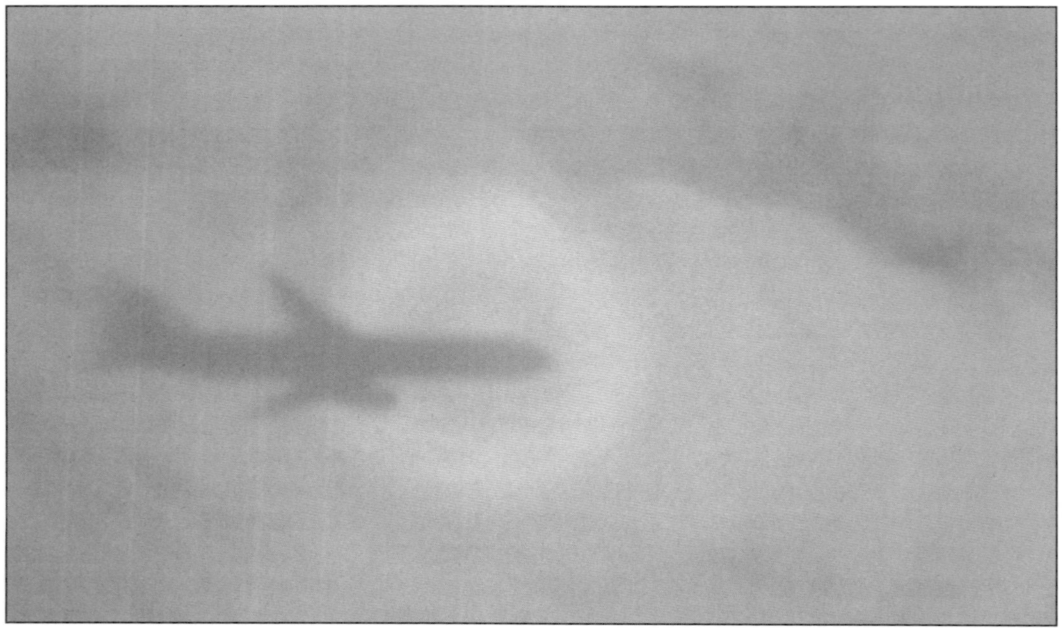

Photo: Rosane Araujo, 2011

It is I, a thinking universe of flesh and bone, wishing to pass.
(Pessoa, 1983: 67 *Saudação a Walt Whitman* [Greeting to Walt Whitman])

Each way of thinking expresses an epoch. However, just as Rossi pointed out that "[t]he form of the city is always the form of a particular time of the city, but there are many times in the formation of the city" (Rossi, 1995: 57), there coexists, simultaneously, several visions and understandings of the world, of man, of life. And that is particularly true at a time of change like ours, when we watch the constant reformulation of the very understanding of what is human[42], as well as the new ways of being, existing, living and thinking.

In this chapter we will talk about the settling of the modern notion of the subject[43] (seventeenth century) – understood as the foundation of the action and knowledge, and the identification of this notion with that of "I" – which lasted three centuries. This means that during this period we have the consolidation of modern thinking and all the corollaries thence resulting, such as: the idea of *I* as reference center; the idea of identity; the idea of knowledge as relation between subject and object; the separation between subject and object, etc.

We will also show the separation of the identity of the concept of *I* from the concept of the subject, which takes place with Freud in the end of the nineteenth century, and the dissolution of the concept of the subject and the transformation of the concept of *I*, which becomes the result of the complexity of unconscious determination.

From then on we will see some thoughts that present reasoning which are centerless and without fixed points of reference; the dissolution of any supposed separation between subject and object; that knowledge is produced by several instances and is not guaranteed by any divine instance or by a subject; inclusive, relativizing reasoning which take into consideration risk, uncertainty, etc. Rather than being restricted to a specific concept, when we articulate this concept, we articulate a certain way of world understanding that has considerable consequence for all fields of thought.

It is necessary to emphasize that this chapter that contains some important authors' books' reviews, does not have the pretension of delving deeper into the work of the relevant theorists, this is not our focus, but, rather, using the concepts as a passageway, almost a generic filing of the questions. Our specific goal is to show a certain relativization of the concept of *I*, as well as some reasoning that present a broadened and complex way of thinking which, when applied to the urban, helps us to understand the complexity of the concept of the city today, and the need for conceptual formulations increasingly more consentaneous with our times.

4.1 René Descartes

4.1.1 Cartesian Philosophy and the foundation issue

Philosopher and mathematician René Descartes (1596–1650) is acknowledged as one of the main authors of modern rationalism. His contribution to philosophy is essential due to the effort in establishing the true bases of knowledge, the introduction to the concept of subjectivity, source for the philosophical, political and judicial thinking of modernity. As mathematician he conceived the coordinate system, which was fundamental for the development of modern calculus. He conceived a philosophy in which mind and body are distinct realities: the mind as "mental substance" (*res cogitans*) and the matter as "corporeal substance" (*res extensa*).

Philosophy seeks to know what are the principles, or the Principle, that is in the essence of everything; a principle, whatever it is, that will contain the means to explain everything that happens. It is worth saying that, beyond knowledge, in order to explain it one seeks its founding principle in a universal and *a priori* way. This foundation, this "beyond", is thought by philosophy according to the concept of "being", regarding the demands of unit, identity, permanence, that is, the separation between accidental and substantial, between provisory and permanent.

Without method there is no true knowledge, and the main task of Cartesian philosophy is to grant order to the act of knowing, finding its foundation and, therefore, its validity. Three points summarize this method: (1) the alleged suspension of all certainties and knowledge; (2) the search for an absolutely certain principle; (3) the apprehension of the subject as the correct foundation. Therefore, the unique case that makes Descartes' philosophy innovatory is exactly the radicalization of the issue of foundation, as it questions the validity of the very foundation and the proposition of the subject as principle. The subject, conceived as author and center of all valid acts of knowledge, of all thinking activity, is allegedly the indubitable principle of philosophy, the criterion from which other truths can be constituted.

4.1.2 Subject as foundation: *I*-substance

Descartes' method needs a foundation, an indubitable starting point[44]. Descartes finds this foundation in the certainty of the "I think". This is the discovery of the *cogito* which resists doubt and becomes the first experience of certainty.

The substantialist presupposition, of Aristotelian background, is indispensable in order to demonstrate the *cogito*, without interruption of the Aristotelian logical-linguistic apparatus and *sine qua non* condition for the emergence of the concept of subject, such as it was established by modernity. Likewise, the three conceptual elements of *cogito* – hyperbolical doubt, consciousness and the reflexivity of consciousness – are also established by Aristotelian thinking. The suspensive power of hyperbolical doubt gives in before the presupposition of the existence of thought; the acts of thinking become acts of a subject: "I think"; and the reflexive operation stops being exposition in order to involve an alleged "self", ultimate essence of the thought.

In Aristotle the category of substance[45] has two meanings: substratum (*sub*) of the phenomena which would be, at the level of the being, the ultimate reality; and the permanent unit of this substratum (*stare*) which supports all characteristics of a thing. For every change it is necessary to assume "something" that does not change, relating to which the change may be identified – *hypokeimenon* (substratum) in Greek, *subjectu* (thrown underneath) in Latin. Therefore we have a principle of permanence that overlaps physical, logical and metaphysical demands. What is real to Aristotle is made of substances, subjects of each and every predication, exactly because they are supports of the attributes or qualities. The progressive assimilation of the several meanings of the term subject, turning into a necessary reference for different domains is noticed ever since Aristotle. In grammar, for instance, there is the subject/verb relation. In logics, subject is the instance upon which the function of predication is applied, whereas in philosophy subject is the being endowed with the qualities, the essence or the foundation of what is.

With Descartes the substantialized subject expressed in *cogito* is subject of the knowledge, *res cogitans*[46]. Among the consequences of this identification, stands out the need to attribute to the subject logical and ontological anteriority in relation to the object the conceptual mark of modern idealism. From Greek *hypokeimenon* to modern *subjectu*, the "substance whose essence or nature is only thinking"[47] individualizes itself in an "I" (*ego*), converted into ontological criterion, identified to the subject of the acts of thinking, author of these thoughts.

According to Descartes, a thought is a property; therefore, there is a substance to which this property belongs: "I". What supposedly allows Descartes to use the pronoun "I" is not only a grammatical convenience, but also the double belief that every act of thought supposes a subject and that every subject exists, substantially, as such.

4.1.3 Subject as a first-person consciousness

Descartes announces modern individualism[48] when he states "I am, I exist". It is not a matter of particular individuals, but specifically of the thinking subject, considered as sole certain reality. Therefore, Cartesian individualism expresses itself in the proposition of *cogito*, defined as act of thought performed by an individual, *ego cogitans*, radically independent, separated from other existences, such as the body, other minds or other individuals. Besides that, all thoughts of this subject are essentially determined by properties of this mental substance, besides being immediately accessible only to the subject of these thoughts. The subjectivity that is stated is that of the thinking individual, understood as independent substance, indivisible and irreducible.

However, the notion of subject will only appear completely when this individual is thought as capable of being "conscious of his thoughts". This step implicates the acceptance of two presuppositions. The first supposition defends that the reference to oneself is always exercised in the first person and that "I" is considered as instance or homogeneous mental unit, capable of immediate transparency towards itself. The second presupposition asserts the identity between thought and consciousness. From the conjunction of these two presuppositions rises the concept of *self consciousness*. The Cartesian *cogito* expresses the state of consciousness of he who says "I think", a state which, for Descartes is, necessarily, an act of a conscious being – to think about itself in the first person.

The indubitable statement "I think" is the consciousness which someone has of being subject of his acts of consciousness; that is, being conscious of something is to be conscious that oneself is conscious of something. All our ideas are related to the "I" who thinks and this is the proof of existence of he who experiences in "himself" these ideas.

4.1.4 Subject of reflection

The Cartesian intention is to make reflection an operation that belongs to consciousness, capable of establishing its unit as subject. The act of reflection on consciousness is not different from the very consciousness he realizes, nor, therefore, from the thought itself. The idea that guides this description is that the reflection consists of the movement that makes the thought coincide with the subject of the thought, for the reflection is the consciousness of the very act of thinking.

The Cartesian subject – substantialized in its existence, taken as first person – determines that reflection be an operation of self-reference, for reflexivity of thought constitutes the thought as its own reference. This circular movement defines, from then on, the operation of reflection.

4.1.5 The Cartesian I: *I-subject*

Cartesian rationalism joined with Aristotelian substantialism in order to originate the modern notion of subject understood as foundation of the action and of knowledge. Therefore, in Descartes, the modern constitution of the subject is the key to equate fundamental questions for modernity, such as the unit of man and his autonomy. But this subject, apparently abstract and disconnected from corporeity and from the experience, becomes concrete and gains content when it is identified to the individual "I". This radical and substantialist individualism, as affirmation of the mental substance (*res cogitans*) in the first person (*ego cogitans*), characterized modern idealism.

For Cartesian philosophy the notion of *I* is summoned to grant reality to the new conception of subjectivity that emerges. With that, we observe the overlapping of the notion of *I* to that of subject. The substantialist interpretation of the thought (*res cogitans*) binds to the statement of this mental substance's individuality: "I" becomes individual substance entirely isolated from other substances or *I's*.

Here we see the thesis of the *mental-I* and of the *I-substance*. However it is necessary to attribute to this *I* other determinations and this second moment corresponds to the interpretation of the substance as individuality: *I-individual*. Besides being an individual substance, the *I*, in order to be recognized as subject and author of its ideas, acquires an identity because the substantial *I* is reputedly identical to itself. This reflection operation supposes there is in the self-reference the possibility of founding an absolute and permanent identity of *I*: the *I-reflexive* leads to the *I-identical to itself*, transparent to itself in its mental existence. These progressive determinations that the concept of *subject* in Descartes involves are the steps, not always explicit, that enabled the emergence of the subjectivity problem in modernity.

4.2 Immanuel Kant

German philosopher Immanuel Kant (1724–1804) was the main reference for western philosophy and thought from the eighteenth century onwards. Prominent representant of Illuminism[49], his project followed the lines drawn by Descartes with his theory of knowledge and his ambition for foundations. Kantian philosophy starts with the question about the possibility of science, with the objective of establishing for philosophy the same scientific status that Euclides' geometry and Newton's physics had. With that purpose, he proposes a new way of thinking in philosophy, analogous to that which granted mathematics and physics their status of science, capable "to determine all pure *a priori* cognition".[50]

This issue unfolds in three moments: (1) establishing the existence of *a priori* principles, which are in the base of pure mathematics and of pure science of nature, physics; (2) showing that these *a priori* principles are the enabling conditions (necessary and universal) of each and every knowledge; and (3) showing that these conditions are referred and conditioned by the subjective unit of consciousness (transcendental subject) that enables the knowledge of objects in general. That way modernity assumes more definite contours with Kantian philosophy, once it radicalizes the Cartesian principle of subjectivity, consolidating the fundamental value attributed to the concept of subject. The idealist position[51] will be assimilated and developed by Kant, resulting in his *transcendental idealism*.

4.2.1 The Copernican revolution and the critical project

Kant compares his philosophic project to the inversion performed by Copernicus in astronomy, when he makes the Earth revolve around the Sun. There are two senses for this analogy. In the first, in the context of a theory of knowledge, *revolution* means to understand the process of knowledge, no longer regarding the nature of the object, but rather regarding the subject's power of cognition. For Kant, it is about excluding any reference to Aristotelian realism, according to which knowledge results from the correspondence of the thought to the nature of things. For Aristotle, concepts reproduce the inherent structure of the object[52] itself and the knowledge should come from the given reality of things in order to establish universal definitions. For this reason the concept is defined as *representation of things* (Cassirer, 1977: 18).

The first step towards modern inversion regarding this conception, as we have seen, was taken by Descartes. Representations are, above all, *mental acts of a subject*. The priority of the subject in relation to the object is, therefore, the remarkable trait of modern philosophy. However, Cartesian philosophy still evaluates human knowledge in reference to the model of knowledge performed by absolute and divine[53] thinking.

The modernity of Kantian thinking proposes that knowledge be a strictly human and subjective representation, independent from any order previous to it, for it has its own organization that ensures legitimacy in all spheres of its existence: cognitive, moral or political. The Copernican revolution announced by Kant results, therefore, in the *autonomization* of the subject, possible only if it considers itself as law of its operations. Therefore the fundamental point of this new model is the consideration of the structure of the mind as source of the conditions necessary to knowledge. In Descartes, subjectivity is not understood as activity that constitutes the object it knows; differently, it regards thinking the subject as thing (*res cogitans*): "I think" is "I-substance". For Kant the issue will be exactly that of "subjectivity", because it considers the subject itself as the condition necessary to knowledge in general.

We have seen that, with Descartes, the subject is the modern name of the philosophical project; its function is to be the foundation capable of leveraging philosophy and subsuming all other regions of human activity, including, above all, modern science. But it is only with Kant that the subject takes on, in fact, this ambitious function, because it is up to the subject to legislate over the theoretical and practical spheres, in other words, to establish limits for human reason and to arbitrate on its legitimate and illegitimate use. It is about subordinating science to philosophy – which, according to Kant, lies on the plane of *a priori* and necessary cognitions – for the validation of any sort of knowledge.

4.2.2 The Kantian transcendental subject

Kant will analyze the basic structures of knowledge according to the equivalence between judging and knowing, but it will also be from judgement that he will conceive the concept of the transcendental subject. In general, judgement is defined, ever since Aristotle, as logical function that attributes and relates a predicate to a subject, determining, for instance, what quality belongs to an object. In this sense, the basic structure of judgement is understood regarding the grammatical form proposed in the subject-predicate relation. However, the question enclosed in the "Copernican revolution" – whether subject itself can determine the knowledge without subordination to the experience (hence the *a priori* judgement) – takes a qualitative leap in relation to the classical logics and to the precedent theories of knowledge. According to Kant, in order to judge, it is necessary a set of "installed"[54] concepts in the subject who performs the act of judgement and, for that reason, it is the subject who determines the conditions of the predication, that is, determines all we can say about the world.

But to what subject does Kant refer? Actually, the Kantian subject intends to be the set of rules by which phenomena may be known. In this case it concerns the subject of knowledge. This fundamentally modern project seeks to demonstrate that the subject of knowledge is the *a priori* capability of knowing; it is the *transcendental subject*.

However, how does one situate the Kantian subject in the face of its predecessor, *cogito*? For Kant, the transcendental subject is distinct from Descartes' substantial subject (*res cogitans*). One first distinction concerns the formal aspect of the Kantian subject. It concerns consciousness as a unifying logical function, a formal subject that can only be apprehended in its activity.

A second difference relates to the very idea of objectivity. The transcendental subject, in Kant, is the very voucher of the objectivity, the function attributed to God in Descartes' philosophy. The fundamental Cartesian idea, according to which all relation with reality involves the representation of the subject, will be radicalized by Kant, for whom knowledge is strictly the subject's production.

Both cases, Cartesian and Kantian, concern: (1) thinking knowledge as relation between subject and object; (2) situating the subject as principle of knowledge; (3) overlapping two distinct concepts, such as that of consciousness and subjectivity; (4) attributing to the reflexivity of consciousness the capacity of founding a *self* recognized as subjective unit and identity – in Kant, consciousness as *a priori* unit, would guarantee the identity of the transcendental subject, which cannot change to guarantee the regularity of the experience and, therefore, its possibility.

Thus Kant does not refuse the Cartesian premise of "I think", but seeks to validate it by transforming it into the formal condition of all experience. In other terms, the subject, in its legitimating function, does not need to be a being, which means granting this figure of "I think" a transcendental statute. Therefore, Cartesian subject-object duality is "interiorized" and each one of the terms becomes the pole of a single relation, constituted by the transcendental subject.

The Kantian subject is defined by the following aspects: (1) *formal*, because it is understood as an empty structure, a pure form, without contents; (2) *a priori*, because it is prior to the experience; (3) *transcendental*, because it is condition of each and every possible experience; (4) *objective*, because it concerns a common and universal condition to all human individuals; (5) *reflexive*, because it is capable of examining and judging its own activity; (6) it is situated between *heterogeneous planes*, the empirical and the transcendental, the theoretical and the practical; and (7) *autonomous*, because it is capable of determining itself in accordance with a law of its own.

4.3 Sigmund Freud

4.3.1 Freud and Psychoanalysis

In a letter to Binswanger, Freud (1856–1939) spoke about something he had started and which would occupy mankind for a long time. This novelty, affirmed by Freud, meant a baffling revolution that echoed in several fields of thought, situating psychoanalysis as indispensable reference for other fields of knowledge. The mutation brought by psychoanalysis proposes a new reflection that considers the plenitude of experience appropriate for the *unconscious*, "unconscious" understood as *concept* that asks for an appropriate theory: psychoanalysis. Even though the processes Freud considered were not unknown before him, psychoanalysis renewed not only the formulations about the unconscious, but also established a new paradigm[55] for the study of the mind.

In general terms, the principle of subjectivity is overcome by psychoanalysis. The belief that the *Ego*[56] is something stable and substantial that remains identical to itself throughout the diversity of its experiences is refused – the *Ego* is, rather, the effect of complexity of the unconscious determination. With psychoanalysis it is no longer possible to defend the idea of man as base and support (foundation) of the knowledge and of himself. There is no longer knowledge understood as the control of objects by a sovereign or autonomous *subject*.

For Freudian psychoanalysis, it is no longer about subjectivity, neither the particular one, of each individual, nor the transcendental, universal subjectivity of man. The experience engendered by the *unconscious* revokes reasoning that affirms any centering or fixed point of reference. The belief in foundations is dethroned, the *Ego*, rational and methodical, is displaced, no longer belonging to any subjectivity, psychological or transcendental. The great binary divisions and the exclusions that characterized the preceding thoughts are replaced. Beyond the nature-culture duality, Freud places the problem of *civilization and its discontents* as the origin of this dualist belief. The mind-body distinction loses its meaning with the proposition of the "limitrophe" concept of *drive*, at the same time that the study of the processes of identification undoes the opposition between individuality and collectivity, and subjective interiority becomes a myth in face of the affirmation of psychical reality.

Freud's opposition to a philosophical concept of mind is well known.[57] His minimum thesis, that with which he starts psychoanalysis, denies the primacy of consciousness – not only in the field of knowledge, but likewise in that of consciousness itself – and sustains that, in psychism, the *Ego* is only an instance, part or effect of the unconscious. The nineteenth century presented different forms of critique to the idea of a privileged place for the *I*.[58] However, the position of psychoanalysis not only causes the revision of the idea of man as center of the world, but also challenges the very idea that the world has a center or a unit. Therefore, not only the privileging of the *I*, but a certain way of thinking by foundations, characteristic of the western thinking, is kept in check.[59]

The term *psychoanalysis* was first used by Freud in an article in 1896[60] and received successive definitions. One of the most known is in the entry *Psychoanalysis*, written by Freud, himself, for an encyclopedia:

> Psycho-analysis is the name (1) of a procedure for the investigation of mental processes which are almost inaccessible in any other way, (2) of a method (based upon that investigation) for the treatment of neurotic disorders and (3) of a collection of psychological information obtained along those lines, which is gradually being accumulated into a new scientific discipline (Freud, 1976c[1922], v. XVIII: 287).

On several occasions Freud defined what he called the "corner-stones"[61] of the psychoanalytical theory. Therefore, upon concluding *The Interpretation of Dreams*, he reaches these three crucial points for psychoanalysis: the existence of unconscious processes; the primacy of desire in psychical life; and the broad reach of the process of repression. Despite the extent of Freudian work and the countless conceptual changes, we observe the permanence of these three basic references, generating particular criteria for the approach of the mind. Therefore we have the recognition of the *unconscious*, not only in the qualitative sense, but also in the *topographical* sense; the concept of *repression* and the psychical *dynamic* it implies; the concept of *drive or instinct*, the condition for considering sexuality as the privileged field of human relations, governed by psychical *economy*. These references organize a theoretical *corpus* called metapsychology[62], which situates psychoanalysis as something more than a simple therapeutics of neuroses. These conclusions led him to a new order of investigations and are decisive steps for the consolidation of psychoanalysis as a new theory of the mind.

4.3.2 Unconscious and consciousness: the Freudian topography

Usually there is no hegemonic and definite position regarding Freud's findings. However, when the previous discussion regarding subjectivity is analyzed, there is no doubt regarding Freud's refusal to align himself to these perspectives. Freudian thinking did not follow the routes established by philosophy, nor accepted, partially or fully, the discussion about subjectivity. Concepts such as *ego, consciousness* and *subject* are considered by psychoanalysis as absolutely distinct and, even, suspicious notions. Actually, each one of the established presuppositions regarding the principle of subjectivity was ignored by Freud. Freudian psychoanalysis moves away from any dialectic between subject and object – the term "subject" does not even exist in Freudian vocabulary, while the object is destitute of any subjective content and deprived of its philosophical significances. Psychoanalysis does not affirm the death of the subject, nor does it call for the return to the original and unspeakable being; it does not support the principle of subjectivity, even if removed from the logic of identity. It does not acknowledge processes of *self-reflection* as inherent to consciousness, or appeal to the notion of *synthesis* in order to conciliate the dualisms established by philosophy, such as that between the empirical and the transcendental dimension.

Freud declared psychoanalysis as the third narcissistic wound[63] imposed to "mankind".[64] This statement condenses the theoretical developments crucial to psychoanalysis regarding the unconscious, and delimits, in a precise way, the references to any reflection concerning it. For psychoanalysis there is no more room for conceptions – philosophical, religious, anthropological, etc. – about *man* as thought from personal and exclusive attributes. It is not about a central issue, nor a preserved presupposition, because, through psychoanalytic thinking, no humanism is reached. The interdependence between humanism and the concept of subjectivity is not accidental, because it is already known that modern thinking was raised on a solid humanist base which situates human nature or the condition of humanity as the ultimate foundation.

Freud caused greater reaction to the thinkers of his time not for affirming the unconscious (others had already done that), but for showing that its radical determination[65] excluded the possibility of delimiting it by any *ism*. What is usually called Freud's "theoretical turning point", in the 1920s[66], happened with the introduction of the concept of the *death instinct*. With that, the unconscious starts to be governed by a determination that extrapolates any condition established up to that moment, because the experience engendered by the unconscious is neither founded nor regulated by any *a priori* subjective condition. When Freud formulated his theory of the unconscious, he disturbed the most sensitive spot in philosophical – and also religious, moral and psychological – thinking when he questioned the idea of man as subject, whose unit would be assured by consciousness.

We have seen that this category of self-conscious-individual-human-subject is the intersection of beliefs and notions which served as the base for a long tradition of thinking. According to these presuppositions, the subject is that which performs unity in the face of the diversity of experiences, is that which incorporates the unit of moral acts, the unit of religious aspirations, the unit of political practices, the geo-political unit of human groups, etc. It is not by chance that tradition presents the consciousness as the ability or function of unification or synthesis. For that, it was necessary to interlock notions such as subject, consciousness and the individual.

Even though it was not initially made by Freud, "the division of the psychical into what is conscious and what is unconscious"[67] is considered by him as the "fundamental premiss" and used to define metapsychology as theory of the mind (Freud, 1976d[1923], v. XIX: 25). Freudian metapsychology is his theory that leads us beyond consciousness, elaborated with the purpose of researching and explaining the movements of mental life, conscious and unconscious. The psychoanalytical theory was developed by Freud as a means to consider the existence of gaps in conscious acts. He introduced the unconscious in order to deal exactly with these gaps. This thesis is reaffirmed at the beginning of his classic text, *The Unconscious* (1987b[1915]).[68]

However, it is a mistake to think that psychoanalysis, when proposing the idea of unconscious, denied the existence of consciousness, for in psychism there is a specific system for consciousness: that called *conscious perception*. Freud considers consciousness as a fact that performs a specific role in psychism, determining, quantitatively and qualitatively, the external and internal perceptions. Another point is the critique of the philosophical conception of consciousness. In this case Freud is ruthless: "We must learn to emancipate ourselves from the importance of the symptom of 'being conscious'" (Freud, 1974[1914], v. XIV: 221).

The target of this criticism is the model of consciousness as a centered unit. Against this conception, Freud proposes an "apparatus" that involves different systems with diverse working principles. In the so-called *first topography*[69], the system comprises the *unconscious,* the *preconscious* and *conscious*. In the *second topography*, this apparatus comprehends the *Id* (the *it*), the *Ego* and the *Superego*. This apparatus is not a centered unit but a set of instances constituted by the game of repression. The de-centering of this topography is such that it is impossible to think the existence of a subject. The *Ego*, which referred only to consciousness, converts into the unconscious part. For this reason, consciousness is incapable of seeing the difference between systems, given that it is only a system among others, whose entire group is submitted to the unconscious dynamic.[70] Behold a topography without center[71], where instances do not have unity and are only constituted in relation to other instances.

Freud attributes to psychism a causality by relations, where there is primacy of relations and not subjects or original individuals, who would work as supports or *substratum,* as ultimate cause. He called this type of causality *overdetermination*. This sort of determination thought by Freud goes beyond individualities, refuses permanent foundations, because the experience of the unconscious is that which takes place in the absence of center.

Ever since psychoanalysis, the unconscious is thought according to other logics. The so-called *unconscious formations* are examples of a logic in which the relation precedes and determines the terms. It therefore concerns a *relational logic* which makes any substantialist approach to the mind (or body) indefensible. This relational logic also explodes the classic model of contradiction. Hence Freud's known statement that in this [unconscious] system there is no place for denial (Freud, 1987b[1915], v. XIV: 213). Therefore, the so-called unconscious formations (Freudian slips, wits, dreams and symptoms) are organized according to a different principle of the cause and effect relation, of the contradiction principle and the Euclidian notion of space.

Since *Wit and Its Relation to the Unconscious* (written 1905), inventories everyday examples of how this articulatory principle of the unconscious works. Among the available resources there are the symmetrization of the enunciations, in which true and false propositions become equivalent; the reversibility of the sense is expressed in the continuous fluctuations of the sense of the words, with the possibility of involving opposite or antithetic meanings. We have, therefore, a production that is organized from the possibility of transience between meanings, ideas, affections and, above all, transience between mental instances. As we have said, psychism presents itself in the form of a modular system integrated by a complexity of functions which are dynamically interconnected without any central regulation.

To centralize would be to relate the world to a (one) *self* who makes the dimension of interiority appear, accessible to consciousness through *self*-reflexivity: consciousness of self. And also makes appear an exterior world, reconstructed by this interiority. Therefore the determination of a center, accompanied by a reasoning of interiority/exteriority, defines this center as *self*. But consciousness, thus understood, would be a nature that is compact and closed to relational existence, an undivided therefore individual *I*, which finds in the (physiological) notion of body the guarantee of its indivisibility. The representation of body as this guarantee of individuality and unit meets, in a renewed way, the demands of substantialist thought which always presupposes an underlying reality, *hypokeimenon*, as guarantee of the thought. We have a psychological conception of the body, defined as support of the whole set of systems, apparatus and organs that respond for the several mental functions. From this equivalence between individual and body results the definition of the individual as indivisible and integrated unit, headquarters of physiological and mental functions. In psychoanalysis, this relation changes in such a way that it becomes impossible to speak of the individual or considering the body as psychological unit.

Since Freud, consciousness is deprived of any self-reflection process, because consciousness cannot coincide with the totality of the mind. Its only possibility is to establish a reference to itself through some association or connection, always complex, of ideas which would be capable of expressing it.

4.3.3 Ego: *das Ich*

The *Ego* is not the ruling instance of consciousness, nor is consciousness the fundamental quality of the *Ego*. Attentive to this displacement, Freud uses the ambiguity of the German word *Ich*, including in its field all significations attributed to this term, in order to name what we call *I*. Thus proceeding, Freud intended to widen the conceptual field for this ordinary term. In general, the *Ego* is defined as an ideational mass, partly conscious and partly unconscious, a pole formed by ideas.

This double belonging to conscious and unconscious processes allows a mediating function to the *Ego*. The modular conception, adopted by Freud in the second topography in order to represent the mind, attributes to the *Ego* the role of mediator, organizer or manager of conflicts. Besides, due to its belonging to the perception-consciousness system, the *Ego* performs the function of liaison to the world and to the so-called internal states and is also capable of controlling the motor action. It is curious to notice that the countless functions attributed to the *Ego* may be classified in two large antinomic groups: regulating functions and defensive functions. This double condition does not allow thinking of the *Ego* as an autonomous instance, because it will always be fragmented in its functions. Freud attributed a specific terminology to this fragmented condition: *spaltung*.

Freud considers that the *Ego* is not original: "I may point out that we are bound to suppose that a unity comparable to the ego cannot exist in the individual from the start; ego has to be developed" (Freud, 1974[1914], v. XIV: 93). There are at least two ideas involved in this thesis. The first concerns the complex aspect of the *Ego*. It concerns a function constituted by the multiple convergence of formations, that is, *Ego* is part and is constituted by a necessarily relational field of existence. Therefore, any individuality that may be highlighted will be precarious, for it is not possible to infer any unity. The second idea affirms that the *Ego* is the result of a process of progressive differentiation. Freud will call this process *narcissism* and it will have the body as starting point of this process: "The ego is first and foremost a bodily ego; it is not merely a surface entity, but is itself the projection of a surface" (Freud, 1976d[1923], v. XIX: 40). This statement definitively removes the concept of *Ego* from the idealist-subjective field.

4.4 The systemic thinking of Ludwig von Bertalanffy

Ludwig von Bertalanffy (1901–1972), with a background in biology, studied at the University of Vienna where he received a Doctorate in 1926, and taught there until 1949, when he emigrated to Canada. In 1967, while writing the introduction to his writings' selection that was published under the title *General Systems Theory,* Bertalanffy observes the popularity of the term "system" which, at that moment, had already invaded not only several scientific fields, but also slang and mass communication media (Bertalanffy, 1973: 17).

The idea of system had become a current notion in order to specify every form of organization (companies, schools, processes of automation and production engineering, living beings, societies, etc.), whose behavior was described as mutual interaction or interdependence between its component parts. The fundamental characteristic of this relation was the production of a totality whose properties and performance were irreducible to the elements taken separately. Any system would be, therefore, a complex entity, identifiable by a set of particular interactive relations where the operation's global resultant exceeds the local reasons of its components. In other words, the totality of the "system" depends primarily on this interactive dynamics, but none of its elements, individually taken, explains it. Any change in the individual component produces transformations to which the system will not be immune; likewise, the behavior of the parts differs when studied separately and when treated as a whole.

Urban space allows several applications of the idea of system. From the road grid to public services, passing by the very idea of urban project, the "systemic" aspect of these realities becomes evident in the interdependence they maintain in relation to each other, always generating more complex effects than when we take them separately.

What does systemic thinking contribute to the comprehension of this process? On one hand, it allows considering the city from the logics of a dynamical totality, which has the function of the interactivity and of the communication which are established between its constituent elements, generating effects that exponentially[72] surpass them. However, what interests us the most is to explore systemic thinking as a conceptual tool capable of expressing aspects of the process of transformation of the "I" to which we refer; a process that has being ongoing since the last century and that is shown, today, as a promising line of analysis for the comprehension of contemporary urbanism.

The fundamental operation of systemic thinking, such as formulated by GST (as we will, henceforth, call the General Systems Theory), dwells less in the operation of identifying the systemic "entity" than in its comprehension as global process – that is, a whole which is more complex than its parts considered separately and irreducible to them, capable of subdividing or even hierarchizing itself into subsystems or being, itself, a subsystem of another more complex one. What is important is to maintain the logic according to which "the whole is more than the sum of its parts", because, "constitutive characteristics are not explainable from the characteristics of isolated parts. The characteristics of the complex, therefore, compared to those of the elements, appear as 'new' or 'emergent'" (Bertalanffy, 1973: 83).

In sequence, we will introduce, in general, a little of the history of the concept of system according to the conceptual development of the GST. The epistemological and conceptual details may seem, at first, strange to our theme. But they are necessary because they reveal aspects of the concept of system which are fundamental, according to our study, in order to accompany the process of decentralization and fragmentation of the notion of "I" which we suppose to be correlated to the process of conceptual and semantic transformation of the idea of city, as well as of complexification of its functions. Besides, the epistemological vocation that the concept of system has for operating in the crossroads of knowledge offers us epistemic support for the construction and demonstration that "the city is me", supplying information for the understanding of "Person" that may, conversely, support the contemporary experience of city.

In two papers of his *General Systems Theory*, Bertalanffy reviews the conceptual panorama he found when he started his studies in biology and whose critique, formulated by him since his first texts in the 1930s, constitutes the core of GST. Two approaches prevailed: mechanicism and vitalism. On one hand this meant, for research in biology, considering the living organism as an aggregate of parts and partial processes analytically reducible and explainable in isolatable causal series, being the problems relative to its organization considered as secondary or even irrelevant. This was the mechanicist approach.

In the other hand, there were, parallel to the attempts of providing a theoretical scenario that would be harmonic with the dynamics of the organism, which were dependent on a certain vitalism still *en vogue*, influential principle in science throughout the nineteenth century. The theories of vitalist characteristics defended a vital "principle" or "force" which explained the specificity, if not, even, the exceptionality, of the living being in face of the inanimate matter subject to the laws of corruption and dissolution. There should be a given "principle of conservation", responsible for the harmonious balance of the living body. Ultimately the existence of every living being (cell or organism) witnessed the natural, permanent and immanent tendency of life to act, accomplishing in the living being its necessary purpose and permanent demand. From this epistemic scenario resulted a mechanicist conception whose scope was the reduction of the "vital phenomenon" to its minimal entities and to its isolated partial processes[73], submitting the physicochemical functioning of the living being to the same laws of the inanimate matter, but without necessarily eliminating the "vital force" that justified its development and specificity.

Going against the flow, Bertalanffy began to support a vision "which emphasizes consideration of the organism as a whole or system, and sees the main objective of biological sciences in the discovery of the principles of organization at its various levels" (Bertalanffy, 1973: 29). This point of view, which he called "organismic", acknowledged the need to study not only parts and processes separately but privileged the problems "found in the organization and order unifying them, resulting from dynamic interaction of parts, and making the behavior of parts different when studied in isolation or within the whole" (Bertalanffy, 1973: 53).

The second important aspect in the notion of system, and thence resulting, was the bid in the reasoning of isomorphism (capable of being mathematically modeled, or not) as a theoretical-methodological strategy of approach to systems. This means that the systemic logics of GST – with its emphasis on the problems of order, organization, totality, differentiation, etc. – not only pointed out the structural similarity of the models, their relations of equivalence and the isomorphism of their concepts and laws, but also encouraged their transference from one field of knowledge to the other, or the creation of new theoretical models where they were needed.

Some considerations can already be made. First, we stress the heuristic value of the notion of system that, starting from the biological issue of "organism", achieved an abstract and broad formulation of an "interaction dynamics", henceforth applicable as a model in several fields, taking into consideration the conceptual specificities of each one of them. Second, and operationalizing such abstraction and range, the very notion of system became sympathetic to the reasoning that enabled the generalized transportation of this "interaction dynamics" and its use wherever a totality expressing itself in the exponential production of effects resulting from the interaction of its parts was distinguishable (not taken separately, but rather in relations of interdependence). In this sense, Bertalanffy's systemic thinking, on one hand, explored the generalized use of isomorphism procedures and, at the limit, made analogy evident as heuristic instrument constitutive of any knowledge.[74] On the other hand, he contributed to calling attention to the high price we pay for the maintenance of irreducibility of borders and the thoughts of separation, as bear witness, until today, the compartmentalization of knowledge and their usual closure.

It is enough to remember that the concept of city, when reduced to its physical and geographic aspect, excludes other possibilities of understanding the urban, which enriches itself and becomes more complex when conceived as political space, as network or as mobility of goods, information and people. Placing the city in historical perspective is already an epistemic exercise of relativization of disciplinary borders, because the forms of the cities reflect the logic of the societies which they shelter: ancient cities conceived under the pressure of religion and of military control and protection; medieval cities with walls and corporations organized around squares, stables, fountains, and expressing sympathies and dependences characteristic of the feudal world; modern cities, characterized by specialized social bonds, based on rationalization and functionality; the contemporary city, articulating itself, for instance, in the perspective of de-location, in the sense that the locations of residence, work, leisure and the logic that presided over their choosing are changing, losing the traditional space-time constraints and entering the reflexive logic, with choices conditioned by the level of mobility and communicability and leading to the feeling of ubiquity and multitemporality (Ascher, 2001).

Thus, GST revealed itself as being a very creative scientific proposition because, in asking about the "general system laws which apply to any system of a certain type, irrespective of the particular properties of the system and of the elements involved" (Bertalanffy, 1973: 61), it stimulated the introduction of new categories of thinking, new conceptual models of interdisciplinary character, resulting in a greater integration of sciences through the search of principles that enabled the transversality of knowledge. Finally, it drew attention to something the scientific and academic community in general used to comfortably forget, that is, the waste of theoretical effort in different fields due to the fact that identical principles had been discovered "several times because workers in one field were unaware that the theoretical structure required was already well developed in some other field" (Bertalanffy, 1973: 56–57).[75]

Our work shares the idea of GST's transversality of knowledge. In fact, we are transporting to the field of urbanism a problematization which, not having emerged there, may contribute to elucidate and enrich its cognitive asset when exploring the possibilities of the hypothesis "the city is me". Somehow, and we hope to be able to demonstrate it, there is isomorphism between the contemporary idea of city – with the technological, cognitive, epistemic, social, economic, political transformations that give visibility to its polysemic transformation – and a new concept of *I*, free from individualizing, centralizing and disjunctive reasoning that characterized its emergence and consolidation in the West, ever since the Greeks. In terms of GST, "I" is a systemic operation which dynamically totalizes – it would already be inadequate to say "centralizes" – a structuring and functional complex, open to the possibility of exchange and transformation.

The openness of the system, in opposition to its constitution as closed system, is another fundamental characteristic of GST. When reflecting about the nature of the systems, starting on the parameters he found in the study of living organisms, Bertalanffy proposed the hypothetical model of "open systems", in opposition to the "closed systems". This difference is thus defined by the author in an inaugural paper on the theme, dating back to 1940: "We term a system 'closed' if no material enters or leaves it; it is called 'open' if there is import or export of material" (Bertalanffy, 1973: 167). When establishing such distinction, the author had in mind the processes of traditional physics, isolated from the environment and characterized by the reversible kinetic equilibrium, offering as example the physicochemical reactions that may occur in closed containers with a given number of reagents. These are considered systems closed to the exterior, and always contain identical components (Bertalanffy, 1973: 167, 63–64). In contrast, the open systems, of which the organism has always been the main example for Bertalanffy, present stable states in a continuous transformation of material and energy components because the organism responds to changes in the medium by dynamically self-regulating. For that it may take several paths, as long as the purpose – its adaptation and equilibrium restored through transformation – is reached.

In short, an open system – a machine, bacteria, a human being, human communities, a city, a company, a school, a factory, a family – exhibits the following characteristics.

- The whole is larger than the sum of its parts and possesses properties that exponentially surpass those parts taken separately; a city, for instance, is a systemic totality that presides over the sum of the services, information, people and assets that constitute it; likewise "I" is a systemic totality that presides over the sum of biological, cultural, linguistic, psychical components that form it.
- There is interdependence and interactivity between component parts of a system, including exchange and reciprocal influence with the surroundings. Between what the system is (its properties and components) and what it is not (the surroundings), a new notion of border is built, more malleable, prone to change, with sufficient porosity to tear down the old "wall" that surrounded the city and served as conscientious enclosure to "I", revealing them as dynamical and mutable.
- Systems form subsystems and may, in turn, be subsystems of more complex systems, existing interaction between them in hierarchic chain; a city's transportation system may be considered a component subsystem of its road grid which, in turn, integrates a country's road mobility network.
- Systems work with self-regulation and control, transforming through their intrinsic capability of permanent regeneration and adaptation to the long process of exchange with the environment, compensating eventual losses caused by entropic tendency which is also intrinsic to them: the urban fabric is always renewable, in direct proportion to the exchanges it performs, just as the systemic notion of "I", which includes border with porosity.
- Systems may reach their goals through several different means. This principle is known as equifinality.

Not everything is aprioristically system. In other words, the application of the concept of system creates a compatible scenario as systemic reality that will be known. The problem becomes having criteria that indicate the operation through which a system reproduces and differentiates itself. That the system indeed proceeds that way was the most general inheritance left by the systemic thinking of Bertalanffy's generation. It was up to Humberto Maturana and Francisco Varela to propose a *how*. That is what we will see next.

4.5 The systemic thinking of Maturana and Varela: the concept of *autopoiesis*

The concept of *autopoiesis* was proposed by Chilean biologists Humberto Maturana (1928–) and Francisco Varela (1946–2001), whose theoretical work is well known by the international community dedicated to the study of systems in general. Our goal here is to show how the advance of conceptual reflections in the systemic theory offers more tools to explore the process of decentralization and fragmentation of "I", increasingly conceiving it as network of interactions, without a fixed point of command and intelligibility. Besides that, a thought taken from these authors is fundamental for our study, that of *circularity*, from which we have to consider the inseparability between the human being and the world (therefore, between *I* and the city). There is not a way of understanding them separately; they are both part of a same dynamics: we build the world that builds us during this time in common.

We will take hold of the concept of *autopoiesis*, originally from the field of biology, in order to explore its propaedeutic possibilities in the field of urbanism, with the meaning that this latter receives in our work: the conception of the city as equivalent to the network which a *Person* is. This network has infinite range in its components and in the complexity of its connections, and functions as radical possibility of relativization of any information, with the possibility of considering them indiscriminately. This epistemic effort is compatible with paradigms of knowledge developed since the second half of the twentieth century which considered communication, information, the questioning regarding the nature of transformations, its non-linearity and unpredictability; which did not step back in the face of unlikely passages between models of knowledge and fields of knowledge seemingly distant; which problematized, diluting, making ambiguous or even dismissing, irreducible differences between nature, life and artifact, as bear witness, for instance, cybernetics, the several theories of self-organization, of emergence, of complexity and of chaos, and the studies about the unconscious that took into consideration these epistemic guidelines, as is the case of the New Psychoanalysis.[76]

4.5.1 Unity, closure and coupling

The paradigm of autopoietic systems became public in 1973 with Maturana and Varela's book *De máquinas y seres vivos*[77], which enunciated the structural foundation of this epistemological proposition: wherever there is circulation of "information" and "sense" for an "autopoietic being", it processes them from the "interior" because it is an operationally closed system (Dumouchel & Dupuy, 1983: 141). The autopoietic being corresponds to a network of production, transformation and destruction processes whose components permanently reproduce, through their interactions, the very network that produced them. Thence results "a spatially defined unit, limited by a boundary that it is, itself, capable of engendering" (Dumouchel & Dupuy, 1983: 142). In other words, autopoietic systems engender the organization that defines them as unity and permits distinguishing them from the environment, clipping the system from something that does not merge with it.

We asserted at the end of the previous section that the systemic thinking, in the formulation of GST, conceived the idea of system from the dynamics of the relations with the surroundings, hence the "open" and "closed" classification which qualifies a system according to its interaction and transformation properties. It is as if the inside/outside differentiation was fundamental data in order to understand the dynamics of the system and its relation to the surroundings. It seemed to be sufficient to conceive that there are limiting boundaries of a system, given that there are inputs or information exchange, which transform the dynamics of the states of the system, keeping it as such.

However, with Maturana and Varela we see a second inflexion in systemic thinking, because the idea of *autopoiesis* ignores the "open system" *vs* "closed system" opposition in favor of a notion of order and organization that postulates "closure" and "self-containment" as immanent values to any relation, abstracting, as from the domain of the living, the general conditions for existence of transactional space which generates transformation with conservation of autopoiesis. In other words, there are nothing but relations and its terms are immanent to the very autopoietic system, which is, at the same time, producer and product[78], somehow differentiating from that which the system is not, from a surrounding that does not merge with it, a surrounding which is, at the same time, *sine qua non* condition of the interactivity dynamics. The network has boundaries that *integrate and result* from the very autopoietic organization. Hence the circularity between, on one side, "a network of dynamic transformations that produces its own components and that is essential for a boundary", and, on the other, "a boundary that is essential for the operation of the network of transformations which produced it as unity" (Maturana & Varela, 2001: 54).

System and boundary are made operationally equivalent, resigning the comfort of the previous distinctive option between "open" system and "closed" system. This new systemic paradigm thus proceeds in conceiving an invariant that classifies and allows recognition of a special type of system: those autopoietically organized. It is this organization that explains the existence of exchange and structural transformation which, in turn, permanently retroacts over the system itself, changing it and, in the same act, confirming it as autopoietic. Something happens in the dynamics of the system that cannot be explained by the mere fact that there is an *input*; in other words, there is clearly a system, a surrounding that does not merge with it, exchange information, change in the dynamics of the states of the system, and the possibility of observing and mapping this process. The system transforms itself, by endogenous reason or intrinsic competence, *beyond* the external causality calculated as contact and coupling between two different units.

Let us consider, for instance, urban traffic jams. In the circumstances of maximum flow without obstruction, it just takes an insignificant obstacle to paralyze the system. We immediately think: there must have been an accident. However, continuing on the route towards our destination, we observe that "nothing" has happened. We are so addicted to a reasoning of external and previous-to-the-system causality – in this case, urban traffic – that we hardly conceive situations that, upon reaching a point of unpredictable mutation, transform, without apparently showing identifiable and linearly explainable reasons. It is a fact that, often, there are particular causes, but they are so dependent on the network that produces them as event that it is practically impossible to attribute them some privileged explanatory value. The particular cause does not explain "anything", for any other would serve as reason or would have produced the same effect (Dumouchel & Dupuy, 1983: 144).

Let us also consider the digital networks, which allow attaching the most diverse personal and cultural experiences around the planet. Communities which are formed there follow the autopoietic and self-organizing dynamics because they define themselves according to the very space of interactions that delimits them as particularity on the network. Well, the urban space changes due to that. The city that the *Person* is qualitatively conforms itself to the nodes and connections that dynamically configure it. Thus, my neighbors are the friends with whom I interact on the internet, regardless of geographic distance, the physical neighborhood or the condominium or street that corresponds to the address of my permanent residence. This neighborhood is self-organizing according to diverse interests which find correspondence and connectivity on the randomness of the network but which, once in contact, organize interactive landscapes where businesses, affections, musical interests, studying, sex, opinions, criticisms, comments and all sorts of information exchange may result in a recognizable autopoietic unity. It is important to remember that, whatever the interactive elements of the network may be, there is no direct equivalence between the geopolitical reference and the self-organized networks that intersect and relativize it as a physically and politically recognizable boundary.

We will subsequently introduce three basic ideas of autopoietic systems definitions: unity, closure and coupling. From each of them we will explore aspects of the autopoietic organization that contribute to build the idea of the city as resultant of the interactions network a *Person* is.

Let us start with the principle of *unity*. There is an organization that characterizes the autopoietic being – in other words, a type of relation that, if and when it happens, allows identifying it as such. In this case, what allows us to distinguish an autopoietic system is the fact that it produces itself continuously, its defining organization being called the autopoietic organization. It is worth stressing that *poiesis* is a word from the Greek and means "production". Therefore the principle of *autopoiesis* means what is common to all the systems in which the means that allow them to continue their existence or to produce themselves are, at the same time, the means that define them as such. We know that a city, physically and geographically speaking, results from, among other things, a series of planning actions, such as laws that define zoning areas; public initiatives to revitalize given neighborhoods and urbanize others; policies of decentralization and distribution of services; etc.

However, along with this planning action, there are communities (virtual or not) which are formed in an unplanned way, on sidewalks, at parties and night clubs, in bars or at the beach (very often with evident physical marking of their boundaries). They are autopoietic unities in the sense that they are produced by self and continuous movement of agglutination and dispersion, whence result sufficiently particular characteristics in order to define them as a "system" that differs from the surrounding. Thus, the city that I am is formed and transformed on and by the network that is weaved for me in the flow of connection and dispersion interests and that define me in an *ad hoc* way. From an autopoietic perspective, this means considering *I* as an existential resultant of organization and stability that is molded in the process of its own production and transformation – the communities I attend, the bonds I establish (with the qualitative variation thereto implicit), the spaces where I wander (virtual or not) – being its boundary a function of its mutant competence.

Hence the principle of *closure*. Every closure is operational, in the sense of the endo-determined dynamics of transactions that take place between a system and its medium, as it is the structure of the system – that is, the number, the nature and the properties of the concrete components which, due to their options of modification and variation, materialize the autopoietic organization at each moment – that determines what responses the system is fit to give to the disturbance caused by the surrounding. Human crowds gathered at popular events, such as shows for instance, exhibit endo-determined dynamics because changes in their behavior may be unleashed by non-specific noise or disturbance. The system changes, generating, as effects, new states (the calming of spirits or, on the contrary, their exacerbation).

From the point of view of the system, the transformation process is "blind" because there is no way to specify in advance either the effects the environment is capable of activating or the changes that the system is capable of producing. Consequently it is *a posteriori* that we witness alterations, mutations and adaptations. And if there is (or was) modification and the system continues to be identifiable in its operational independence it is because the autopoietic organization was, then, and continues to be preserved. In short, *autopoiesis* is the invariance: the organization; the ability to be operated, its endo-determined structure; the closure, a self-referential function that creates openness.

This is the reason why Maturana and Varela propose the principle of *coupling*: the recurring and, very often stable, transaction between system and medium according to the congruence that is established between them, given that the closure of the system is self-referential. In this sense, there is a not irrelevant background factor in the process, which generates another level of circularity: being structural-coupling selective, due to the demand of commensurability between system and surrounding, its repetition ends up conditioning, throughout time, selectivity criteria through the recurrence of reciprocal "choices" between system and medium.

Therefore, at each moment, coupling is a possible emergence of the alternatives which acted in the production and conservation of the systemic relations between autopoietic unities. Just as our immunological system, which modifies in the presence of some pressure unleashed by the surroundings (exposure to a virus and the immunity that develops from that), the city that a Person is results from the game of permanence and instability paced by the repetition of the transactions that move it. This creates cultural standards, behavioral habits, stable series of interests. But the endo-determining structural condition, which is a permanent stimulant factor, places the transaction at a space of unpredictability, producing differences in time. Here, the process is also "blind", because there is no predetermined direction that directs its resultant of variation and diversity. If there is invariance, it is, as we have said, the very autopoietic organization that, in its necessary conservation function, acts as a sort of minimum ontological reference in whose interior systems are produced.

The idea of *autopoiesis* has contributed to the reflection about new conceptions of world, system, observer and "I". The self-determined perspective of the system as complex and diversified internal coherence that produces, as network of interactions, its own limits and boundaries, through immanent organization capacity, implies at least two epistemological advances. First of all it reinforces the abandonment of the causal and linear logics, otherwise an exercise demanded by systemic theory in general. As input or operational closure, we are dealing with dynamic processes that produce effects which exceed the restricted intelligibility of their separately-taken components. More than that, we are dealing with systems that show unpredictable behavior as a result of the plasticity of their structure, given their autopoietic organization, that is, their immanent competence to perform and specify themselves at the same time (Maturana & Varela, 2001: 56).

Second, the autopoietic paradigm means yet another blow to the representationist habit, which conceives reality as a (re)introduction of mental or empirical contents to a *subject* (of knowledge) which apprehends them due to innate or learned reason, as if there were a world outside our experience, as if we could separate subject-object. On the contrary, *autopoiesis* means building the world, making it emerge along with and due to the reciprocal specification that is established between a unity and its universe (environment or medium). Therefore, the actions of a person transform the world he/she inhabits (or better yet, the world he/she *is*); conversely, the transformed world retroacts, equally transforming its players, without it being possible to identify linear causalities or previous hierarchies in the process that happens in circularity.

This leads us to another basic principle of this theory, according to which "every act of knowing brings forth a world", that is, "all doing is knowing and all knowing is doing" (Maturana & Varela, 2001: 31–32). With this proposition, Maturana and Varela insist on the existing sequence between action and experience, between a particularity of being and how the world seems to us. In other words, my experience of the world produces the world I know and my knowledge of the world results from what I experience from it. It is not possible to know where the dividing line is between what we experience as the world, with all its regularities and randomness, how we act in the world and are affected by it, and the knowledge thence emerging. The proposition "the city is me" is compatible with such statement. If life is *autopoiesis* and *autopoiesis* is knowledge, then the same principle will be present, from cell to language, going through all the complexity of our behavioral, neuronal, social and linguistic domains.

4.5.2 The human knowledge

Knowledge has a necessarily reflexive character, when we include the human complexity of expressing it through language, an instrument with which the circularity between living, knowing and acting is exhibited. The network of linguistic interactions facilitated by the emergence of language – which, at the same time, continuously renews it – creates infinite recursion, bringing forth *a* world in the direct correlation of the reflexive capacity provided by the same language, in a "cognitive circle that characterizes our becoming, as an expression of our manner of being autonomous living systems". (Maturana & Varela, 2001: 264). The ensuing comments should be considered as detailing of the notion of autopoiesis, which we assess as important for they grant the due epistemic scope to this concept and its pertinence to the reflections about the contemporary city.

There is a key-characteristic in language that makes it a decisive element of human knowledge, life and action: it enables "those who operate in it to describe themselves", including their circumstantial situation (Maturana & Varela, 2001: 232). Language does not only allow describing and organizing events, situations, relations, feelings, in a semantic range that is, up until now, incomparable in the living world. The fundamental is that it places man in the position of "observer", because "descriptions can be made treating other descriptions as if they were objects or elements from the domain of interactions" (Maturana & Varela, 2001: 233). Therefore, describing the description evokes simultaneous knowledge of knowing and of the known: someone describes (observer) descriptions of descriptions (domain of interactions) which retroact over the observer as an undistinguishable part of oneself[79].

Thus, what we speak, how we speak, behave, imagine, feel, think, establish relations with other people (family, friends, professional colleagues, etc.), with our pets or other behavioral domains (other living beings), these examples or any other that involve human presence constitute recurrent linguistic interactions that permeate our entire existence. Thus, given that these interactions are couplings, it is not possible not to recursively include the fact of knowing that we know and that we make descriptions; that is, it is not possible to know without acknowledging the knowledge, nor describing without acknowledging the act of describing. Thus, language brings as correlation the awareness or the reflection of the act about itself, given that "we are observers and exist in a semantic domain created by our operating in language" (Maturana & Varela, 2001: 233). And it is not possible to know and reflect on the knowledge outside of language.

We are biological beings, which implies situating the emergence of language in the human species as result of an evolutionary history that, at the limit, involves the entire living system on the planet. However, from a more focused perspective, this equally implies situating such emergence as the result of complexification (whose process is historically impossible to follow) of behaviors, gestures and habits selected and repeated in the social experience and transformed, adapted and conserved in it, until the moment that the linguistically-constructed and socially-shared and acknowledged self-reference emerged. Thus, *I is continuous recursive description, "it enables us to conserve our linguistic operational coherence and our adaptation in the domain of the language"* (Maturana & Varela, 2001: 254, my italics).

For this reason we are also something more than just biological beings. The social dynamics – incremented in and by the evolutionary history of the living – has launched and does launch us on a network of social and linguistic couplings responsible for the emergence of the consciousness phenomenon.

In this perspective it does not make sense to speak of consciousness as the inaugural moment of human identity, in the Cartesian way of a substantialist consciousness, unique and, as subject, creator of a world that presents itself to its questioning and in relation to which it (consciousness) places itself in transcendent position. Nor does it regard considering consciousness as transcendental operation logically prior to knowledge, as its universal and necessary condition, in the Kantian way. It is not "something" that is inside the skull or that flows from the brain. It is an operational stability, recursively created and maintained in language, sharing, for this reason, its infinite plasticity.

From Maturana and Varela's contribution we can conclude that the concept of autopoiesis, originated from an epistemological reflection in the field of biology, contributes to the reconsideration of what may be "I", displacing it from the traditions of the substantialist or transcendental subject, from oppositions between representation and world, which are epistemic positions that organize our existence and our way of knowing as if everything were distributed in a previous "inside" and "outside", a definitive and irreconcilable "internal" and "external", in an irreversible, incommunicable and mutually exclusive "yes" and "no", in isolated parts that have no interaction nor connection to the whole, in obedience to a linear and predictable logic. On the contrary, in light of autopoietic organization, "I" is pure recursive operation, whose recurrence stabilizes and creates communicational coherences in the several social and linguistic couplings that participate in it and whence it results. Therefore, "the city is me" is a statement that is conceptually supported due to the fact that we inhabit the necessarily recursive universe of language. If there is such statement, then it denotes an action and a knowledge. Legitimating it is another story.

4.6 Gilles Deleuze and Félix Guattari's *rhizome*

French philosophers Gilles Deleuze (1925–1995) and Félix Guattari (1930–1992), commenting upon the experience of writing together the book *O Anti-Édipo* [*Anti-Oedipus*], put forward questions that will gain theoretical and practical consistency in the concept of *rhizome*:

> The two of us wrote *Anti-Oedipus* together. Since each of us was several, there was already quite a crowd. Here we have made use of everything that came within range, what was closest as well as farthest away. We have assigned clever pseudonyms to prevent recognition. Why have we kept our names? Out of habit, purely out of habit. To make ourselves unrecognizable in turn. To render imperceptible, not ourselves, but what makes us act, feel, and think. Also because it's nice to talk like everybody else, to say the sun rises, when everybody knows it's only a manner of speaking. To reach, not to the point where one no longer says I, but the point where it is no longer of any importance whether one says I. We are no longer ourselves. Each will know his own. We have been aided, inspired, multiplied. (Deleuze & Guattari, 1995: 11)

The change of understanding of what is *I* contained in the statement "We are no longer ourselves. Each will know his own. We have been aided, inspired, multiplied" becomes evident in the philosophical scope of *Mil Platôs* [*A Thousand Plateaus*] (1995), through the definition of concepts of multiplicity and rhizome, such as outlined by Deleuze and Guattari. In this book, the authors affirm the "book is an 'assemblage'. It is a multiplicity – but we don't know yet what the multiple entails when it is no longer attributed, that is, after it has been elevated to the status of a substantive" (Deleuze & Guattari, 1995: 8). The central understanding is that multiplicities are *the* reality and not the unity, any totality, or any idea of subject. The interest is on a thing's circumstances, where concepts should express the happening and not the essence. What interests is saying "in what situations, where and when … how", in what circumstances something happens (Deleuze, 1992: 37–38).

From this understanding, subject and object are not distinguished. The authors use as example a book where it is not possible to determine any subject or object, if we take into consideration the whole wide array of external correlations and connections present in its elaboration; the book is considered a sort of intermediation and, therefore, is unascribable.

It no longer concerns thinking in terms of hierarchic subordination, whose model is the tree and the process of arborescence, with its fixed base originating multiple branches. In this universe, the organization and dynamics of practices and knowledge, as a root that grows and develops vertically, are individual points and knots of a structure, which relate to each other for a reason of necessary reciprocity, binarity and opposition. Far is far, near is near, outside is not reversible with inside, public and private are clearly distinguishable and mutually exclusive. In a rhizomatic regime, on the contrary, any point may be linked to any other one, any element may affect or befall any other one, without previous order or value, without centralized and fixed coordination, on an open map: "connectable in all of its dimensions; it is detachable, reversible, susceptible to constant modification" (Deleuze & Guattari, 1995: 22)

The idea of a rhizome allows us to apprehend the contemporary reality as multiple and decentered, an open and infinite arrangement of fragments that are autonomous and inter-connectable on a network and without fixed point of convergence. That is what the rhizome metaphor indicates: originally from botany, it is an underground stem that grows and ramifies horizontally.[80] Some characteristics of the rhizome are relevant to this discussion:

- Principles of connection and heterogeneity – the generalization of the connection possibility where "any point of a rhizome can be connected to anything other, and must be" (Deleuze & Guattari, 1995: 15).
- Principle of multiplicity – the multiple is treated as substantive. Here we face the existence of any unity, there is no subject nor object, but only determinations, magnitudes and dimensions that change in nature when they grow. Multiplicities are defined by the outside: "by the line of flight or deterritorialization" (Deleuze & Guattari, 1995: 17).
- Principle of asignifying rupture – a rhizome may be broken, shattered at a given spot, just as it may start again on any of its lines. Lines of segmentarity stratify, territorialize, organize, but also deterritorialize. Segmentary lines become lines of flight causing the rupture of the rhizome and these lines often tie back to one another.
- Principle of cartography and decalcomania – a rhizome is not amenable to any structural or generative model. Making a rhizome is building an open map with multiple entryways and susceptible to constantly receiving any modifications.

As cognitive tool, the rhizome is useful for us in order to think of urban space as a complex grid of social, political, cognitive, technological relations in a 'fluid' state. Its rhythm is that of multiplicity and connectivity. Its dynamic is that of reticulation. Its meaning is given by the movements of deterritorialization and by the processes of reterritorialization, in constant becoming, denoting the nomad and plastic character of the rhizome. Such a concept allows us a plural approximation to contemporary reality, as different, multiple and decentered instance, an open arrangement of automaton fragments that are inter-connectable on a network and without a fixed point of convergence.

4.7 The cognitive ecology of Pierre Lévy

Pierre Lévy (1956–) is one of the most representative authors of critical thought on digital culture. New technologies and their broader cultural implications have been at the heart of his work since the 1980s, his conceptual investment falling upon the cognitive transformations of the dissemination of digital technology. The historical course of the technological leap we have experienced did not go unnoticed by him, which allowed him to create intelligibility schemes of the human course in the relation with his own technological creation, while conceiving a notion of "human" and his cultural avatars (aesthetic, political, economic, ethical, urban, etc.) within the perspective of "a human way of being, which is technical" (Lévy, 1999: 16).

His texts emphasized the means by which new technologies are changing culture in depth and considering digital information technology as a symptom of an "anthropological mutation", comparable only to that of the Neolithic (Lévy, 1993: 16).[81] The broadness of this mutation spills out beyond the "technical" logics of digitalization and information technology, because they "affect not only the fields of information and communication but also our physical presence and economic activities, as well as the collective framework of sensibility and the exercise of intelligence" (Lévy, 1996: 11) converging "towards the constitution of a new medium of communication, thinking and work for human societies" (Lévy, 2003: 11).

Since his pioneer work, *La machine univers: creation, cognition et culture informatique* [*The Universe-Machine: Creation, Cognition and Computer Culture*] (1987), Lévy has as trademark of his work the drawing of attention towards the need for new paradigms of more effective thinking in the treatment of this "new change" (Lévy, 1987: 7) brought from the 1980s. Hence the question: "What does culture become when communication, teaching, knowledge and the most part of cognitive activities are mediated by devices of automatic treatment of information?" (Lévy, 1987: 7) And we add, for the purpose of our work: What does the city become when culture is thus transformed? What does "I" become, when such devices push towards the pulverization of the subject, the desubstantialization of the body, the deterritorialization, the generalized relativization of spaces and borders?

The objective of this section is exactly that of discussing such questions. We will use as a reading key two propositions of discussions on intellectual technologies explored in *As tecnologias da inteligência* [*Les technologies de l'intelligence*] (1993) and *A inteligência coletiva* [*Collective Intelligence*] (2003), with the support of other texts such as *Cibercultura* [*Cyberculture*] (1999) and *O que é o virtual?* [*Becoming Virtual*] (1996). We refer to what the author called three poles of the spirit, which are primary orality, writing and information technology, and the four anthropological spaces which are Earth, Territory, Commodities and Knowledge.

Our intent is to show how the city constitutes an expression of mutations and cognitive and social adjustments throughout history, demanding to be thought today, in accordance with the new panorama of digital culture. Conversely we expect to demonstrate how technological mutations – which can be followed throughout human history, according to the route proposed by Lévy – fell upon different ways of conceiving "I", from the individual fixed in a territory, which is his house, village, native language or geographically and physically delimited city, to the virtuality or acceleration of the "heterogenesis" of the human, his "becoming other" (Lévy, 1996: 12), confirmed in the diversity of materialization plans, existence and meaning of human activity which the convergence of new technologies enables. We, at last, remember the author's warning: it is not about establishing successive and causally-sequenced chronological *eras*, or evolutional and cumulative chronological stratus. At each time and place the three poles of the spirit and the four anthropological spaces are present, with variable intensities and speeds (Lévy, 1993: 126; 2003: 125–30).

4.7.1 The couplings of space-time

Primary orality and earth: this is the first era of spirit and anthropological space when the primacy of social and individual memory are expressed as writing and recording as support for the information that weaves together the cognitive network of a random human group and builds a common space of meanings. Primary orality is the manner of organization of a memory "embodied" in rituals, gestures, dances, narratives and other skills that enable the members of a community to observe, listen, repeat or imitate the contents that give wholeness to the group, while granting its identity (Lévy, 1993: 84; 2003: 131).

In turn, earth is the narration-space or memory-space (Lévy, 2003: 150), constantly re-elaborated by these social strategies. It corresponds to the space of proximities and exclusions that is molded according to the identity links that connect individuals to each other, and these to the cosmos: consanguinity, community of tasks, beliefs, mythical ancestors, totemic deities. But it is not just about that. Relations established with the environment and the physical spaces – mountains, rivers, trees, rocks, animals, stars, geological and meteorological phenomena, as well as the perceptions of temperature, pressure, moisture, heat – participate in the significations that repeat, in their cyclic rhythm, the marks of fixation, stabilization, organization and continuity of human communities. Along with them, gregarious behaviors of cohesion and social organization, that humans share with a series of other animal species, work for this stability and continuity.

This last argument is absent from Lévy's considerations, at least explicitly. While the author speaks about the Earth as "a cosmos in which humanity communicates with animals, plants, landscapes, locales, and spirits" (Lévy, 2003: 115), we prefer to specify, widening the scope of this "communication", showing more indications of its configuration and dynamics, pointing out some properly ecological and ethological elements that enter the composition of the networks of significations that constitute this communication. This did not go unnoticed by scholars of the city such as Lewis Mumford. In terms of the historical emergence of the city, it concerns considering certain analogies between human culture and animal ethology, as is the case "of the most primitive kind of permanent human settlement, the hamlet or village", which serves the task of "defensive isolation" (Mumford, 1991: 11–12)[82] and can, from this perspective, be considered a true niche of protection, reproduction and feeding, maintaining a similarity to animal strategies for the provision of the same functions of protection, mating, reproduction and caring for the offspring. They are human social spaces that intertwine several significations, amongst which these ethological vestiges, rearranged by culture, analogous in their functionality to gregarious animal behaviors of defense and protection in face of predators, see the formation of family groups for protection of the offspring, recognition and protection of congeners and attack against individuals strange to the group.

In short, we are involved in a space-time – primary orality, Earth – where hypertexts are close to one another, significations are closed and the speed of metamorphosis is low. We use the hypertext metaphor according to Lévy's indications: universes of sense built and remodeled on the inside of a random communication process, in its several ranks, but also socio-technical processes and any other phenomena or spheres of reality "in which significations are at stake" (Lévy, 1993: 25, 70–73). For him, the basic operation of sense attribution is the association or the connection of one text to another. In turn, text is understood as the "knitting" of things; verbs and names sewn together by language and their symbolic and cultural unfolding. Therefore, "hypertext" is already the initial condition of any meaningful place we wish to indicate or to isolate on the network of significations that constitutes us, in ways of being; rank and perspectives always more or less undefined.

When we deal, therefore, with the polarity constituted by primary orality or by Earth as hegemonically structuring anthropological space, we are operating in a network whose transformation potentialities are dammed or obstructed by the barely malleable and repetitive nature of the elements and of the dynamics that constitute it. It regards human groups as dependent on orality and on social memory embodied in living people, and whose available knowledge is hardly undissociable from practices, rituals and specific narratives that build their identity spaces. In their functionality they are still very dependent on alliance and separation strategies that mobilize cosmic forces, physical phenomena, repertoire of gestures, expressions and behaviors that ensure the group and the social space constructed by it as enclosed world, center and production of centralization of significations. It is, moreover, a physically-delimited nomadism which accompanies the migration trails of herds, the salubrity and feeding possibilities according to favorable physical sites, and the ecological dynamics of the seasons (Lévy, 2003: 149–50).

Writing, the second era of the spirit, is coextensive with territory and trade – other structuring anthropological spaces, besides Earth. Writing is one of the most expressive intellectual technologies of human cognitive ecology, bringing in its wake millennia of organizing hegemony of the powers and knowledge of civilizations. In a strong analogy of significations, writing is correlated to agriculture as a technology of settlement, fixation and separation. Writing deterritorializes speech, separating it from the living breath and, attaching it to an inert substrate, sedentarizes it (Lévy, 2003: 142). But, concurrently, it produces other displacements, because its speed increases, and it gains the historical rhythm of the filing and control of information, henceforth subject to the endless game of powers in order to establish the "true" meaning or the authority that decides about the origin and fate of men – the practice that is usually called interpretation and that comes to occupy a preponderant place in the process of communication.

What were once strategies of the designation of belonging and concomitant exclusion – branded bodies, repertoire of gestures, expressions, behaviors strongly assured by the ecology of direct physical cohabitation – are transferred to the written text and the potentially endless network of comments, debates and interpretations that it enables. As Lévy states, "reading leads to conflicts, founds rival schools, offers its authority to alleged returns to the origin, as happened so many times in Europe after the triumph of printing" (Lévy, 1993: 90). Thus, independent from human mediation in the context of the characteristic narrative of orality, writing permits another level of displacement between the stock of identity information that social memory is and the individuals and groups molded by it because, henceforth, knowledge is available to be filed, consulted, and compared as it differs in space and in time.

For this reason it can be said that history – in the linear and cumulative sense, tributary of the logics of origin and finality and of the proliferation of the "versions" of truth as results of power relations – "is an effect of writing" (Lévy, 1993: 94–95). Its most eloquent symbols are the domestication of animals and seeds, the city as space of social domestication of men, including the social division of labor, and the State as police authority of this process. Furrowed earth, raised walls, engraved steles, registered taxes, established calendars are just a few examples of settlement in space and demanding perpetuity in time. The Earth, thus probed and gridded, becomes Territory, and now we can ask each individual – turned into an inhabitant of some geographic, social or psychical place – what is your address? What are you?, which can be answered by identities of territorial type, such as the family, the house, the domain, the city, the province, the country, the native language, the profession, the social or institutional status, the university degree, the rank, the property, the anatomic sex and its transposition in linguistic and cultural gender, the age: "everything that organizes a space in terms of borders, ranks and levels" (Lévy, 2003: 132), crystallizing belongings and exclusions.

Comparatively, we see here a way of enunciating the notion of the modern subject, which is nothing but a psychical and cognitive *territory*. The interiority of *cogito*, supported by the assumption of possessing an attribute that, naturally belonging to it, cannot be thence separated without rupturing its substantial unit: the thought. *I am, I exist*, the formula of Descartes' *Meditations*, which we have already considered, is the conscientious correlative to all aforementioned closure operations. From "my thoughts", a sort of translucent and self-reiterative box, I confirm being a permanent support, a thing, a substance that "doubts, understands, affirms, denies, wants, refuses, and also imagines and senses" (Descartes, 1979: 95). Every idea of subjectivity – regardless of how torn, deterritorialized, pulverized, differed and differentiating it is – keeps the Cartesian trace of this closure operation, bearing the mark of what *one is*.

In completing this section, it is necessary to consider a relatively-recent process that granted more speed to the social and cognitive space-time fabric, as well as to Earth and Territory. We are talking about what Pierre Lévy called the "Space of Commodity", whose organizing principle is the flow: flow of energies, raw materials, merchandise, capital, labor, information and which is nothing but the deterritorialization movement that capitalism brings, transmuting "into merchandise everything it draws into its orbit" (Lévy, 2003: 119). With merchandise, identities are deterritorialized because the generalized mercantilization process displaces sociabilities and identity certifications, which are redefined by the circuit of manufacturing, the circulation and consumption of things, information and images (Lévy, 2003: 119). Surpassing in speed previous spaces, the new ordination of the flow does not suppress the Territory, but subverts it and subordinates it to the mechanisms of production and circulation. Wealth is measured by the control of flow, and not just by the exploration of the borders.

This "media space" (Lévy, 2003: 144) multiplies, by fragmenting, the available supports for information recording, filing and transmission. Sound, image and texts, are infinitely reproduced by books, press, photographs, records, cinema, radio, tapes, television, fax, mobile phones: "people, things, technology, capital, signs, and skills are renewed, endlessly, circulating within commodity channels" (Lévy, 2003: 151), on networks of communication, transportation, distribution and production of goods. The city, for instance, is constituted as network that makes unintelligible the old city-countryside territorial distinction. In its place we have the urban, the "city whose center is everywhere and whose circumference nowhere" (Lévy, 2003: 152).

4.7.2 Virtualizations

In the sequence of the explanatory process, Pierre Lévy considers a third era of the spirit, which he calls the *digital network* or *informatic-mediatic pole,* and a fourth anthropological space he calls *knowledge space.* Both are situated in the field of social and cognitive transformations enabled by new digitally-based technologies. Both belong to the more general process of constitution and expansion, via digital networks, of "a global *cyberspace* in which elements of information are in virtual contact with one another and with anyone" (Lévy, 2003: 11), in a progressive process of convergence and minimalism of functions. For this reason, we will consider the digital network and the knowledge space from the perspective of virtualization, that is, from the broader dynamics of mutation (of identities), of displacement (of references' center of gravity), of permanent problematization (of solutions already given towards the fluidification of any established distinction), of indetermination, of interactivity, of deterritorialization, all characteristics of the new digital technologies. If it was possible to explore the "space-time couplings" that outlined the dynamics of fixation, the establishment of borders, exclusion and non-passage, all of which condition the performance of people, collectivities, and communication processes, we now turn to those dynamics which, under the logics of virtualization, promote in culture a sort of decoupling of the ordinary physical or geographic space from the temporality of the clock and calendar (Lévy, 1996: 21), making classical space-time escape to its "realistic" common places, the place unit making way to the synchronicity, and interconnection replacing the time unit.

Let us start from the idea of cyberspace, which harbors this space-temporal relativization, leading, in Lévy's work, to the cyberculture and to the cybercity. The etymology of the prefix *cyber*, that came to us from the modern rearrangement of the Greek noun *kubernetes*, meaning pilot, helmsman and, figuratively, director, boss, governor, is already common knowledge and has become reshaped in the coinage of the word *cybernetics*, a field of investigation molded and disseminated immediately after the second world war. Mathematician Norbert Wiener (1894–1964), who had launched Cybernetics in 1948 as a new science that aimed at the comprehension of the essential unit of natural and artificial phenomena through the study of communication and control processes in living beings, in machines and in social processes, in 1950 wrote *The Human Use Of Human Beings: Cybernetics And Society*. In cybernetic heritage, writer William Gibson coined the word cyberspace, which indicated, in his science fiction novel *Neuromancer* (1984), the universe of omnipresent digital networks, to which humans connected directly via the nervous system, which allowed them to visualize data and programs and to work on them, defying the real universe. The term spread very rapidly among the users of digital networks.

Pierre Lévy gives his own definition of cyberspace as a "communication space made accessible through the global interconnection of computers and computer memories", with emphasis on digital technology because it conditions the information in its "plastic, fluid, calculable, real-time, hypertextual, interactive and, yes, virtual" character, which is "the distinctive characteristic of cyberspace" (Lévy, 1999: 92, 93). The network thus constituted includes not only the material infrastructure but also, and above all, the universe of information that it possesses, permanently connected to the social and cognitive performance of the humans that feed it and navigate it.

A culture thus conditioned becomes *cyberculture*, that is, a non-universalizing socio-technical and cognitive environment whose function is hegemonically presided over by material and intellectual techniques, by practices, behaviors, attitudes, knowledge, ways of thinking, values that develop in a relation of co-pertinence and co-determination with cyberspace (Lévy, 1999: 17).

We said "non-universalizing".[83] In what sense? Let us recapture the characteristics of the previous cognitive regimes in order to, in contrast, clarify the non-universalizing aspect of *cyberculture*.

Orality, Writing, Earth, Territory and Commodity correspond to intellectual technologies and anthropological spaces that provide more-or-less stable and stabilizing sense units. If I am a member of a tribe or of a closed and self-centralizing community, I am restricted to and compulsorily identified by its religious, social, technical repertoire, by its institutional and behavioral standards, which transcend the order in which I am inserted, orienting it from "outside" or from "above". The intra- and inter-groups exchange opportunities tend to follow a circuit determined by the very tribal border, disciplined by immemorial custom, by deities, by magic. Since the end of the nineteenth century ethnographic researches describe societies that function based on principles of reciprocity and redistribution – a systematic and organized give-and-take of valuable objects, often transported over great distances – which sews up social and religious solidarities on a network of reciprocal obligations and which, in turn, punishes and marginalizes those who infringe its codes of honor and generosity (Polanyi, 1980: 59–69).

If I am a user of writing, especially after the invention of the printing press, I navigate on more abstract hypertexts, removable from their emergent contexts and rearranged according to strategies of power and knowledge that support and feed on the infinite hermeneutical activity that assures them as distinct knowledge-producing units, and settled on authorities fighting for hegemony, to whom are attributed powers of permission, sanction, management and control over the lives of individuals and collectivities. In each generation, more nodes and links are added to these hypertextual libraries, asserting the territorialities and proliferating the rivaling game of establishing the "correct", "true", "valid for all", "objective" version of knowledge, behaviors and values.

If I am a user of mass media, if I access radio, television, movies, press, phonographic production (in ancient LP and CD formats), books, attend rock concerts, theater plays, football matches or watch their transmission on television, I am part of a movement that connects me to the flow through some large-scale common denominator, which gathers millions of people through the logics of the best seller, the largest audience, the show of the year, the Academy Award winning movie, the idol of football or of the stages of national and international pop scenarios. Human herds kidnapped by the concentration of the *media*, in a double sense: by the monopolization of technical and industrial media (the *mass media*) by a few economic groups, a phenomenon that became evident especially from the 1970s and 1980s onwards; and by its reverse, the precarious availability and access to alternatives, because there simply was no way to have a partial, anonymous and networked contact with other producing centers and information users.

Telephone contact depended on a physically-fixed device installed in residences and public spaces, a situation gradually liberated by the mobility of cell phones, which, until the end of the 1990s, transmitted only speech. The radio station to which people listened was geographically local and its shows often placed users in contact with each other through letters, a practise taken up by newspapers and magazines, which also used the PO Box. Taking pictures involved the operation of buying film and, afterwards, having the photographs developed at a specialized facility. Watching broadcast and cable television, the latter still scarcely available and at prohibitive cost, was a collective domestic family activity at more-or-less established times and with a standardized set of options. Newspapers and magazines, national and international, circulated on paper and, often, difficult to find when they were not within their local geographic circuit; and there was also the distinction between the mainstream, the official, the popular, the "best selling", and the underground, the "trash", the "alternative", the "subversive".

Cyberculture pulverized all these poles of concentration, totalization and universalization, dissolving or relativizing borders until they became indiscernible, by placing everything and everyone in connection and interactivity, in an unlimited and unfiltered way, in a seamless landscape, without the contrasts of *mainstream* vs *underground*, and in which the "professional" content as well as the "amateur" one, the "official" as well as the "pirate" started to be consumed without much discrimination (Anderson, 2006).

It is a fact that today we live a quotidian existence that has significantly changed in relation to that which was conceived in the 1990s, when the texts we are considering were published. Then, people began to deal with the scenario of popularization of domestic use of computers; internet (dial-up); access to data over distance, their transference, sharing and construction through online tutorials, electronic conferences and *groupware*; e-mail; CD ROMs and DVDs as enlarged and mobile supports to store and save information (text, image, sound).

Today we have even more dynamic and fragmented devices that accelerate virtualization, such as broadband or wireless internet access; online access to entire movies, which, in turn, can be burned onto a DVD-R at home, freeing memory space in the computer and allowing the broadcast of the content at any place that has a computer or a television and DVD; *iPods* and simpler flash drives, which load text, sound and image (photograph and video), besides recording sound, accessible on the device itself or through any computer with a USB port and compatible software; the popularization of music (mp3), text and image-sharing programs; cell phones which are digital photo and video cameras, as well as microcomputers that transmit sound, text and image, besides accessing the internet; more recent devices already available on the market, merge the functions of cell phone with wide screen *iPod* and internet access with browser and e-mail, using as a new interface a multi-touch screen and a new program that enables the user to use the device with nothing but the fingers[84]; instant message programs and virtual relations, such as on Orkut; virtual spaces such as You Tube where videos and personal information are shared, sites that allow entertainment downloads, classes, lectures, conferences, not necessarily connected to official university programs; general user content, anonymous or not.

These are just a few examples that allow us to exponentially widen the reach of Lévy's arguments, following the logics of virtualization. Certain intuitions of the author are confirmed such as, for instance, the statement that "cyberculture is a wholesale collection of heresies", because, unlike previous separations, "its borders are fluid, moving, and provisional" (Lévy, 1999: 238). Its common spaces are occupied by anyone who produces, disseminates or investigates what interests him/her, giving him/her the initiative, in a regime of high partiality and using network dynamics, in forms such as *photologs* and *blogs*, You Tube or search engines with browsing filters such as Google Scholar. At last, infinite interconnection and interactivity point towards the end of monopolies on public expression; the growing variety of modes of expression; the progressive availability of search and browser engines which annuls the previous hierarchy of information; the development of virtual communities and interpersonal contacts regardless of physical and geographic barriers; the relativization of political, economic and technological restraints to the worldwide expression of cultural diversity and to the exchange of information, to which the several file sharing programs that permanently dilute the market power of intellectual property bear witness (Lévy, 1999: 239–41).

In the light of these dynamics, certain concepts, expressions and ideas brought forth by Lévy are potentialized. We can finally consider that which interests us more closely – the concept of cybercity – animated by the more general processes of desubjectification, desubstantialization and deterritorialization to which we refer.

The central idea in the proposition of cybercity is to think of the articulation possibilities between two qualitatively different spaces: territory and collective intelligence, the latter having cyberspace as support. We have seen how different these spaces are physically and topologically: territory is adscript to a center and its limits, organized by systems physically or geographically close; cyberspace is co-presence of a point on the network relative to any other, moving at very high speeds. Besides that, from the point of view of social processes, territory is a space of separations and hierarchies, whereas cyberspace works on the transversality of relations and in the fluidity of contacts.

Therefore, it is not about eliminating or replacing a form (the territory) to the benefit of another (cyberspatial functioning), but, rather, to "compensate, at least to the extent possible, for the lassitude, inertia, and unavoidable rigidity of the territory with its realtime exposure to cyberspace" (Lévy, 1999: 195).

Cybercity would be the result of collective intelligence processes applied to territory, optimizing its resources by the plasticity of cyberspace, effectively building a cosmopolitan space or *polycosmos*, a space of metamorphoses of relations and of appearance of ways of being, which would facilitate the expression of uniqueness, the weaving of social bond through reciprocal apprenticeship and the unfettered navigation of knowledge (Lévy, 1999: 196). The subjects of classical space-time would no longer appear "as solid figurines placed within clearly demarcated territories, but as nomadic distributions streaming through a moving space" (Lévy, 2003: 137). In other words, cybercity is the dwelling space of "immigrants of subjectivity" (Lévy, 2003: 14), who inhabit, therefore, all media with which they interact.

4.8 Complex networks

Several authors have dedicated themselves to studying the network phenomenon. The discoveries in this field surprise us because they do not always follow linear reasoning. Albert-László Barabási, physics professor at the University of Notre Dame, is a researcher who has dedicated himself to demonstrating what networks are, how they form and develop. His 2003 book has an enlightening title: *Linked: how everything is connected to everything else and what it means for business, science and everyday life.* The innovative discoveries are so many that he appoints them as propellers of a new scientific revolution (Barabási, 2003). The emergence of complexity[85] has placed us in the face of a new reality, at whose core is the comprehension that we live in a small and interconnected world in which systems as different as the economy, the cell, the postal and road system, air traffic, the language and the Internet present similar behaviors, and can be used to explain each other. Actually, this is only possible because these different systems have a common organization: that of the networks.

We can consider that "networks are everywhere": from the brain as a network of nerve cells connected by axons, to societies – a network constituted by people connected by bonds of friendship, family, profession, etc. – and all the way to language, which is a network composed of words connected by syntactic standards.[86] Complex networks are defined as having a very large number of connections, and as not presenting a predictable standard in their structure, and that each node can bear a different amount of links.

4.8.1 Random networks

In the theory of random networks we have the formation of clusters, which are densely interconnected networks formed from the progressive addition of links and the junction of nodes that form a huge agglomerate, characterized by the fact that each node has, on average, one link.

Let us take, for instance, the "small world" hypothesis developed by Stanley Milgram, social psychologist at Harvard, who articulated the idea that a person can be connected to any other in the world through five links at the most. Through a study[87], he found a relatively small value for the existing distance between any two people in the selected space of study: 5.5 people in average. Despite this work being inconclusive due to the small number of letters that reached the final destination, the interest that arose from such idea comes from the fact that even large dimensions can be connected by a very small number of links.

Another example very much used in social networks is the following: if you know approximately one thousand people, who also know about one thousand people (didactically using the hypothesis that they are unknown to each other) – you will be just two handshakes away from one million people, and just three handshakes away from one billion. Following this reasoning, the entire population of the planet will be just four handshakes away from you. Thus we live in a *small world*, in which two people can be easily connected despite the almost six billion nodes of the circumscribing network.

However, the standard of the random networks does not apply to many of the situations which are evidenced in everyday practice. For instance, in the case of cities, very often we see that its commerce prefers to concentrates on certain streets, to the detriment of others, maintaining no correspondence to a democratic resultant regarding all the streets of the city. These situations follow another standard, that of scale-free networks.

4.8.2 Scale-free networks

Albert-László Barabási, Réka Albert and Hawoong Jeong, from the University of Notre Dame, initially aiming at the functioning of random networks, joined, in 1998, a project of the mapping of the World Wide Web. Unlike their expectations, the result of this research showed a differentiated model, where a very small number of web pages had a huge number of connections while a very large number of pages, approximately 80 per cent, had less than four links.

This disproportion is the characteristic of the scale-free networks structure, which also explains many situations of our everyday life, where the most connected nodes tend to be the most searched. Therefore, the scale-free networks present a model where a small number of nodes show an enormous concentration of connections to other nodes and a very large number of nodes with few connections. This model introduces a new element: the connectors, or *hubs* – nodes with an exceptional number of links which are present in several systems.

The topology of scale-free networks also determines two other characteristics: the resistance to failures and the liability to attacks. Unlike what happens on a random network, scale-free networks do not disintegrate easily when a given number of nodes, different for each network considered, is withdrawn from its structure. On the contrary, they show an amazing readaptation and reorganization capability, which makes them extremely robust. Hubs are responsible for this connectivity maintenance, given that the probability of a failure happening in just one of the numerous small nodes is far greater than in a hub. However, the price that is paid for this robustness is extreme vulnerability to coordinated attacks. Difficult as it may be, the action of crippling several of its hubs simultaneously would have a devastating effect on a scale-free network, comparable to the simultaneous shut down of a country's main airports or to the simultaneous blocking of a city's main streets and avenues.

These and other studies related to networks bring new understanding about the phenomena around us. We can conjecture that our interconnected universe is not random, nor average, let alone democratic. However, if there are great advances in the comprehension of networks topology, there is still much to investigate about internal mechanisms and the dynamics that take place in such peculiar structures. For urbanism, these new perspectives can bring progress for the comprehension of the different processes and mechanisms that interconnect, granting a new understanding of the articulations that are at stake when we consider the concept of city.

Such developments already allow applications which help understand the dynamics of everyday lives of people and urban centers. One of them would be the possibility of classifying contemporary citizens according to the degree of connection each one has. Considering the urban networks which are interpenetrated by informational space, we can relativize the social bonds concerning the geographic belonging to a city. From this perspective, on our society's network we would have those citizens with an exceptional number of links – including connections to many people in different places of the world –

while most citizens have only a few links. This organization is also present on the network of connections each person bears, which is not only translated in terms of social bonds or geographic connections, but also in several situations. Therefore, a few people are highly influent social characters – they have more acquaintances, more professional contacts, more opportunities, more information, several tastes, interests and consumption possibilities, etc. – whereas most people would only have a reasonable number of such connections. Scale-free networks are an integral part of our reality, and act decisively in several areas of our urban lives. They express our relationship with the space of the cities and with the several networks that form it, whether social, informational, affective, ecological, political, of transportation and displacement, etc. Thus, we constitute ourselves as the cities we daily cross, as sets of flows, relations of power and strength. Just as the city, we are also networks of formations, power fields constantly at stake, as we connect to the spaces, in an imbricated and interdependent way. These are the relational situations that blur the limits and dissolve the borders that separate us from the city.

4.9 Summary Chart

DESCARTES (1596-1650)
France
- I – individual substance isolated from other substances or I's.
- I – substance = I – individual = Mental – I: subject and author of its ideas.
- Supposed identical to itself: absolute and permanent identity of I.
- Overlapping of the notion of I to that of Subject: substantial Subject.
- Knowledge is relation between subject and object.
- SUBJECT – OBJECT. Process of knowledge as from the nature of the object.
- Assesses human knowledge in reference to the model of knowledge performed by an absolute and divine thinking: theocentric model.
- Mind and body are distinct realities: mind as "mental substance" (res cogitans) and matter as "corporeal substance" (res extensa).

KANT (1724-1804)
Prussia/Germany
- Autonomization of the subject.
- Subject as law of its operations.
- Kantian subject set of rules by which phenomena may be known.
- The subjective unit of consciousness (transcendental subject) enables knowledge of objects in general.
- Subject of knowledge is the a priori capability of knowing.
- Transcendental Subject.
- Knowledge is relation between subject and object.

- SUBJECT – OBJECT. Process of knowledge as from the subject's ability to know. The structure of the mind is the source of the conditions necessary to knowledge.
- Knowledge is strictly human and subjective representation, regardless of any divine order: anthropocentric model.

FREUD (1856–1939)
Austria

- Ego has the role of conflict mediator. Performs the task of liaison to the world and to the so-called internal states.
- Ego is not something stable and substantial that remains identical to itself throughout the diversity of its experiences.
- Ego is effect of the complexity of the Unconscious determination.
- Decentering of conscious Freud proposes an "apparatus" that involves different systems with different working principles: the id (it), the ego and the superego.
- Man is no longer foundation of knowledge and of himself. It is no longer about subjectivity, neither particular, of each individual, nor transcendental subjectivity, universal to man.
- There is no longer knowledge understood as domination of objects by a sovereign or autonomous subject.
- The experience engendered by the unconscious revokes reasoning that states any centering or fixed point of reference.
- Mind-body distinction loses meaning with the proposition of the "limitrophe" concept of instinct.

LUDWIG VON BERTALANFFY (1901–1972)
Austria

- I is systemic operation that dynamically totalizes a structuring and functional complex, open to the possibility of exchange and transformation.
- I – is a systemic totality that presides over the sum of the biological, cultural, linguistic, psychical components that constitute it;
- City – systemic totality that presides over the sum of the services, information, people and goods that constitute it.
- System – all forms of organization whose behavior is described as the interdependence between its component parts (road grid, living beings, societies, etc). Systems may be open or closed and are delimited by boundaries.
- General Systems Theory – set of particular interactive relations where the global resultant of the operation exceeds the local reasons of its components.
- Analogy as heuristic instrument constitutive of any knowledge.
- Function with self-regulation and control, transforming themselves through their intrinsic capacity of permanent regeneration and adaptation throughout the process of exchange with the environment.

HUMBERTO MATURANA & FRANCISCO VARELA (1928– ; 1946–2001)
Chile

- I – existential resultant of organization and stability that molds in the process of its own production and transformation – the communities I attend, the bonds I establish, spaces where I circulate -, its border being a function of its mutant competence.
- I – is pure recursive operation, whose recurrence stabilizes and creates communicational coherences in the several social and linguistic couplings which participate in it and of which it results.
- Autopoiesis: network of production, transformation and destruction processes, whose components permanently reproduce, through their interactions, the very network that produced them.
- Autopoietic system – continuous production of itself.
- There is nothing but relations and their terms are immanent to the very autopoietic system, which is, simultaneously, producer and product.
- Boundaries that integrate and result from the very autopoietic organization.
- Circularity: inseparability between human being and the world (we could say, therefore, between I and the city).

GILLES DELEUZE & FÉLIX GUATTARI (1925–1995; 1930–1992)
France

- Rhizome: theory of multiplicities. Acentered, non-hierarchical and non-significant system which is defined solely by the circulation of states from one point to any other. Option for nomadism; disclaim to ontology, to foundation, to end and to beginning; the choice of being "between".
- Multiplicities - detached from any unity, totality or dualism, without subject or object, acentered. Are defined by the outside, change nature when connecting to the others.
- Principle of connection - any point of a rhizome can be connected to any other.
- Heterogeneity - connections take place between very diverse ways of coding.
- Asignifying rupture - a rhizome can be shattered or broken at any spot, and restart on any of its lines, or even another line. Process of deterritorialization and reterritorialization.
- Creating a rhizome is to build a map as from experimentation anchored in reality. Open map, built, detachable, reversible and connectable in all of its dimensions, with multiple entrances and exits, susceptible to receiving constant modifications. It regards performance, not competence.

PIERRE LÉVY (1956–)
Tunisia

- Digital informatics - it is me anthropological mutation: affects information, communication, the bodies, economic functioning, collective settings of sensitivity, the exercise of intelligence.

- Three poles of the spirit: Primary Orality, Writing, and Informatics.
- Four anthropological spaces: Earth, Territory, Commodities and Knowledge.
- Primary Orality / Earth - it is me close hypertexts, closed significations and low metamorphosis speed.
- Writing - correlative of agriculture whereas technology of sedentarization, fixation and separation. Deterritorializes the speech, separating it from the living body, and sedentarizes it by rewriting it on an inert support.
- Space of Commodities - it is me the organizing principle is the flow: of energies, raw materials, merchandise, capital, labor, information.
- Third era of the spirit - digital network or informatic-mediatic pole. Knowledge space. Social and cognitive transformations allowed by new digital-base technologies.
- Worldwide cyberspace where every element of information is in virtual contact with each and everyone. Cyberculture - pulverized the poles of concentration, totalization and universalization.

ALBERT-LÁSZLÓ BARABÁSI (1967–)
Romania
- Different Systems (city, economy, cell, road grid, air traffic, language and the Internet) organized by networks, present similar behaviors, may be used to explain each other.
- Complex Networks - mold large systems, many connections whose structure does not follow a regular pattern, given that each node has a different number of links.
- Random Networks - approaches the complexity as from randomness. Democratic universe in which averages prevail.
- Scale-free Networks - systems that reveal an enormous number of nodes with few connections, and a few nodes (hubs), which are irradiation and convergence poles, with a huge number of connections to other nodes. Resistance against failures and vulnerability to coordinated attacks.
- Our interconnected universe is not random, nor average, let alone democratic.
- Just like the city, we are also networks of formations, power fields constantly at stake, as we connect to the spaces, in an imbricated and interdependent way. (We could say that these relational situations that blur the limits and dissolve the borders that separate us from the city).

4.10 Considerations

We have presented a few understandings of the concept of "I", from the understanding of the concept of subject, as well as from some forms of thought articulations.

Thus, we have seen in Descartes the modern notion of subject, and the understanding of an embodied subject identified to an individual *I*. With this overlapping of the notion of *I* with that of subject, and the configuration of a subject conceived as author and center of command of somebody's acts and thoughts, we have the individualism that characterized modern idealism.

Before Kant, it was supposed, when explaining knowledge, that the subject sought on the very object the understanding of the latter and the object was considered a substance in itself (Reale & Antiseri, 2004: 352). Kant, in an innovative way, inverted this relation between subject and object, and stated that the object is constituted by the subject, that "about things we do not know *a priori*, except what we place in them ourselves and, therefore, the foundation of *a priori* synthetic judgements is the very subject with the laws of its sensitivity and of its intellect" (Reali & Antiseri, 2004: 352). The great importance of this displacement is that it results in the understanding of autonomization of the subject and, consequently, the conception of the Kantian transcendental subject. In this situation, the subject takes itself as controller of its operations, and is the one who produces understanding of the object. But what interests us mostly is that, up until this time, we are specifically dealing with discernible and separated subject and object.

As we have seen, in Freud there is a complete revolution of the entire understanding of *I* that had been constructed up to that moment. The belief that *I* is something stable and substantial that remains identical to itself throughout the diversity of its experiences is denied – *I* is, rather, the complexity effect of unconscious determination. For Freudian psychoanalysis, it is no longer about subjectivity, neither particular, of each individual, nor the transcendental, universal subjectivity of man. The experience engendered by the *unconscious* revokes reasoning that affirms any centering or fixed point of reference. The belief in foundations is dethroned, the *I*, rational and methodical, is displaced, and no longer belongs to any subjectivity, psychological or transcendental. The position of psychoanalysis not only causes the revision of the idea of man as center of the world; it contests the very idea that the world has a center or unity. Therefore not only the privilege of the *I*, but a certain way of foundational thinking, characteristic of western thought, is kept in check.[88]

In continuance of the broadening, decentering and dissolution of the concept of "I", we have the contribution of other contemporary authors. With GST we have the introduction of that which, today, is considered commonplace through the understanding of networks, which is the interdependence, the interaction and the properties of organization in a systemic and relational way. This reasoning is particularized by the understanding of *autopoiesis*, where the concept of circularity makes producer and product undistinguishable; there is no separation between subject and object, whence we can already conceptually think the inseparability between city and I.

The concept of rhizome allows us to apprehend the contemporary reality as multiple and decentered, an open and infinite arrangement of fragments that are autonomous and inter-connectable on a network and without a fixed point of origin and convergence, where Multiplicity takes us to the comprehension of the huge number of factors that affect us and constitute us as social beings. However, Lévy's hypertext and collective intelligence place us directly in the informational environment of virtual networks that have been analyzed and characterized by their configurations that may escape any predictability.

Our objective is to understand that, just as the urban "being" has gone through deep modifications – in a growing dematerialization process ever since the medieval city, where the wall ceased to be not only the boundary between city and the space that does not belong to it, but also its conceptual safety, defining its "very being" (Lepetit, 2001: 252), and from the advent of the industrial city, in the nineteenth century, to the contemporary city with the dematerialization of the borders which, replacing the wall, gradually forged the definition of urban in an increasingly larger perspective of communication and mobility of goods, information and people (Ascher, 2001). Likewise, the "urban" being who, as inhabitant, interacted with this progressively-dematerialized urban space, also experienced, in the same process and at the same time, the vertigo of decentralization and multi-belonging, being forced to leave behind the place of undivided and permanent subject, and become chief-coordinator of its own actions.

Our intention in this chapter was to supply data that enabled the following of the process of decentralization and the fragmentation of the notion of "I", while, in chapter 2 we tried to show the process of semantic and conceptual splintering of the idea of "city". It is worth asking at this point whether the fluid state of the modern urban space could still shelter any "subject" or "individual", inhabitants of the Cartesian planned city, according to functions that are specific and non-interchangeable. We probably can no longer imagine ourselves in the shoes of the citizen who performs exclusive roles in family, leisure, work, in seasonal tourism; someone who depends exclusively on cable communications, on the road map or on the printed newspaper. Conceptualized as *individuals*, we bore the self-image of being an undivided spot, minimum and irreducible unit sustained by the corporeal figuration, whose individuality is apparently assured to us, unquestionably, by the specular image. Atoms of the social fabric, numerically different and individually valued, in the core of this existence we once probably felt untouched and protected from the advancements of the public sphere, and at the same time ready to celebrate social achievements as victory of the individual.

Nothing very different happens when we establish ourselves as *subjects*, in the good and old western tradition. From ancient to modern, we have built the idea of subjectivity from the idea of self subsistence and of a unifying consciousness of that, which affirms its identity in time, an essentially immutable base provided with purely accidental and changeable characteristics – perceptions, tastes or affections. Whether or not guaranteed by divine act, the fact is that, for centuries, we were oriented by the notion of subject as substance capable of existing by itself, the substratum, *sub-jectum*, the foundation on which we built the image of self as commander of our acts and thoughts.[89]

In the next chapter we intend to present the concept of I = *Person* with the Pole of formations that constitutes it, becoming a network which, today, can no longer be described in the limited terms of horizontality (I – you) or of verticality (absolute transcendent with defined face) relations, including the corollaries thence resulting. We intend to show the pertinence, adequacy and functionality of the proposition *the city is me* for contemporary discussions that are happening in urbanism. For that we use a supporting theory capable of supplying us the heuristic tool to construct the thesis *the city is me* and authorizing us to think, given the properties of *Person,* what is *I,* inhabitant of this informational urban space, *videoptical* and *videophilic,* non-stop, globalized, controlled, digital, instantaneous, e-topical and distopical, in short, the equivalence *I = Person,* built on the terms of the New Psychoanalysis, the conceptual base for this reflection, conceptualization and demonstration. This is what we will see next.

Chapter 5

The Concept of *Person* According to the New Psychoanalysis

Mosaic: Isadora Dantas

We have reached the point of particular interest for this study. With the objective of demonstrating the pertinence and adequacy of the proposition *the city is me* for the contemporary discussions that take place in urbanism, we will specify the concept of *I* which grants base and support to our hypothesis and which was originally formulated by the *NovaMente* theory or *New Psychoanalysis*[90], developed as from the 1970s by Brazilian psychoanalyst MD Magno. Our intention is not to present the framework of this theory – for that, there are many published works[91] and several master's and doctorate dissertations and postdoctoral papers presented – but, rather, to point out some characteristics of the concept of *I* brought by this theoretical-clinical apparatus. It is self-evident to assert that the presentation of part of a theory involves a reduction. Therefore, for a broader understanding, we suggest that research be done into the original work.

As we have seen, the notion to which we currently refer as *I*, the subject, the individual or even subjectivity is a heritage of the Greco-Judeo-Christian matrix. Originally *hipokeimenon* in Greek and *subjectum* in Latin, subject would denote something underlying, which would be "under". Otherwise, the subject is also the notion developed from grammar – something or someone that the sentence is about, that has attributes and predicates and can perfectly be something. Therefore, we end up non-critically absorbing this notion, which is imposed on us, everyday, by several means, be it through belief in separation between body and soul (*subjectum* as a little man who expresses himself inside us), be it through the practice of language (Greek and Latin heritage) with its reflexive function, with its grammatical subjects and its distinction between subject and object. However, on the other hand, we have also seen that several authors have abandoned the notion of subject, and are increasingly presenting a more acentered, relativizing, relational, systemic notion without distinction between subject and object. However, whether from habit, or because of grammar, or language, we still talk as if we were in the seventeenth century, while the functioning of practices of existence in the contemporary world move increasingly farther from any of the characteristics of the past and theories considered as "extremely advanced" already start from a new configuration and, as we have seen, are creating several new concepts to deal with the new reality. For this reason, in order to define our concept of city, we sought a concept of *I* which is compatible with the ongoing transformations.

In this theory, the notion of subject is rethought and bypassed, giving way to a new proposition that moves from the notion of individual, as well as from current conceptions from which subject is approached. In its stead, the term *Person*[92] – "process without subject, in the sense of without any center of enunciation" (Magno, 2010: 116) – is proposed as a sign of distancing in relation to the usual denominations, heavily loaded with connotations that have been crystallized for centuries in the tradition of Christian philosophy. But this is not the only conceptual difference; if it were, we could use other concepts from other fields which are already thus configured. For this reason, we intend, throughout this chapter, to show more characteristics of this concept of person brought forth by New Psychoanalysis which authorize us to forward the thesis: the city is me.

For the development that interests this work, we will stress that, according to New Psychoanalysis, the concept of *I* is equal to that of *Person* and may be defined (Magno, 2010: 99–128; Magno, 2009) by the following attributes (which we will later develop): (1) by the conjunction of Primary Formations + Secondary Formations + Original Formation, which in their articulations constitute a network; (2) a Pole with Focus, Fringe and Background; (3) *Persons* are *Idioformations* of the human case; and, (4) *Person* is in the order of Being and *Há* in the order of *Haver*.[93] Our intention is to articulate the items above in order to enable a given understanding of this concept.

5.1 The equivalence *I* = Person

The concept of *Person*, such as developed by Personalism, encompasses a number of meanings that range from the basic etymological notion of "mask" up to the broader notion of man (as in mankind), going through individual, subject, relation, community, and differentiation. When exploring the concept of *Person*, making it equivalent to that of *I*, Magno makes a radical displacement, granting an original understanding to this concept, betting on the greater intelligibility this may bring to the handling of contemporary discussions, where the issue of city is immersed. The target is the creation of a conceptual space compatible with the contemporary perspective of information, network, connectivity and flows, closer than the psychoanalytical field conceives as being the non-tectonic movement of the unconscious or of psychism. The author himself draws attention to the fact in 1992, in his Seminar *Pedagogia Freudiana* [Freudian Pedagogy]:

> I would actually say that Freud's speech, due to his epoch, to the theoretical collections he made, is entirely tectonic. It is an architecture with ground, with force of gravity ruling the flying buttresses, the domes, and above all organizing the foundations on a terrain that is actually not very regulated by his own speech, borrowed from an archeology which is a little ancient. It is as if the Freudian system were a geocentric apparatus: everything is gravitationally directed towards the base, towards the center of a planet. (Magno, 1993: 3)

The reformulation experienced by psychoanalysis under Jacques Lacan between the 1950s and the 1970s is seen by Magno as a displacement from this geocentrism towards a heliocentrism, as Lacan rendered movement to the psychical forces, even if granting linguistic focus to the ellipse of his heliocentric system. He says:

> … it seems to me necessary and urgent to assemble an absolutely non-tectonic, nor geocentric, nor heliocentric apparatus, but which could – and there the blow may cease to be Keplerian and become Einsteinian, if you will, as metaphor – become centered on a radical relativism of the energies that support the great system of the thinking universe of psychoanalysis (Magno, 1993: 4).

One of the aspects of non-tectonic psychoanalysis is the way it conceives that *I* equals to *Person.* On one hand it acknowledges that the efforts of previous psychoanalysis in abstracting the old Freudian notion of *Ego*, moving on to the abstractive conception of *Subject,* are no longer sustainable. In the face of the contemporary idea of information – translating pole of the formations[94] which present themselves in any order, be it digital, analogical, mechanical, computational, quantum, but also linguistic, artistic, poetic – it becomes likely that the idea of *Subject* is not enough for the network and for the flows of (in)formation. Here, there is not, as was believed throughout the twentieth century, a definitive distancing from the Ego ballasted on figurative appearances of the body. On the contrary: given that the human configuration is a body which, when it opens its mouth, focuses, we imagine it to be a Subject. But where? This is only "an expansion without definite place" (Magno, 2005: 95). On the other hand, the contemporary formation as networked, informational, *videoptical* and *videophilic*, non-stop, globalized, controlled, digital, instantaneous, e-topical and distopical, etc., which may be approached as an expanding network, without center or definite place – is compatible with the concept of *Person* which will permit performing the necessary displacement for the construction of the idea that *the city is me.*

First of all, we believe the current usages of the notion of *Person* can create a "friendly interface", better situating the desired displacement. Therefore, when we consider a *Person,* "we forget that it is a mere *carrefour*, mere confluence of a huge amount of things, including the corporeity that is over there, with its habits and biological particularities" (Magno, 2005: 97), an open network that disappears when we limit it to a scope that individualizes or subjectivizes. At the same time, the notion of *Person* – when carrying the burden of the reasoning of individuation, subjectification, subjectivity, subject, identification, etc. – allows for consideration of the other face of the coin. Because

> I can only perceive this supposed subjectivity when there are closures that eliminate any *herenow* possibility of communication. We then call subjectivity that which is, actually, particularity of a closed set of formations. (Magno, 2005: 97)

In other words, every operation of individuation or subjectification is a reduction of the broader possibilities of the idea of *Person*, and indicates an operation of repression, that is, exclusion and non-connection. From another point of view, the notion of *Person* allows certain displacements, on a vector that is particularly appropriate to our work of demonstrating that *the city is me*. The existing conceptual commitment between *Person* and "community", through the vector of *openness to the relation* that the concept usually bears, makes the equivalence *I = Person*, which is an open network of (in)formations, a good tool to understand what might be the city (finally) transformed in civilized universe, that is, *oikouméne*.[95]

Therefore, we understand by *I = Person* the infinite set of formations and interests with competence of connection (to other formations and interests), constituting the network or fabric that affects and moves us, nowadays increasingly more qualified in the sense of behaviors and attitudes that take into consideration (the availability of) *mobility, connectivity and communication*. Some examples may help.

Let us think about the professional network that constitutes the characters and fragments of characters that we assume in our everyday life: at the office, on visit to clients, in reports we need to present, in conferences to which one is appointed at the last minute, on team activities, in the classroom, at the counter, whenever we are required to integrate new information and get rid of the previous, in order to grant flow and speed to the actions and tasks for which we are responsible.

The communication theorist Marshall McLuhan had already in the 1960s pointed out the aspect of "all-now" of the world in the "age of electricity". With the idea of "Global Village", he insisted on the fact that men were, henceforth, intertwined with each other by the electric circuits system which made information "pour upon us instantly and continuously", so that "instant communication insures that all factors of the environment and of experience coexist in a *state of active interplay*" (McLuhan, c1969: 91, my italics). Thus, the "age of electricity" made us acknowledge, once and for all, the level of interaction present among our culturally constructed artifacts and the "natural" devices of which we are spontaneously constituted. For this reason, McLuhan could speak of electronic technology as an extension of our central nervous system, globally broadening the effects of this extension, as something that affects the whole psychical and social complex of the planet (McLuhan, 2007).

With the new supports for the recording, transmission and processing of information, the world at the beginning of the twenty-first century is extending McLuhan's intuitions with remarkable speed. Concurrently, the treatment some concepts have received highlights new aspects of the idea of the cultural artifact as extension of man and helps us understand the equivalence *I = Person*. It is the case, for instance, of the idea of *hypertext*, such as developed by Pierre Lévy (Lévy, 1993: 28–42). Technically speaking, a hypertext is

a set of nodes linked by connections. The nodes may be words, pages, images, graphs or excerpts, sound sequences, complex documents that may, themselves, be hypertexts. The information items are not linearly connected, as in a rope with knots, but each of them, or the most part, extends its connections in a star-like fashion, in a reticular way. Browsing a hypertext means, therefore, drawing a route on a network that may be as complicated as possible. Because each node can, in turn, contain an entire network. (Lévy, 1993: 33)

In other words, we are treating *I* as a network that behaves as hypertext, without borders between hearing/visual capacity and manipulation of aural/written documents, involving "body", words, images, memory traces, affections and sensations, also determined by the social, political, cultural, aesthetic network, etc. which constitutes this *I* in which it is dynamically inserted. As Lévy himself acknowledges, "hypertext may be a valid metaphor for all spheres of reality in which *significations* are at stake" (Lévy, 1993: 25).

We can, however, take one more step. Let us consider an activity such as "writing". We have the text on the monitor screen; the software employed; the processor speed; the notes written on paper; open books under consultation; stored information memory; keyboard and hands writing; the wind coming in from the window and the landscape it portrays; the thirst and the glass of water; the car passing by; the cricket that sings at the end of the afternoon; the icon and/or the sound signal that warns of incoming e-mail in the inbox; the flow of meaningful and meaningless words and sentences that invade the focused attention; intentions and desires of signification which, without us noticing it (!), monitor and invade our reflection activity, processing and writing... Where is *I*?

The state of active interplay (McLuhan) or hypertext (Lévy) that constitutes the network *I* = *Person* reveals itself, ultimately, as a processing without subject, without a communication "actor" (to use Lévy's terms), without a control center and without an owner. This network happens *regardless* of what we volitionally know, feel, remember, forget, hear, see or control, because it is the versatility of the field in which we move that transforms us, at each time and in each case, into versatile *Persons,* that is, with talent in and for a given activity. *I* = *Person* is indistinctively all the network possibilities, in its materialization (organic, digital, mechanical, analogical, quantum) and organization (horizontal, vertical, reticular), in a set that opens towards the infinite, suspending space and time. Through a psychoanalytical approach, we can add that *I* = *Person* is also a set of formations invested due to interest of exacerbating and extrapolating its given or imposed limits, that is, with availability to be affected by Hyperdetermination.[96] The abstractive vector of technology shows us this:

What has the so-called science done, that operates through technique? What does it, or knowledge in general, do if not trying to invent keys which grant access to files that are closed? Be it the structure of the atom, or of human cerebral formations, or that of stars, etc., it is about inventing keys to break into files. Scientists are *hackers*: they want to break into what God would have closed ... knowing is the invention of keys, picklocks, with which to break into locked files. (Magno, 2003: 79–80)

Consequently, dealing with I = *Person* involves considering an infinite network of formations, where passages happen (locked files are opened). But also, as the opposite vector, dealing with I = *Person,* involves considering an infinite network, in which enclosed formations have the rest (of the network) excluded from them, fighting over powers of hegemony and of centralized authority (the network paralyzed due to the closing of files).

This equivalence, considered from the understanding of the concept of *Person,* as we will see next, will permit the establishing of this concept of I as parameter for the understanding of the concept of *city*.

5.2 *Person* = Primary Formations + Secondary Formations + Original Formation

The proposition of working with *formations*[97] constituting the network which is I = *Person* can offer us a discerning criterion of what exists as constitutive of the world we inhabit, liable to being approachable through characteristics such as quantity, materiality, complexity, composition, emergence, or, in a few words, as porosity and as a binding capacity which make available larger or smaller connectivity between formations. Thus a formation is, through the relations it establishes, always relational. And these relations may be of exclusion, reciprocity, alternation and/or complementarity. Depending on the approach or the understanding, we stress more or less one or several of these characteristics. Therefore, considering that everything that exists presents itself as formation, we will make small and precarious distinctions, so that we may think recognizable modes of organization. Such abstraction allows us to go a step further and that is what interests us: considering each and every formation as available "information" for connection with others, which immediately takes us to the idea of formation as *bondable information.*

For a broad understanding of the ways of organization of the Formations into Primary, Secondary and Original, we will clarify how these distinctions are thought in the theory of New Psychoanalysis.

5.2.1 Primary Formations

As *primary formation*[98] we understand every formation or set of formations that we intuitively associate with the idea of "nature", and which corresponds to the given or spontaneous formations, which we will call spontaneous artifice.[99] It concerns what, as "nature" or spontaneous artifice, we can list as organic/inorganic; living/non-living; formations of the known or yet to be known Universe, at macro or subatomic order; formations of the planet we inhabit, in its mineral, vegetable or animal design; in the order of living organisms (man included), its genetic constitution and associated devices of ecological connection, etc.

On the level of our "corporeity", for instance, belonging to Primary, are the set of formations involved in the vital regulations that maintain the homeostasis or homeodynamics of the organism, artifices appointed to automatically solve, without the need for specific reason, the basic problems of life, such as finding, incorporating and transforming energy (a metabolic process with chemical and mechanical components), maintaining the internal chemical balance compatible with the vital process, maintaining the structure of the organism repairing its deterioration and defending itself from external agents of disease and physical damages, etc.

This "biotic architecture" is the autosomatic constitution, that is, the Autosome[100] of primary formations. In living beings, it presents itself as immediately articulated to "programs" or "models" of behavior which biology, since Darwin, has posited as ethology of species.[101] Thus, the human body, on a primary level, besides being constituted as autosome, has an Ethosome inscribed, a way of referring to the behavioral component embedded in the living that determines it, on a scale of larger or smaller complexity, with larger or smaller elasticity, to perform tasks destined to ensure its survival as an individual and as a species.

On the level of willingness or openness to primary bonding of the human species, for instance, we are affected by a set of formations which, from early days, establish themselves from the sensorial and perceptive point of view, through which the child and those with whom he/she interacts build very strong bonds. They are behaviors of proximity, contact, interaction or expediency – imitative or not – that create behavioral standards, without necessarily being possible to identify the *content* of the information exchanged through the possible signals emitted by the interactive set. Therefore, mimicry, gestures, touches, squeezes, odors, flavors, vocalizations – that a maternal relationship establishes, for instance (Vieira, 1983) – are constitutive of our network of (in)formations which symptomatically mark us, which we carry for the rest of our lives and which, therefore, integrate our daily performances.

Thus, if we were "orthodox" Darwinists, we would be happy to differentiate the primary level of organization from that which exists strictly in the order of the living matter, with its genetic, morphological, ethological components, etc., and we would privilege this level of the analysis of the approach to human relations, or a biological, social, linguistic, urban level... If we were physicists in love with the possibility of discerning the minimum structure of matter, living or not, we would dedicate our time to researches in the field of quantum mechanics, attentive to the possibility of coherently joining the results of these researches with cosmological speculations about the "origin" of the Universe. But that is not the case.

The approach we bring from the constitution of what is $I = Person$ as a network of (in)formation includes the physical and/or biological data as a constitutive element of the Pole[102] of the symptomatic network that determines us, coherent with the postulation of a fringe zone which is infinite in its ability to be scrutinized and discerned. This posture, therefore, tells us that it is necessary to consider as a datum of analysis of the relations between formations the primary level of its organization, which participates, as biotic architecture and behavioral program, in the decisions that created culture, institutions, cities, established powers, etc. When considering, one case at a time, the level of commitment of the Primary in the performance of man, this posture also helps us to deal with the new research data which, in biology, neurosciences, computer sciences, are showing us the possibilities of mutation of this same biotic architecture and this behavioral program.

Our attention, then, turns to this second order of articulation and intervention that constitutes the space we inhabit: the art or *techné* that transforms the Primary, simultaneously feeding back on its own creations.

5.2.2 Secondary Formations

By *secondary formation* we understand the formation or a set of formations manufactured thanks to the articulatory competence of the mind, capable of moving and creating beyond the spontaneous or "natural" datum. In other words, it concerns the articulatory capability of the human species, which includes its linguistic performance, its historical, artistic, institutional, technological accomplishments, etc. If, on one hand, this means greater flexibility in relation to primary determinations (let us remember, for instance, the idea that our technologies are extensions of our body), on the other hand, the relations of bonding which are given to us on a secondary level tend to work as if they were *imprintings*, to use the old term of ethology. After all, the brand that culture imprints on us is so strong that it is as if we worked with a new behavioral program which gradually attaches to the first or *primary*.

We call neo-ethology this symptomatic functioning performed according to behavioral programs of culture. Let us consider, for instance, the learning of a language and the difficulty in shifting from the native language to another one learned in adulthood. Not only can we conjecture as to the involvement of our primary competences on the performance of this task – in terms of brain functioning, for instance – we also need to account for the inhibitions and difficulties inherent to the situation of already being symptomatically settled in a language. A *secondary* way to get around the problem is by inventing money. Therefore, when we travel, even though we might have difficulties expressing ourselves in the local language, if we have money, we quickly find a "translator" that will perform the necessary exchanges, momentarily neutralizing the situation of initial failure. Likewise, technology operates as an increasingly more neutral and invisible "middleman" in the sense of creating conditions for us to move on the symptomatic network that constitutes the space we inhabit. Technological devices for communication and information transmission (text, sound, images), related to work, leisure, domestic life, are creating new living habits, transforming the city which is the space constituted by this network of (in)formation.

5.2.3 Original Formation

Original formation is the basic structure of the mental functioning of the species.[103] Using the topological space as parameter, it is understood that the mental performance may be *from any side* because *there is only one side*, and everything we think, create, destroy, desire, accomplish is inscribed in this "Moebius band" which is the Mind. Thus the original formation is directly related to this mental competence of being potentially capable of reversing whatever is presented, always unilaterally. This mechanism that grants the possibility of reversing whatever is presented, taken as mental functioning model of our species, is named by New Psychoanalysis as *Revirão*.

We are, therefore, at the core of the psychoanalytical understanding of the issues regarding questions related to *I = Person*. Why? Because this thinking considers that the *singularity* of the *Person* consists exactly in its ability to be affected by *motivations* that may *extrapolate* and *exceed* the limits which design a given relation and, in so doing, may inaugurate a new situation. In topological terms, we would say that for every presenting situation, we can request its reverse and, as on a Moebius band, accompany the transformation on this unilateral surface. I will find out that I have "changed" place, "changed" sign (+/-), but I continue on the same surface. Thus, the "other side" of the question, as it is popularly said, is always a qualitative relation of position: in each situation I find a duality, an alternative. This capacity of reversing whatever shows up denotes that our psychism is structured like a mirror. Therefore, according to the functioning of our mind, whatever we think or imagine, its reverse or enantiomorphous may be thought and imagined.

To add the questioning, I can ask about the reverse of all situations, because my mind does not definitively settle itself on given configurations. That way, if I bear a "corporeity" capable of vital adjustments, I also bear the psychical movement to reverse the repetition of this adjustment and I can invent a technological gadget that refrigerates air according to my "taste". Between the *primary* datum of temperature adjustment and the *secondary* datum of technological invention – Primary and Secondary in the sense that we mentioned above – a third place is postulated, one of neutralization, that enables invention and creation, which we call *original*.

It is due to originally having availability for relation that we circumstantially perform connections. But it is due to its *drive* nature – in the Freudian sense – that this availability or openness to relation becomes absolute. Any formation may be reversed to any side: boundary may be reversed into flow; sexual reproduction may be reversed into biotechnological production; growth may be reversed into destruction.

This becomes evident in the history of mankind, given the permanent production of means and artifices to reverse a given context: if we cannot fly, we invent the airplane; if we are not resigned to the dark, we invent fire and the electric light; if we get sick, we invent medicines to reverse the physical condition. All these alleged hindrances are considered *modal impossibilities*, that is, are liable to reversibility. Regardless of how difficult it may seem, the reversion of a situation is a matter of time, investment, and knowledge to be acquired.[104] What does *I = Person* gain from this? The possibility of mutation of its discontents through invention and creation: the quantity and the quality of information available to be accessed increase, alternatives multiply, solutions for problems appear, the symptomatic network enriches. The only absolute impossibility is to reverse the experience of *Hei*.[105] In other words, it is absolutely impossible, regardless of how much we want it, to have as experience that of being outside this *havência* [continuous present]. The absoluteness of the relation is the exasperation of wishing to "leave" and this being impossible.[106] In very simple terms, we do not have as fundamental experience anything different from this *havência* – we are alive. Not even dying, because death does not configure itself as an experience. The experience of being "not alive" is impossible.

5.3 *Persons* are *IdioFormations* of our case

The capacity to make this *Revirão* apparatus work – and this event is observed whenever a new articulation that did not fit into the ordinary configurations of world appears – is called Hyperdetermination. It is worth saying that hyperdetermination is the last-instance determination capable of indifferentiating[107] and suspending the given determinations and inaugurating a new situation and a new articulation. This possibility is available to any of us, because it is assumed that we bear this *Revirão* as a functioning model of our mind.

For New Psychoanalysis, this characteristic will define a concept of species, according to which, what qualifies us as a species is the fact of having this Original, this model of mental functioning. This is the Hyperdetermined species, that is, with a last-instance determination, which is the fact that the possibility of *Revirão* was inscribed. To this species, New Psychoanalysis gives the name of Idioformation.

This species is named Idioformation, regardless of the bases of its corporeal constitution, that is, regardless of its primary constitution being carbon-based (like ours) or any other. Said differently, the concept of *idioformation* is defined for any species that bears the *Revirão*. Or yet, IdioFormation is "any formation primarily and secondarily symptomized, but which has *the eventual availability to be moved by HyperDetermination*" (Alonso, 2005: 79, italics in original).

This concept expands the comprehension of the human species to a broader category, in which the acknowledgement of belonging to a species does not take place through corporeal configuration (and this eliminates all differences of color, background, body with head torso and limbs, biochemical base of constitution, etc.), nor by inhabiting a given planet (this includes the possibility of other beings, of another galaxy, etc.), but rather due to the fact of bearing *Revirão* as the possibility of mental functioning. Therefore, "Idioformations are formations that eventually exist in *Haver* and are co-moveable by Hyperdetermination" (Magno, 2007: 109). The term *Person* is formulated from the extrapolation of the biotic level, defined as the "Idioformations of our case" (Magno, 2007: 109) – of the human-being case.

5.3.1 *Haver*

After the descriptions of what are Formations, it is convenient for us to have a general understanding of the context of these articulations. For that purpose, it is necessary to describe a central concept of New Psychoanalysis which is the concept of *Haver*.[108] The range and abstraction of this concept have cosmological vocation, given that it is a neutral conceptual extension of "everything there is", of what *há* (meaning: whatever exists in the universes), researched by several routes and fields, which have been seeking to understand its basic structure and functioning, whether by an algorithmic, a quantum, an organic, a complex method, or other route. However, as a psychoanalytical concept, the concept of *Haver* (used as a noun) remains connected to the Freudian postulation of traumatic experience of the impact of being in the world and the concomitant acknowledgement, irreducible to any means of description, of the impossibility of evading it, even if this is desired.

Haver includes all, whether or not we acknowledge it: is all that *Há*. Therefore, it is redundant to say that we are referring to any level of *havência* said natural or artificial, solid, liquid or gaseous, real, virtual, concrete or abstract, matter or energy. This concept encompasses *all that is available and that may show up*: animate/inanimate; organic/ inorganic; alive/not alive; physical and/or chemical; on macro or subatomic order; formations of the planet we inhabit, in its mineral, vegetable or animal design; on the order of living organisms (man included), its genetic construct and associated devices of ecological connection; the plethora of cultural artifacts already produced and yet to be produced; the determinations operating there, of historical, cultural, political, material, aesthetical background, from civilization to an individual account. The range is total, so that everything that *Há* is formation of *Haver* and there is nothing apart from that.

Another approach is the rough, traumatic experience of each and everyone of *Haver*, of being present here and now. The fact is that there is no universal understanding of this event, of what we are doing here, and there is no possibility of evasion, of escape, from this *havência*. Not even through death is it possible to have some experience different from this one, because we will not be present at our decease. Regardless of how much we wished to leave, to move on to the other side, it is impossible, "*há*, we are part of *Haver* and it is impossible to move on to *não-Haver* [not-*Haver*]"(Magno, 2009:17).

Our species has invented several apparatuses in the attempt to understand this event, but there is nothing that can be said from this place. When we remember this, we are reminded of our ever-present loneliness, we remain in a position of radical indifference, which New Psychoanalysis calls *Absolute Wharf*.[109] This place (this experience), also called *Real*, is the place of absolute loneliness, of fundamental horror generated by the consciousness of this unspeakable position, because we live in a continuous present and condemned to eternal life. Outside this position, we are in the regime of overdetermination – "the term is used by Freud, meaning that everything is overdetermined and many are the determinations which lead our lives towards certain sides" (Magno, 2004: 49) -- immersed in the order of the *Being*, of our routine, of the production of world, of ideas, of articulation, of construction of everyday life, of the most diverse attempts to create means and articulations of existence in the world.

5.3.2 The *Person* "is" in the order of "Being" and "há" in the order of "Haver"

The *Person* is constituted by *Haver* and by *Being*. More precisely, it is a character in the daily work with the *Being* – in its everyday existence in the world -- and bears the traumatic experience of *Haver* – bears the extreme experience *Há*, with the possibility of exasperation of the Absolute Wharf. Such distinction shows that *Haver* is a radical experience in which one is "absolutely present, but in abyss, infinity, eternity, and even in anguish, in total exasperation" (Magno, 2008:103). There is nothing to be said about this place, it is pure experience, pure trauma and the absolute silence, given that it is unspeakable and, when we try to speak (we are already out of that place) it is a translation, or rather a reduction that will never capture the radicalism of this experience. On the other hand, given that it is impossible to remain at this place of absolute binding, smaller and diverse bonds make the *Person*. In this sense, if we consider our existence in the World, this *I* in its implications in the World, the *Person* is there, in the regime of *Being*, of speech, of creativity, it is existing. In this context, this theory equals *Being* = *Having* – that is, "I am what I have", or rather, "I am the assemblage of my properties" (Magno, 2009: 56). When we are in the regime of the *Being*, we exist with our properties and our relations in the world. It is also in this place, in the order of *Being*, that we have the possibility of equivocation, given the mental movement of *Revirão*; it is there, in this place, that we are in the regime of the production of the world. In short, it is in the order of *Being* that all events of the world take place.

Thus, *Persons* are formations that exist in the order of *Being*, therefore building and producing World, and are moveable by *Haver*, by *Hyperdetermination*, by the radical trauma of *Haver* with no alternative of an "outside", of a *não-Haver*, regardless of how much that insists on being desired.

After these considerations, we can move on in the understanding that *I* = *Person* is the set of *primary* and *secondary formations, originally* moved by the willingness of *não-Haver*, which, while absolutely impossible, forces us to find exits, doors, passageways, connections, for our symptoms, potentially making the network that constitutes *I* = *Person* diversify and enrich, reducing the discontent but never putting an end to it.

Starting by considering the formations at stake (primary, secondary, original), there is a great difference from the concept of *I*, because it assimilates the articulation of the network, the hypertext, the multiplicity, but is not reduced to these concepts. We see, therefore, that *Persons* are formations composed by data traditionally considered as natural, plus the cultural data, which, in turn, are increased by a specific mental performance given that it bears the logics of *Revirão*, the availability for Hyperdetermination. This concept splinters any closed configuration and creates a scope which sets the *Person* always *in process*, therefore making it impossible, except for cut-outs and closures, to determine the extension of a *Person*.

5.4 Person is a Pole with Focus, Fringe and Background

In general terms, the concept of *Person* points to the network formed by an immense and complex agglomerate of formations resistant to their own transformation or change which form Poles, "configured as formation and as resistance" (Magno, 2007: 113). These Poles are bearers of two main characteristics: Focus and Fringe. Therefore, in a large formation configured as Pole, we have a focal zone, which we can define from its greater force, and the fringe, which no one knows where it ends. For this reason, whenever we cut out a random formation, we will be removing from it what we do not know, thus mutilating its fringe.

Thus the notion of *Person* involves intricate relations which place powers and force fields[110] at stake. Given that the pole does not have delimited borders, it is impossible to scan its entire configuration. Therefore, what we perceive more clearly are the focuses (Magno, 2007: 113–17), and all that we do not know – but which, even so, fully act on this network of relations – is situated as fringe. However, as the fringe is acknowledged, the focus widens, so that it becomes impossible to define where the *I* ends.

Therefore it can be affirmed that the task performed by us daily in our several forms of interactions consists in dealing with a focal region and its fringeness. To the pole, with its focus and fringe, is added the Background, from which the focus and the fringe are substantially built, even if, apparently, they show themselves as different (Magno, 2007: 195). The concept of background sustains the assumption that *Haver* is homogeneous and that, in it, differences emerge through processes of discontinuity, which make the formations which we encounter everyday apparently different.[111]

Structurally it concerns a distinct pole with focus and fringe that shows up on a network which is conjecturable as infinite. Given that it is situated on a network, every pole has infinite implications, towards all sides, with the other connections of this same network, which is full of intersections we call nodes.

The compositions of *Persons* pass through their specific relations with given physical, geographic spaces, other *Persons*, their relatives, friends, their fields of interest, their professional, personal, romantic activities, etc. These connections compose the *Person*. Here there is a polarization with focus and fringe. For instance, despite living in a given city, geographically speaking, it is certain that only parts, pieces of that physical space that forms the city, have some significance to each resident. These are the spaces from which they trace relations of continuity and acknowledgement: the routes they take everyday, the stores, restaurants and entertainment places they usually attend, etc., structure the fundamental bonds which are part of the network that constitutes a *Person*. In this sense *Person* refers to the network to which one connects, in the sense that what exists are formations referring to other formations and, within this reasoning, it does not make any sense to speak of me or oneself, but it is rather formations speaking of formations. (Magno, 2007: 129).

The conception of *Person*, while multifaceted, implies replacing the notion of boundary by intricate relations of force and powers which, despite being resistant, are, nevertheless, mutable. Hence, the focalizations may displace and frequently do so. Therefore, the emergence of our several characters[112] is nothing but a change of focus that we often associate with a change of personality. Add to that that a *Person* has availability to Hyperdetermination and *Revirão*, which allows the *Person* to include in its formations the reverse of that which is assumed as objectively given and, consequently, we have the new, the creation.

I equivalent to *Person* is a complex formation, composed by Primary, Secondary and Original formations which *consider*[113] each other, so that the change in one of them inevitably changes the resultant of orbiting. Hence, the *Person* is a dynamic network – characterized by intricate interactions between symptomatic formations, on one hand, and the possibility of *Revirão* on the other – so that it is only possible to think of it as variable resultant, considered in each case and at each moment. Let us also add that a *Person's* fringe tends to the infinite in the extent of space and in the direction of time (Magno, 2007: 187). In this sense, a radical difference is established between the philosophical notion of the individual – as indivisible and fundamental element of society – and the notion of *Person*, which would tend, on the contrary, to encompassment.[114] The possibility of the spreading of focus means, ultimately, the possibility of expansion through access to Hyperdetermination.[115]

The dissolution of the habit of thinking in terms of irreducible boundaries is indispensable to this approach of the concept of *Person*, as it also involves the idea of Knowledge (Magno, 2003: 59–66 and 2007: 141–45), "this because *Person* is also constituted by its knowledge, which is precarious and changes with time" (Magno, 2007: 141). Such perspective reinforces the abandonment of the classical distinction between subject and object to the detriment of *consideration* (or transaction) between formations, so that knowing is not an act of a subject. It is a matter of including oneself in this relation, this orbiting between formations, which results in knowledge. In this perspective knowledge rises from a summing up, from transaction among formations, so that "all we have is transaction and its performers" (Magno, 2007: 150), who may be the *Persons* considered simply as formations, at stake.

It is in this sense that I can also affirm *the city is me* because whatever we may identify or discern takes place in this relation of orbiting between formations. This implies a radical rupture of the supposed boundaries that would delimit these two instances so that the idea of city is encompassed by the concept of *I*. Thus, in our everyday life, we are not the agent subjects who make conscious decisions in a passive environment that simply surrounds us. We can consider cities as formations that constitute a *Person* in a certain way. The *Person* is an *utente*[116] formation, which is the same as "user". "And a *Person* who uses is nothing but a *Person* in use, that is, who is being used, in other words, in exercise" (Magno, 2007: 151). Therefore, once the dichotomy that would place a division between subject and object is dissolved, we understand that there are no boundaries between assemblages of powers and forces that are set in relation to geography or to a given territory and its inhabitants.

5.5 Negative definitions of *I = Person*

We started our argumentation stating that, in this theory, *I* is equivalent to *Person*, stressing the polysemy of this notion. We can now reorganize this semantic field, proceeding to negative definitions with which we expect to clarify further our comprehension perspective regarding the problem of the contemporary city. We will present these definitions in short topics.

Person is not individual.
In a technical definition, the notion of individual is related to a recognizable and given unit that, in philosophical language (Mora, 2001: 378), is numerically distinguished from the other individuals of the same species (e.g. "any man", "any tree") by its individuating characteristics. It is the matter-form composite constitutive of the physical world in which it is born, grows and dies; a unit which is numerically identifiable and quantifiable and materially indivisible. The notion of individual is often associated with the human being considered separately, with body (animated or not), considered as the closure thereto attributed, resultant, in turn, from an act of discretion, that is, an act of separation. It is as if we separated some "piece" or formation and called it an individual through this separation.

When we speak of individual, what commands the assimilation is the physical unity. Thus, the human body, as individuation benchmark through an operation of discretion or separation, is only a set of formations. Throwing it onto the network of formations, we dissolve the reasoning of individuation through corporeity. We have, listed in a random corporeal discretion, a plethora of formations in the order of gestuals, syntax, grimaces, semantics, modulation of voice and all the other formations that are excluded in such consideration. Therefore, the fringe of any individual, when taken into account, suspends discretion. The naming of the individual always takes place after the separation which, in turn, always takes place after an act of repression. Once again the posture of indifferentiation promoted by McLuhan's idea of the medium as message and that of technology as extension of man help us think. After all,

> the ear favors no particular "point of view." We are *enveloped* by sound. It forms a seamless web around us … Where a visual space is an organized continuum of a uniformed connected kind, the ear world is a world of simultaneous relationships. (McLuhan, 1969: 139, italics in original)

When we speak of individual, what rules the assimilation is the physical person considered as unit. Here there is a cut that removes from the concept of individual the compulsory exchanges and interactions that it [the individual] maintains in the world. Even without trailing McLuhan's path, treating technologies as extensions of our body and staying within the immediateness of our biological needs, we ask: where does the human body end? Is the oxygen in the atmosphere a part of my body? Does my body exist without oxygen? Well, the human body, as individuation benchmark is only a set of formations which integrate *I = Person*.

Person is not subject.
The notion of subject was ineffaceably associated with the properties of subsisting within self, to knowing that one is subsisting, being identical to oneself in time, regardless of its modal or accidental variations. The idea of subject as substance capable of existing by itself, having the qualities of support, substratum, *sub-jectum*, foundation, an existing mental thing that recognizes itself within itself, also operates through an act of discretion, focusing on the opposition between a mind that knows and an object to be known and electing it as fundamental quality of the subject as a central basic position or sub-position (as the name says), a sort of central command station of somebody's acts. It is from this attribution of a center for enunciation of thought and action, strongly anchored in the human capability of speech, grammatically articulated in the subject-verb-predicate phrasal arrangement, that the idea of subject can be sustained.

Thus, it is not about denying cuts, operations of closure, exclusion and repression on the network of formations that constitutes *I = Person*. It is simply about acknowledging that some formations are used in a privileged way as an expressive interface of a closure's commotions and affectations where several sorts of discretions converge. The power and wealth of this interface may be so large that other formations name it *subject of something* as focus which is nothing but *effect* of operations of repression and of the habits thence resulting. Once the relation of powers is changed, this impression of unity dissolves. The Internet is the *princeps* example: chats dissolve sex as anatomy, gender and chronology; electronic commerce and social network dissolve geographic borders, not to mention the widely varied array of available *online* contents.

Person is not permanence
Permanence is the duration, here and now, of the formations at stake, due to the resistance, which will have their closure undone or relativized. Permanence is acknowledged as such in time, producing, as effect, the belief that we are the definitive headquarters of something. More than that: each and every calculation of permanence depends on the artifices and supports for the storage of information, be it the organically-constituted memory or its technological extensions. When we forget that, we have the feeling of Personal identification as headquarters (we would be the headquarters responsible for events, thoughts, actions, choices, attitudes,

moral principles, memories, remembrances and insurmountable and unshareable impressions, etc.).

Thus, digital machines, computer hard drives, photographs, music, telescope images, information processors, e-mails, *blogs*, movies, work environment, leisure spaces, financial, commercial, erotic or parental transactions, tastes, linguistic skills, visual, tactile, acoustic, aesthetic preferences are some examples or aspects of the network of formations we access on their storage bases, which also constitute a *Person* at a given space-time and in a given correlation of forces.

5.6 Without frontiers

Various arguments can be made[117] that weaken or even rule out any possibility of sustaining the idea of subject or individual. The problematization of the frontiers that delimit, separate and forge the idea of subject or individual is the gist of this question.

- Personal affections are not totally incommunicable. Since everyone calls him/herself "I", where is the dividing line between one I and another? To communicate is to make common. When we communicate, we make common anything: an idea, a cold or a symptom. There is clearly permeability between people. Hence, the idea of delimitation is compromised.
- We do not know where the frontier is between interior and exterior. As seen, the notion currently referred to as I, subject, individual or even subjectivity is a legacy of the Greco-Judeo-Christian mold. Originally *hipokeimenon* in Greek and *subjectum* in Latin, subject denoted something subjacent, that is "behind things" or that "lies within". But behind what? Within what? There is no way to define what is inside and outside, or even whether there is an inside and outside.
- We do not know how to precisely discern, in a given realm of knowledge, what is from the subject and what is from the object. The separation of subject and object is imbued with the idea that the former corresponds to an interiority and the latter to an exteriority, which is situated as such in relation to the subject. If we cannot distinguish "inside" and "outside", all reasoning that depends on these concepts is undermined. Knowledge is an exchange of formations; there is no way to separate the order of a subject and the order of an object. Likewise, there is no way to separate person and world.
- We do not know where the frontier is between the conscious and the unconscious. The idea of the unconscious introduced by Freud sustains that, in psychism, the conscious is merely an instance, part or effect of the unconscious. In this sense, all mental processes are of a unconscious order.[118] We do not heed the fact that the conscious is a focalization of something with the repression of the enormous fringe of formations that tends to infinity.

- We do not know where the frontier is between individual and environment or between individual and group. If we define individual as being that contained inside the skin that confers a corporeal image, we have to acknowledge that this does not exist without the most basic worldly exchanges, like air, atmosphere, gravity, etc. The environment is part of the individual, and the individual composes the environment, without the possibility of separating them and assuring their existence. We do not have any way to indicate frontiers, separate or distinguish supposed sides, since they are part a single process. Likewise, any individual defines him- or herself as belonging to a determined group. No matter how strong the illusion of separation, when analyzing it from the viewpoint of pole with focus and fringe, any isolation is a fiction, because there is an infinite network that constitutes the person, with which the idea of limit is also infinitely dislocated.
- We only accept the term *subject* in a logical-linguistic sense. Subject is also a notion developed from grammar – that which acts, which has attributes and predicates and that can perfectly well be a thing. Hence, we uncritically absorb this notion, which is imposed on us daily in various ways, whether through belief in the separation between body and soul (the *subjectum* as a little man expressed within ourselves), or in the practice of language (inherited from Greek and Latin) with its reflexive function, with its grammatical subjects and its distinction between subject and object. So, that which says "I" can be considered, within grammar, to be the subject of a sentence, but this cannot be confused with a person. The most we can say is that "I" is the first person singular.

In short, as we have seen, in New Psychoanalysis, the concept of *Person* breaks up with delimitations and boundaries, whether individual, corporeal, physical, geographic, mental, intellectual or psychical. Likewise, it does not make a subject/object distinction or separation. What we have are interactions of the concerning formations at each moment, which denotes a process without center of enunciation.

For New Psychoanalysis, whatever shows up as extension, as connection to a given *Person* is prosthesis (of this) *Person* (Magno, 2010: 131). Thus prostheses are clothes, the airplane, devices, streets and neighborhoods, ideas, buildings, a text, a thought, urban agglomerations, the galaxy, etc.; all of this is prosthetic. These prostheses may be spontaneous – natural – or industrial.[119] The idea of body gains another dimension because, as we have seen, it is not restricted to an anatomy which is contained inside the skin. The body, in this case, encompasses the components that guarantee survival through more direct physiological exchanges, as, for instance, oxygen on the atmosphere, going through everything with which we may have direct or indirect, conscious or unconscious contact, even the huge and undetermined fringe zone that constitutes the *Person*. *Person* incorporates (adds) all that to which it binds and to which it is bound; for this reason it is always in process. These thoughts help with understanding that "there is a focal body and a fringe body for any personal instance" (Magno, 2010: 132).

Several physical and geographic elements take part in the constitution of a *Person*; even different cultures may actively participate in the structuring of a *Person*. It is composed by everything and everyone who integrate, interact, have signification, interfere, pressure, affect and articulate the network that constitutes it. Therefore, as *Person*, we constitute and are constituted by this network that includes places of the geographic city where we live, and the entire geography or territory that produce some signification in our history.

Any manifestation or knowledge of a given *Person* will be submitted to the understanding and vision resulting from the network it is. Along with this same reasoning we can ask, for instance: Is there world without *I*? Before *I* existed and after my death, where is the world? Of course I can conjecture that everything was already there and will certainly stay there after my disappearance, but what experience did I or will I have from this? "Anyway, it is other people who die"[120] – when I *pass away,* I am *over,* I cannot even have the experience of death. Likewise, the entire civilization , the big bang, the planet's urbanization, the evolution of the species, etc., which took place before my birth and which constitutes me as DNA, cellular memory, a location in the evolution of civilization, "was given to me ready", whole, at once – when I came to exist. The world, everything included, past, present and future, exists for whom is alive, present.

We can even imagine that there is world for other people, but *Haver,* as experience, does not exist without this *Person* that is called *I* (Magno, 2008: 33).

Each *Person* is the result of an enormous quantity of all affectations that make up its history, the places that made an impression, specific tastes and pleasures, repulses, tragedies and dramas occurred in its life, technological facilitations, financial hardship and wealth, its (in)competences, its corporeity with all significations thereto understood, and whatever else we can list in order to define what composes a networked life. For all this, each *Person* is unique. From this perspective, I can affirm *the city is me,* because there will be as many cities as there are *Persons,* and that is precisely what we intend to show in the next chapter.

Chapter 6

The City is Me

Photo montage: Isadora Dantas

"The" city no longer exists. As the concept of city is distorted and stretched beyond precedent, each insistence on its primordial condition – in terms of images, rules, fabrication – irrevocably leads via nostalgia to irrelevance ... To survive, urbanism will have to imagine a new newness ... We have to imagine 1,001 other concepts of city; we have to take insane risks; we have to dare to be utterly uncritical; we have to swallow deeply and bestow forgiveness left and right. (Koolhaas, 2002: 3)

The understanding of what is city and its architectonics could not be immune to topology. It is evident that urban macrophysics continues to depend on the application of the plane and three dimensional Euclidian logics, without which there are no streets, buildings, houses, gardens, transportation, road system, borders, walls, customs, urban/rural, *geo*-calculated space-time. Likewise, and compatible to this city of Neolithic emergence, we continue to live with the previous symptomatic of kinship, of sexual reproduction of bodies, of subjectivities and identities, of traditional social, judicial and political institutions, all ruled by the bilateralizing and excluding logics of Euclidian mentality which finds great difficulty in operating under the regime of concentration at the focus and dispersion at the fringe, on the polarization transformation and passage between poles.

But it is also evident that the city is no longer limited to its *geo*-metric and quantitative supports, nor to the cognitive skills based on the verbalizing competences of the human species. The range of the accomplishments, conjectures, technological implementations, research programs, etc. has exploded all possibility of supporting the notion of city on a random-border criterion – physical, mental, cultural, ethnic, linguistic, financial, technological. More than that, the displacement of the notion of city is simultaneous to the displacement over what might be its fundamental support: the carbon-based human format, instituted by the heterosexual-family-reproductive-cultural-urban-geographic-couple[121] design.

Once we start from the polysemy of the concept of city, which is presently under heavy fire, we do nothing but affiliate to the theoretical positions that decided to face the challenge of rethinking the problem in a way that coheres with risk and uncertainty, but likewise the potentialities that characterize our epoch. Stating *the city is me* is, therefore, including these ongoing potentialities and transformations.

When we incorporate the concept of City to that of Me in our hypothesis *the city is me*, we do so based on the following articulations:

- The concepts of City and Me – as with any other concept – are historically built products.
- The concept of City, in this study, is not restricted to geography, to Euclidian geometry, to history, to the physical space constituted through its circumscribing boundaries, or to chronological time.
- The concept of Me is not restricted to subject, individual, anatomic body, first person of the verb.
- The concept of Me hereto used, is that contributed by New Psychoanalysis and refers to the Primary and Secondary formations, affected by the Original, which form a network and constitute a pole with focus and fringe. Based on what we have already seen, this *Person* is composed of a network which is conjecturable as infinite and includes, among other formations, parts of urban agglomerations which interact on this network.
- In this concept of Me, there is no center of enunciation, there is no separation between subject and object; what we have are *formations* which consider *each other*.
- The concept of City is one of topologic basis. When thought of as a network of interactions, cities are displaced along with people.
- In the hypothesis *The City is Me* there is a *Person* who makes this statement and this *Person* is the reference that affirms itself as city. This means that what is being said necessarily goes through an experience (of) *Person*. In this case, they are formations that interact and result in a given knowledge about Me = City. Even if anyone can affirm him/herself as City, it is always a unique, singular event, that can only be enunciated one by one.
- We employ New Psychoanalysis' idea of pole with focus and fringe, for it seems to be compatible with the technological movement and the increasingly more abstractive vectors that show up each day. From research in robotics to the investigation of the quantum world, from the internet to artificial intelligence and nanotechnology, the network of "significations" is no longer coupled solely to the traditional biological and cultural devices to which we are used.

Consequently, vectoring the problem as from the *I* which is conceptualized by New Psychoanalysis is giving emergence to a concept of City which goes beyond, in its inclusive possibilities, the contours of man's format, concerning biological and cultural competence. The city of which we speak embraces all emergences of human formation, including, and above all, the technological, which, secreted by this formation, seems to threaten its existence, but which, on the other hand, can provide it with unparalleled qualitative mental leaps. It embraces all information, from quantum to digital (and its promising connection), from mechanical to analogical, with all the *inhabiting* potentialities thereto. It embraces all cultural compositions and re-compositions which are happening within the territory of the city. It, at last, is *Me* as *network of formations*, computable, conjecturable, even if unapproachable (here and now).

Thus, stating *the city is me* is to definitely integrate with urbanism the effects of topological mentality. The emerging transformations – on the already-known repertoire of communication and information technologies, of the radical relativization of mobility parameters, communication and neighborhood, with the collapse of traditional borders – already make the city function in a regime of non-tectonics. It is the current state of the network of formations in the world which is constituting *I = Person* as place.[122] In other words, *I = Person* as network makes the place, not the opposite.

Places, previously geometrical and of Euclidian competence, have become topological places, demanding, each time and at each *situs*, appropriate consideration and analysis, because there is no (longer) distinction between the network, the *Person* and the space forged according to the formations and transformations that symptomatically compose this space. Inhabiting is to constitute, at each moment, the network that constitutes the *Person*, making space coincide with the symptomatic materiality that qualifies and quantifies it.

Applying the concept *I = Person* contributed by such as New Psychoanalysis, there is no distance capable of separating *I* and City. There is no *a priori* city, external to us, in which we are inserted. Similarly, we are not out of a city which we consider as such. On the contrary, the pole that constitutes me, with its focalization and fringe extension, partially coincides with the city.

If we understand the poles as distinct, we should treat them with *ipseity*[123], a term that refers to the principle of difference, the unique character of a formation of *Haver* which distinguishes it from all others. In this sense, "my singularity is the world I am" (Magno, 2008: 35). And the city I am is not the geographic city in which I live, but rather the city that lives in me. We are not just a body, a thing, an address, but a *city-me*, full of the most diverse fragments – geographic, personal, local, virtual, affective, sensorial, genetic, historical, etc.

The city is configured according to the network that I am and, at each change of this network, the city changes and, in turn, transforms me, too. I can only bear witness and enunciate while I configure myself within the very process, while I am the process. Then: the city is me.

6.1 The city is me: pole, focus, fringe

We wish to reaffirm that, as pole, focus and fringe, the space in which moves *I = Person* – from where we have started in order to state *the city is me* – is the space constituted by all the accessible formations here and now, configuring and unconfiguring space and time (past, present and future). Likewise, the communication which takes place as network of formations *I = Person* is the communication established as network of connected formations, accessible here and now, consciously or not. Therefore, the images of planet Mars, or of the most distant known galaxy which satellites access are *my* images and configure *me* as network connected to the Universe. The experiences with stem cells and their amazing plastic and undifferentiating capacity are my experiences: plasticity and undifferentiation *integrate me* as qualities. But also technological space which includes this information and which was transformed because of it, constitute the network on which I move and which is me.

The grid or network of formations that constitute *I = Person* demands a way of approaching which, preserving its integration and transformation dynamics, equally permits distinction, differentiation and separation procedures. It is in this sense that we work with the idea of focus and fringe, or focal zone and fringe zone, constituted over organization poles of this network.[124]

From the point of view of formations of any order at stake in a given situation, there is a focal zone and a large fringe zone, intersecting or not, at a space-time, in a group that is infinite in every direction. Every focalization is integrated in a fringe region which is practically impossible to be determined, and this goes for the space here and now, for past, present and future time. There can be no judgement, cut or operation which is not from a focal zone, which does not eliminate – on the contrary, demands it as constitutive of the very dynamics of the network – the interference of the fringe zone.

In terms of city, the situation is no different. This time it is McLuhan who helps us once again. For him, what distinguishes the railroad system from an electrical complex is that the former needs stations, tracks and large urban centers, whereas the latter, because it decentralizes, allows any place to be a center, and can do without large agglomerations (McLuhan, 2007). In other words, according to the network of formations that constitutes the city (that is me), the dynamics between the organization poles of my references also changes. McLuhan saw in electricity a great power of implosion of the restraints imposed by the mechanized world of the bricks of geometrically-considered factories and houses, betting on the expansion of the fringe through electronics.

He was right. After all, it is possible to live in seclusion on the mountains or on a beautiful island, and access, from any of these places, in real time, information via satellite, through the Internet, cell phone or television, in a qualitative and quantitative relation which is very different from that of an inhabitant of an urban center who does not have such resources. Likewise, I can inhabit a large metropolis and dislike the idea of using a car to solve everyday needs (going to the bakery, for instance), because my formations which map distances and the tastes thereto associated include old habits acquired in a childhood spent in the "countryside", where everything was done by foot.

Whatever the examples may be, the reasoning at stake is the operation of separation and eventually of exclusion that the focal zone implies, for it is impossible not to operate focally, which means, at a given circumstance, to exclude all the rest from the focal zone thus constituted. But, at each occasion, we must remember that the floating attention towards what remains inaccessible here and now (fringe zone) and the *ad hoc* operation which cuts concrete situations (focal zone) are not mutually exclusive. If it is a fact that the focus of a situation gives us (the impression of existing) specific judgement conditions, in which we operate through condensing, differentiation and even exclusion, we cannot refrain from including the ramifications or the network of which focus is just a localized and immediately-relativizable effect, once reinserted in the larger scope of the network as focus-fringe set. We then compute, in the idea of *the city is me*, its local and recognizable effects here and now through focalization, but we do not dismiss the dispersiveness of (in)formations we do not access and which, nevertheless, are not less active in the determination of the *design* of this city.

6.2 The urban pole in focus and fringe

Lewis Mumford starts his now classic book from 1961, *The city in history*, by resuming a path which starts with "a city that was, symbolically, a world" and closes with a "world that has become … a city" (Mumford, 1991: 3). In his analysis of the role of city as a "magnet, container, and transformer in modern culture" (Mumford, 1991: 570), he forecast what we currently see happening, beyond the migration of man towards the city: the dissemination of urban culture throughout the planet, regardless of any geographic, cultural, economic or political situation.

Many authors confirm this reasoning. For Octavio Ianni, for instance, from the universalization of capitalism, at the end of the twentieth century, "is observed a simultaneous generalization of the urban way of life, or urban sociability, of urban cultural standards and values … invading rural areas, agrarian ways of life … The agrarian world alters, changes, dilutes" (Ianni, 1997: 80). Two decades earlier, Henri Lefebvre supported the hypothesis of *complete urbanization of society* (Lefebvre 2004: 15, italics in original), in which urban society is the post-industrial society, a planetary society "that results from a process of complete urbanization. This urbanization is virtual today, but will become real in the future" (p. 15). The urban, in Lefebvre's definition, comprises "living creatures, the products of industry, technology and wealth, works of nature, ways of living, situations, the modulations and ruptures of the everyday – the urban *accumulates* all content" (p. 112, italics in original). In the same work he proposes to no longer say "city", but rather *urban* (p. 50, italics in original).

What interests us in the aforementioned manifestations is the evidence of the urban phenomenon as paradigmatic in order to think the field of urbanism. Therefore, city is the urban way of inhabiting/occupying the planet. The concept of city encompasses, today, all the inhabiting relations in the world, with or without a city (geographically speaking) nearby. As we have shown, authors are unanimous in demonstrating that the city has extrapolated the physical-geographical space and has become broad. This way of inhabiting the world has put an end to borders. There are more or less dense urban focuses which do not necessarily coincide with the geographic size. Variables were displaced; it is useless to think about geographic area. Can we determine where the focus and fringe of a city start and end, if we consider all sorts of trades, exchanges, commercial, cultural, financial interactions in which it takes part and depends?

The concept of urban culture manages the planet; that is, the urban way of inhabiting is hegemonic in the world. For this we defended the use of the word *Orbanism* in chapter 3, for it seems to us as more adequate in order to express the issues which are being considered when we deal with the urban, especially within the context of this work. If we wanted to articulate this question, in old terms, we could affirm that the rural way no longer exists. The rural way is determined by the urban way of living. In short: from the urban point of view it lacks a given amount, its deficit is a given amount, because it is on the fringe. What we can analyze is on which level of insertion the *Person* is, but already knowing that all are inserted.

From this understanding, we will approach the urban phenomenon through the concept of polarization, such as proposed by New Psychoanalysis. It should be said that we will work with the ideas of "focal zone" and "fringe zone" (Magno, 2003: 421). The pole[125] is urban, varying its degrees according to its location more or less close to the focus. The fringe will define, according to the distance from the focus, the different degrees of urbanization (see figure below). Starting from this principle, and considering that urban culture was established as paradigmatic throughout the planet, all we can distinguish are the different degrees of urbanization that we will find in the situations/region we will study.

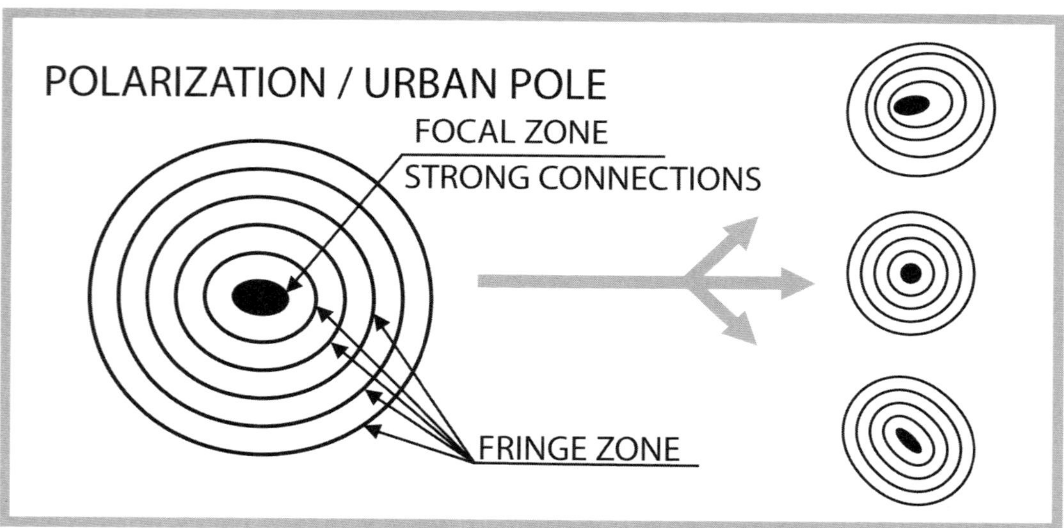

This way, if we establish that the urban pole will be defined by different and strong connections[126] between formations – cultural, mental, political, financial, intellectual, commercial, residential, professional, geographic, informational (whether of electronic basis or not), etc. – the level of urbanization will depend on the level of proximity of the focal zone to the existing pole. In the context of this work, this level refers to the concept of *I* as *Person* such as conceived by New Psychoanalysis, compatible with the concept of Network, with Focus and Fringe, and composed of a plethora of primary formations, secondary formations plus the original formation, which are located not only in someone's body, but in any part of *Haver* (Magno, 2010: 130).

In this sense, each *Person* is the very constitution which will situate it as a given level of urbanization. In turn, the level of urbanization (of) a *Person* does not coincide with the level of urbanization of the urban geometric space it attends. Thus, this geometric space functions only as another one of its connections. Following this reasoning, we can speculate that, in the classic concept of city, it was stated that cities contained people, or that person and city established a relation of subject and object, or that there was a boundary which defined where a person ended and a city began. Now we can suggest that there is no distinguishable boundary that delimits a person who is composed by formations which constitute a network that includes several other formations, physical and geographic spaces.

Therefore, in this transaction of formations, singular cities are formed according to specific trajectories, which, despite being barely detectable – each in its own anguish, loneliness, *havência* [continuous present] – are transmitted by the inscription of the actions of the *Persons* in the world. Therefore, the reference for the understanding of city is changed: the city (of) a *Person* will not be equal to that (of) any other. Regardless of how similar or coincident they are in some formations, the city that a person is will always depend on the resultant of a large set of formations, each with its own vectors. People certainly may share some or several formations: in this case, we can say that they are parts of people who constitute similar cities.

This understanding includes and encompasses each and every *Person*, as from their intrinsic differences. Thus, *the city that constitutes me* – that is, connections, vision of the world, symptoms that filter the information that constitutes me, the utilization of the space I produce, my material condition and the optimization capability of this condition, my (in)competences, my preferences to attend given places, the affective memories associated to the everyday routes, the significations established in given places, the geography drawn by my specific need for daily displacement, my ignorance regarding spaces where I have never been, etc., ultimately the whole array of articulations that are part of my specific history and which constitute me,– *is unique.*

The city (*Person*) in this context is defined by the set of formations – material, geographic, mental, intellectual, informational, historical, etc. – that constitute the dwelling of a citizenship. The city is the circumstances which constitute a *Person*, that is, its selective affinities connected to the network that constitutes it.

The connections between each one's formations bring forth the world, and each *Person* is the result of the confluence of different formations and articulations which constitute the *Person* as the city it is. Therefore, the city is me.

Chapter 7

Conclusion

Photo: Isadora Dantas, 2010

I know I hear some murmurs in the blood each time a bottomless well opens before me and I see a city … if art is a dungeon, this vision is a lesson of freedom. (Tolentino, 2006: 33)

Our objective was to propose a concept of city. We understand that the concept proposed requires a change of vision which propitiates a broader and more precise understanding, especially because we are considering the articulation of this concept from the point of view of our mind's structure, according to the conception of the theory of New Psychoanalysis. That is, a concept of *city* and of *I* compatible with our way of mental functioning and with the hegemonic configurations of the contemporary world.

Different authors we have presented are unanimous in showing that the city has extrapolated physical space, it has become encompassing. City is the way of occupying the world; for that reason we can speak of informational city, global city, ecstacity, city of bits, etc. Likewise, several authors show that the way of occupying the world is urban (therefore, city is the urban way of occupying). They show the generalization of the urban way of life, to the point of no longer referring to the term city, but rather urban. The urban way of living is the contemporary way (with or without a geographic city nearby), and what we have are more or less dense urban focuses. There is no way of life "outside" the urban way; given this amplitude, we can move on to speaking of *Orbanism*, because our considerations encompass the world and the universe as formations of this Person-city.

The city, the world or any space, only interests us and we will only acknowledge it where inhabitable by people. Everything that exists (civilization, etc.) is byproduct of the existence of this species. Therefore, from what can I describe the existence of this city, this urban thinking? From the person. The person is producer and consumer of the urban, and the urban is that which constitutes the set of formations of this person. Within this reasoning there is no possibility of separation between person and city, because they are part of a same process – the urban way of life. What we can analyze is the level of insertion of each person, according to the focus and fringe that constitute it.

When a person moves, he/she carries his/her connections, resources, competences. Each person-city results from an enormous number of variables which change according to the configuration of formations of each one in each situation. The city each person is results from an enormous set of formations. Regardless of how some people may share some common formations, the resultant of all the formations that constitute a person will never be equal to that of another. The title of our book is a universal statement: any person, contemporarily, can say the city is me.

In order to develop this work, we have initially defined what a concept means, which is not identifiable with things, even if it has relations of co-pertinence with reality. From the epistemological point of view we acknowledge that all explanations of world are equivalent, leaving to discussion its power of authority and its power of performance concerning the problems that may be presented.

We have seen the implementation of a concept of city in the Neolithic period, which used as reference sedentarism, geography, soil, chronological time, the domestication of man, the acknowledgement of consanguinity and, consequently, family bonds – the bonds of the heterosexual, reproducing couple. Currently we see the establishment of concepts of city in which this initial base was disregarded or is very unconfigured and relativized. Thus the city starts to be defined from different parameters such as finance, informational and planetary connection capability, nodes and networks, demographic density, level of virtualization, sensorial experience, etc. By going through these changes, the field of urbanism starts to consider the fluid character of contemporary urban space, which includes the malleability of transformation, the frailty and transience in its usages and functions, the flexibility of its use, the simultaneousness of its usages and meanings and the overlaying of information – characterizing an urbanism in fluid state.

Given the technological transformations which currently allow us to communicate, interact, choose, work, be present in real time and over distance, creating "continuous fields of presence" (Mitchell in Castells, 2004: 11), we are multiplied.

The understanding of what might be *I* has been relativized and broadened and, according to the theory of New Psychoanalysis, this concept bears no distinction between subject and object, it is a pole with focus and fringe, resulting from the conjunction of formations which articulate. Therefore it is composed by everything and everyone who integrate, interact, have signification, interfere, pressure, affect, by places that made an impression, the geography frequented, by specific tastes and pleasures, repulses, tragedies and dramas performed by its life, technological facilitations, financial hardships and wealth, (in)competences, ideas, the corporeity that bears – with all significations thereto understood, and whatever we can list in order to define what composes the networked life of a *Person*. For all this, each *Person* is unique, and will always be the resultant here and now of all its resources, factors and characteristics of its story.

The criteria to be used in the evaluation of what is "city" become increasingly more dependent on the person as interaction, location, access and functionality of the resources which it uses when inhabiting.[127] The uselessness of separating the concept of person from that of city comes exactly from the co-extension between what one is, what one has, what is accessed and what is available. Therefore, any city will be liable to being analyzed as from the concerning *Person*.

Thus, when we think about the process of expansion of the human body and mind through technology, it becomes easier to conceive that the city as network is pertinent to the network which a person is. With the "explosion of portable machines that provide ubiquitous wireless communication and computing capacity", people, organizations and spaces interact anywhere and at any time, "while relying on a support infrastructure that manages material resources in a distributed information power grid" (Castells, 2004: 6). Simultaneously, with the advent of nanotechnology and the convergence between microelectronics and biological processes and materials,

> the boundaries between human life and machine life are blurred, so that networks extend their interaction, from our inner self to the whole realm of human activity, transcending barriers of time and space. (Castells, 2004: 6)

If technology witnesses the extension and interaction of the networks that constitute the urban fabric in its diversity, blurring the boundary between human, machine and digital, *the city is me* means that the network of formations that constitute a singularity (= Me) constitutes the city one is. We are the current and virtual connections that configure us as multiple spaces and inhabited times. Just as urban fabric and space are patched by the overlaying of different values and experiences of their social role players, we are the result of vincula which, in a more or less intense way, conform us as the city we are.

There is no distance between the city "I inhabit" and the city "I am". The city each one is is co-extensive to one's urban way of insertion in the world. If urban life, urban sociability and urban culture have become generalized, altering (through increasingly more intangible technologies) the several environments and social practices, we can say that the expanded "city" has found the "person" who supposedly inhabited it, revealing that, actually, inhabiting is to be. In other words, the city of cement, concrete and bricks which was liquefied through technologies/spaces of flows/etc., has found a person, previously contained in the city and who was transformed by the same process of liquefaction.

It is about considering *city* and *me* as the *two* faces of the only possible way of life, according to the predominant, contemporary vector: the urban way of life. *City* and *me* compose the single-faced path of a Moebius band, in which disappear the differences between the concept of space one inhabits and the concept of space one is, because we are the city that results from the infinite set of available connections, identifiable and manipulable here and now.

The city is me resides in the fact that the network society constitutes us as urban beings, without the alternative to access an "outside" which would allow us, in opposition, to situate ourselves in relation to the non-urban.

The city is me resides in the fact that the convergence of city-technology-society has made information and its means of access indiscernible, as well as the social-environmental surrounding and its connection and communication resources, with no access to an "outside" that would enable separating *habitat* and inhabitant.

Our proposal, *the city is me,* is the conceptual formulation that there is no distance/difference between reality and symbolic representation. If we wish, "the city a person is" are its symbolic representations. A *person-city* is also a set of symbolic representations.

It is necessary to think the city from this perspective, placed not as a determined plane outside myself, where I should ask permission to enter, following rules created by others in the context of their specific cities. It is transformation of the way of considering the very geographic city, from which the material structure that surrounds us should consider the city each one is.

We believe that the proposition *the city is me* finds strong support points. Reviewing what we have already presented, we could thus conclude in defense of our work:

1. There is space and, we would dare say, demand for conceptual growth within the discussions performed in urbanism regarding the contemporary city: the moment is appropriate due to the technological movement that is redesigning the concept of city.
2. Explanatory models of the contemporary city, which include interfaces of discussion with other fields of thought, may offer propositions compatible with the reality of this city which no longer has clear walls and works as a corridor – that is, it functions by integrating information from the most different levels.
3. The identification of the city to *I* = *Person* is interesting and productive, because it explains the relational data of this city from the transformation of its inhabitants into parts of the network that constitutes it.
4. The presentation of a concept of city with *I* = *Person* is effective because it presents a way of understanding the transformations through which contemporary thinking is articulating the concepts of space, place, network, function and person;
5. The recapture of the concept of *Person* and its identification to *I* may have enlightening and pedagogical effects: it uses reasoning and terms which are on the agenda, explaining them, however, not only in the region that everyone knows (which is individual, subject, etc.) but in the situations in which usual significations are insufficient.
6. The search for a spot as distant as possible in order to examine a problem may be useful, for we usually "come back" with a new vision and a new approach. Therefore we suppose we are winning in circumspection when applying to urbanism a theory that cares for abstractive reasoning, while simultaneously working concretely with formations.
7. We are speaking about Orbanism, because we consider that the scope of the questions regarding the proposition *the city is me* has no limitations, and is not restricted to any previous determination of space. Likewise it is not possible to draw a line between urban and non-urban, given the fact that there is no boundary that may indicate an "outside" from the urban way of life. The access and the

interaction between formations which compose the person have no previous limits, especially because *Person* is an expanding process.

8. But that is not enough. *I = Person* is the definition of city because there is no longer any distance between who inhabits the place (man), the place (city) and the ways of inhabiting it (the relations of power and the available techniques).

9. Our understanding is that, given that the concepts of city, of urban, of civilization have left the geometric and geographic places, it is necessary to define *Person* in order to define (its) city. Therefore, *any* citizen, *any person* can say *the city is me*.

Our objective was to propose a concept. However, we would like to forward questions which will allow us to search and take a step ahead of this present work and which we intend to develop in further research: How to elaborate the political and administrative management as from this understanding of city? How to think everyday practice in this totally inclusive city? How to administrate the conflicts and consensus as from the understanding of this concept of city? How to create mechanisms of an *ad hoc* administration? What are the skills necessary to the performance of the *orbanist*? This subject is of utmost importance and we will continue it in the future.

Photo: Rosane Araujo, 2011

Bibliography

Abbagnano, N., 2003. *Dicionário de filosofia* [*Dictionary of philosophy*]. São Paulo: Martins Fontes.

Alonso, A., 2005. *A Grande Maneira. Maneirismo e Psicanálise*. Ph. D. Universidade Nova de Lisboa, Faculdade de Ciências Sociais e Humanas.

Alonso, A., 2003. Aspectos do verbo haver e seu uso na Nova Psicanálise. In: *Anais do III Seminário de Institutos, Colégios e Escolas de Aplicação: Educação e Sociedade Contemporânea: Desafios e Propostas*. [publication on cd-rom] Rio de Janeiro.

Anderson, C., 2006. *The long tail: why the future of business is selling less of more*. New York: Hyperion.

Araujo, R., 2001. *A Cidade Contemporânea e As Novas Tecnologias*. M.Sc. Federal University of Rio de Janeiro, PROURB, School of Architecture and Urbanism.

Araujo, Rosane., 2006. *O urbanismo em estado fluido* [*Urbanism in fluid state*]. In: *A cidade pelo avesso* [*The city inside out*], Viana & Mosley. Org. Rachel C. M. da Silva.

Ascher, F., 1995. *Metápolis: acerca do futuro da cidade* [*Metapolis, ou, l'avenir des villes*]. Translated by A. Domingues, 1998. Oeiras: Celta Editora.

Ascher, F., 2000. *Événements nos Dépassent, Feignons d'en être les Organisateurs; essai sur la société contemporaine*. La Tour d'Aigues: L'Aube.

Ascher, F., 2001. *Les nouveaux principes de l'urbanisme: la fin des villes n'est pas à l'ordre du jour*. Paris: L'Aube.

Bachelard, G., 1972. *O surracionalismo*. In: *Lugar em Comunicação* (Translated by Magno, MD.) Rio de Janeiro. Year 1, v. 1.

Barabási, A., 2003. *Linked: how everything is connected to everything else and what it means for business, science and everyday life*. New York: Plume, Penguin Group.

Barabási, A. and Bonabeau, E., 2003. Redes sem escala [Scale-free networks]. *Scientific American* (Brazil), Year 2, No. 13, pp. 64-72.

Beck U., Giddens A & Lash S., 1995, *Modernização Reflexiva* [*Reflexive modernization. politics, tradition and aesthetics in the modern social order*]. São Paulo: UNESP Publisher, p. 8.

Beyssade, J., 1999. Descartes et la nature de la raison. In: Marques, E. da R. *Verdade, conhecimento e ação*. São Paulo: Loyola.

Bertalanffy, L. v., 1973. *Teoria geral de sistemas* [*General system theory*]. Petrópolis: Vozes.

Bourbaki, N., 1984. *Éléments d'histoire des mathématiques*. Paris: Masson.

Bouzon, E., 1998. *Ensaios babilônicos: sociedade, economia e cultura na Babilônia pré-cristã*. Porto Alegre: EDIPUCRS.

Calvino, I.,1972. *As Cidades Invisíveis* [*Invisible Cities*]. Translated by D. Mainardi, 1998. São Paulo: Companhia das Letras.

Cassirer, E., 1977. *Substance et fonction*. Paris: Les Editions de Minuit.

Cassirer, E., 1992. *A Filosofia do iluminismo* [*The philosophy of the enlightenment*]. Campinas: Editora da Unicamp.

Castells, M., 1995. *La Ciudad Informacional; tecnologías de la información, reestructuración econó-mica y el proceso urbano-regional* [*The informational city: information technology, economic restructuring and urban development*]. Translated by R. Q. Muñoz. Madrid: Alianza Editorial.

Castells, M., 1999a [1996]. A Sociedade em Rede. In: *A Era da Informação: Economia, Sociedade e Cultura – vol. I* [*The Information Age: Economy, Society and Culture – vol. I*]. Translated by R.V. Majer. São Paulo: Paz e Terra.

Castells, M., 1999b [1996]. O Poder da Identidade [The Power of Identity]. In: *A Era da Informação: Economia, Sociedade e Cultura – vol. II* [*The Information Age: Economy, Society and Culture – vol. II*]. Translated by K.B. Gerhardt. São Paulo: Paz e Terra.

Castells, M., 1999c [1996]. Fim de Milênio [End of Millenium]. In: *A Era da Informação: Economia, Sociedade e Cultura – vol. III [The Information Age: Economy, Society and Culture – vol. III]*. Translated by K.B. Gerhardt. São Paulo: Paz e Terra.

Castells, M., 2003. *A galáxia da Internet: reflexões sobre a internet, os negócios e a sociedade [The Internet Galaxy: reflections on the internet, business, and society]*. Rio de Janeiro: Jorge Zahar Editor.

Castells, M. ed., 2004. *The network society: a cross-cultural perspective*. Cheltenham, Mass.: Edward Elgar Publishing Ltd.

Cauquelin, A., 1996. A Cidade Contemporânea e a Arte Contemporânea. *Arte e Ensaios, Revista do Mestrado em História da Arte, EBA-UFRJ*, 3(1), pp 31-35, 2nd semester.

Choay, F., 1979 [1965]. *O Urbanismo: Utopias e Realidades – Uma Antologia [L'Urbanisme: utopies et réalités]*. São Paulo: Editora Perspectiva.

Christelle, R. Reconstruction des territoires, projet urbain et anthropologie de l'espace. In: Touissant, J. and Zimmerman, M.(eds.) 1998. *Projet urbain: ménager les gens, aménager la ville*. Paris: Pierre Mardaga Éditeur.

CIAC, *2005 La Ville Virtuelle III: espace public / espace privé*. Magazine Électronique n. 22: June 2005. http://www.ciac.ca/magazine

Coates, N., 2003. *Guide to ECSTACITY*. New York: Princeton Architectural Press.

Da Matta, R., 2003. *A casa & a rua: espaço, cidadania, mulher e morte no Brasil*. 6th ed. Rio de Janeiro: Rocco.

Debord, G. 1997 [1967/1988]. *A Sociedade do Espetáculo; comentários sobre a sociedade do espetáculo [The Society of the Spectacle; comments on the society of the spectacle]*. Translated by E.S. Abreu. Rio de Janeiro: Contraponto.

Deleuze, G., 1992 [1972-1990]. *Conversações [Negotiations]*. (Translated by P.P. Pelbart). Rio de Janeiro: Editora 34.

Deleuze, G. and Guattari, F., 1995. *Mil Platôs: capitalismo e esquizofrenia [A Thousand Plateaus: capitalism & schizophrenia]*. Vol.1. Translated by A.G.Neto and C.P. Costa. Rio de Janeiro: Ed. 34.

Descartes, R., 1979. *Coleção Os Pensadores [Collection "The Thinkers"]*. São Paulo: Abril Cultural,.

Dumouchel, P. and Dupuy, J., (eds.), 1983. *L'auto-organisation: de la physique au politique*. Colloque de Cerisy. Paris: Seuil.

Eliade, M., 1977. *Tratado de história das religiões*. Lisbon: Cosmos.

Eliade, M.,1978 . *História das crenças e das idéias religiosas*. Tome 1. Vol. 1. Rio de Janeiro: Zahar Editores.

Farouki, N., 1996. *La foi et la raison: histoire d'un malentendu*. Paris: Flammarion.

Freud, S., 1974 [1914]. *Uma introdução ao narcisismo [On Narcissism: an Introduction]*. S.E. Vol. XIV. Rio de Janeiro: Imago.

Freud, S., 1976a [1916]. *Conferências introdutórias sobre a psicanálise [Introductory Lectures on Psycho-Analysis]*. S.E. Vol. XV. Rio de Janeiro: Imago.

Freud, S., 1976b [1920]. *Além do Princípio de Prazer [Beyond the Pleasure Principle]*. S. E. Vol. XVIII. Rio de Janeiro: Imago.

Freud, S., 1976c [1922]. *Psicanálise [Psycho-Analysis]*. S. E. Vol. XVIII. Rio de Janeiro: Imago.

Freud, S., 1976d [1923]. *O Ego e o Id [The Ego and the Id]*. S.E. Vol. XIX. Rio de Janeiro: Imago.

Freud, S., 1976e [1924]. *As resistências à psicanálise [The Resistances to Psycho-Analysis]*. S.E. Vol. XIX. Rio de Janeiro: Imago.

Freud, S., 1976f [1938]. *Divisão do ego e os processos de defesa [Splitting of the Ego in the Process of Defence]*. S.E. Vol. XIX. Rio de Janeiro: Imago.

Freud, S., 1987a [1896]. *Observações adicionais sobre as neuropsicoses de defesa [Further Remarks on the Neuro-Psychoses of Defence]*. S.E. Vol. III. Rio de Janeiro: Imago.

Freud, S., 1987b [1915]. *O Inconsciente [The Unconscious]*. S.E. Vol. XIV. Rio de Janeiro: Imago.

Gibson, William, 2003. *Neuromancer*. São Paulo: Aleph.

Godelier, M., 2004. *Métamorphoses de la parenté*. Paris: Fayard.

Grahan, Stephen and Mervin, Simon *Towards the real time city* in *Telecommunications and the city: Electronic Spaces, Urban Spaces*. Available at http://www.eesc.sc.usp. br/nomads/tics_arq_urb/cidtempo.doc. Accessed 23 June 2012

Guattari, F., 1993. [1990-1992]. *Caosmose: um novo paradigma estético* [*Chaosmosis: an ethico-aesthetic paradigm*]. Translated by A.L. de Oliveira and L.C. Leão. Rio de Janeiro: editora 34.

Hardt, M., 1996. La société mondiale de contrôle. In: *Gilles Deleuze. Une Vie Philosophique*, pp. 359-375. Paris: Institut Sintelabo.

Hardt, M. and Negri, A., 2001 [2000]. *Império* [*Empire*]. Translated by Berilo Vargas. Rio de Janeiro: Record.

Houaiss, A and Villar, M. 2001. *Dicionário Houaiss da língua Portuguesa* [Houaiss Dictionary of the Portuguese Language]. Rio de Janeiro: Editora Objetiva.

Ianni, O., 1997 [1996]. *A era do globalismo*. 2nd ed. Rio de Janeiro: Civilização Brasileira.

Johnson, S., 2003. *Emergência: a dinâmica de rede em formigas, cérebros, cidades e softwares* [*Emergence: the connected lives of ants, brains, cities and software*]. Rio de Janeiro: Jorge Zahar Editor.

Jullien, F., 1997. *Figuras da imanência: para uma leitura filosófica do* I Ching, *o Clássico da Mutação* [*Figures de l'immanence: pour une lecture philosophique du* Yi king, *le Classique du Changement*]. São Paulo: Editora 34.

Kant, I., 1985. *Textos Seletos* [*Selected Texts*]. Petrópolis: Vozes

Kant, I., 1989. *Crítica da Razão Pura* [*Critique of Pure Reason*]. Lisbon: Fundação Calouste Gulbekian.

Kerckhove, D. de., 1997 [1995] *A pele da cultura: uma investigação sobre a nova realidade eletrônica* [*The Skin of Culture: investigating the new electronic reality*]. Translated by L. Soares and C. Carvalho. Lisbon: Relógio d'Água, 1997.

Kerckhove, D. de., 2000. *The Architecture of Intelligence*. Basel: Birkhäuser.

Koolhaas, R., 2002. "Qué há sido del urbanismo?" ["Whatever happened to urbanism?"]. *Oeste: cultivos urbanos. Revista de Arquitectura, Urbanismo, Arte y Pensamiento Contemporaneos*, nº 15.

Koyré, A., 1991. *Estudos de história do pensamento científico* [*Études d'histoire de la pensée scientifique*]. Rio de Janeiro: Forense.

Lefebvre, H., 2004 [1970]. *A Revolução Urbana* [*The Urban Revolution*]. Belo Horizonte: UFMG.

Lepetit, B., 2001. *Por uma nova história urbana*. Selection of texts, critical review and presentation by Heliana Angotti Salgueiro. São Paulo: Editora da Universidade de São Paulo.

Lévy, P., 1987. *La machine univers: création, cognition et culture informatique*. Paris: Ed. de la Découverte, 1987.

Lévy, P., 1993[1990]. *As tecnologias da inteligência; o futuro do pensamento na era da informática* [*Les technologies de l'intelligence*]. Translated by C.I. da Costa. Rio de Janeiro: Editora 34.

Lévy, P., 1996 [1995]. *O que é o virtual?* [*Becoming Virtual*]. São Paulo: Ed. 34.

Lévy, P., 1999. *Cibercultura* [*Cyberculture*]. São Paulo: Ed. 34.

Lévy, P., 2003. *A inteligência coletiva: por uma antropologia do ciberespaço* [*Collective Intelligence: mankind's emerging world in cyberspace*].. São Paulo: Loyola. Ed. 4.

Lewontin, R., 2002. *A tripla hélice: genes, organismo e ambiente* [*The Triple Helix: gene, organism and the environment*]. São Paulo: Companhia das Letras.

Lorenz, K., 1995. *Os fundamentos da etologia* [*The Foundations of Ethology*]. São Paulo: Editora da Unesp.

McLuhan, M., c1969. *O meio são as massa-gens* [*The medium is the message*]. 2nd ed. Rio de Janeiro: Record.

McLuhan, M., 2006 [1964]. *Os meios de comunicação como extensão do homem* [*Understanding Media: The Extensions of Man*]. !8th ed. São Paulo: Editora Pensamento-Cultrix.

Magno, MD., 1986 [1981]. *Psicanálise & Polética* . Rio de Janeiro: Aoutra Editora.

Magno, MD., 1990 [1988]. *De Mystério Magno.* Rio de Janeiro: Aoutra Editora.

Magno, MD., 1993 [1992]. *Pedagogia Freudiana* Rio de Janeiro: Imago.

Magno, MD., 1998. Formações e Interfaces: Parangolés e suas Transas. *Lumina. Revista da Faculdade de Comunicação da UFJF*, 1 (1), Jul-Dec, pp. 33-51.

Magno, MD., 2000a [1996]. *Psychopahtia Sexualis.* Santa Maria: Editora da UFSM.

Magno, MD., 2000b [1990]. *Arte e Fato. A Nova Psicanálise - Da arte Total à Clínica Geral.* Rio de Janeiro: NovaMente Editora.

Magno, MD., 2000c [1994]. *Velut Luna: a Clínica Geral da Nova Psicanálise.* Rio de Janeiro: NovaMente Editora.

Magno, MD., 2000d [1995]. *Arte e Psicanálise: Estética e Clínica Geral.* Rio de Janeiro: NovaMente Editora.

Magno, MD., 2003 [2000/2001]. *Revirão 2000/2001: "Arte da Fuga" and "Clínica da Razão Prática".* Rio de Janeiro: NovaMente Editora.

Magno, MD., 2004 [1999]. *A Psicanálise, Novamente: um Pensamento para o Século II da Era Freudiana.* Rio de Janeiro: NovaMente Editora.

Magno, MD., 2005 [2002]. *Psicanálise: Arreligião.*Rio de Janeiro: NovaMente Editora.

Magno, MD., 2006 [2003]. *Ars Gaudendi: a Arte do Gozo.* Rio de Janeiro: NovaMente Editora.

Magno, MD., 2007 [2005]. *Clavis Universalis: da cura em psicanálise ou revisão da clínica.* Rio de Janeiro: NovaMente Editora.

Magno, MD., 2008 [2006]. *AmaZonas: A Psicanálise de A a Z.* Rio de Janeiro: NovaMente Editora.

Magno, MD., 2008 [1999]. *A Psicanálise Novamente.* Rio de Janeiro: NovaMente Editora.

Magno, MD., 2009 [2007]. *A Rebelião dos Anjos: eleutéria e exousía.* Rio de Janeiro: NovaMente Editora.

Magno, MD. 2010 [2004]. *Economia Fundamental. Metamorfoses da Pulsão*. Rio de Janeiro: NovaMente Editora.

Maturana, H. R. and Varela, F. J., 1980. *Autopoiesis and cognition: the realization of the living*. Dordrecht: D. Reidel Publishing Company.

Maturana, H. R. and Varela, F. J., 2001. *A árvore do conhecimento: as bases biológicas da compreensão humana* [*The tree of knowledge: the biological roots of human understanding*]. São Paulo: Palas Athena.

Mazlish, B., 1993. *The Fourth discontinuity. The co-evolution of humans and machines*. New Haven and London: Yale University Press.

Medeiros, N., 2003. O 'Homem pós-orgânico': quarta ferida narcísica? . *Lumina*. vol. 4-5.

Mitchell, W.J., 1995. *City of bits: space, place and the infobahn*. Cambridge: MIT Press.

Mitchell, W.J., 2001[1999]. *e-topía* "vida urbana, Jim, pero no la que nosostros conocemos" [*E-topia: "Urban life, Jim – but not as we know it"*]. Barcelona: Gustavo Gili.

Mora, J.F., 2001. *Dicionário de Filosofia*. 4th ed. São Paulo: Martins Fontes.

Morin, E., 2006. *Introdução ao pensamento complexo* [*Introduction à la pensée complexe*]. Porto Alegre: Sulina.

Mumford, L, 1991[1961]. *A cidade na História; suas origens, transformações e perspectivas* [*The city in History; its origins, its transformations, and its prospects*]. 3rd ed. Tranlated by N.R. da Silva. São Paulo: Martins Fontes.

Nagel, E. and Newman, J.R., 2003. *A prova de Gödel* [*Gödel's proof*]. 2nd ed. São Paulo: Perspectiva, 2003.

OESTE, 2002. Revista de Arquitectura, Urbanismo, Arte e Pensamiento Contemporâneos. N.15: Cultivos Urbanos. Madrid.

Pessoa, F., 1983. *Ficções do Interlúdio*/4: poesias de Álvaros de Campos. Rio de Janeiro: Nova Fronteira.

Polanyi, K., 1980. *A grande transformação: as origens de nossa época* [*The great transformation: the political and economic origins of our time*]. Rio de Janeiro: Campus.

Pont, J., 1974. *La topologie algébrique, des origines à Poincaré*. Paris: PUF.

Prigogine, I. and Stengers, I., 1991. *A nova aliança: metamorfose da ciência* [*The new alliance: metamorphosis of science*]. Brasília: Editora da UnB.

Reali, G. and Antiseri, D., 2004. *História da Filosofia*. 2nd ed. Vol. 1 and 4. São Paulo: Paulus.

Rossi, A., 1995 [1966]. *A Arquitetura da Cidade* [*The Architecture of the City*]. Translated by E. Brandão. São Paulo: Martins Fontes.

Rykwert, J., 2004. *A sedução do lugar – a história e o futuro da cidade* [*The seduction of the place – the history and future of the city*]. Martins Fontes. São Paulo.

Santos, C.N.P. dos, coord., 1985. *Quando a rua vira casa: a apropriação de espaços de uso coletivo em um centro de bairro*. 3rd ed. São Paulo: Projeto FINEP/IBAM.

Sassen, S., 1998 [1994]. *As cidades na economia mundial* [*Cities in a world economy*]. Translated by C.E.M. de Moura. São Paulo: Studio Nobel.

Silveira Jr., P.M. da., 2006. *Artificialismo Total. Ensaios de Transformática. Comunicação e Psicanálise*. Rio de Janeiro: NovaMente.

Singh, S., 2006. *Big Bang*. São Paulo: Record.

Solà-Morales, I. de., (unknown). Presente y futuros. La arquitetura en las ciudades. *Presente y Futuros; arquitectura en las ciudades*. pp. 10-23.

Solà-Morales, I. de., 2002. *Territórios*. Barcelona: Gustavo Gili.

Solà-Morales, I. de., 2003. *Diferencias. Topografia de la arquitectura contemporánea*. Gustavo Gili.

Solà-Morales, I. de and Costa, X., 2005. *Metrópolis – ciudades, redes, paisajes*. Barcelona: Gustavo Gilli.

Tan, K., 2005. Teoría de la ciudad nodal. In: Solà-Morales, I. de and Costa, X. *Metrópolis – ciudades, redes, paisajes*. Barcelona: Gustavo Gilli.

Tolentino, B., 2006. *A Imitação do Amanhecer*. Rio de Janeiro: Globo.

Vázquez, C.G., 2004. *Ciudad hojaldre: visiones urbanas del siglo XXI*. Barcelona: Gustavo Gilli.

Vernant, J., 1990. *Mito e pensamento entre os gregos* [*Myth and thought among the Greeks*]. Rio de Janeiro: Paz e Terra.

Vieira, A.B.,1983. *Etologia e Ciências Humanas*. Lisbon: Imprensa Nacional – Casa da Moeda.

Virilio, P., 1989 [1980] *Esthétique de la Disparition*. Col. Livre de Poche/Essais, no. 4202. Paris: Galilée.

Virilio, P., 1993 [1984/1993]. *O espaço crítico e as perspectivas em tempo real* [*L'espace critique*]. Translated by P.R. Pires. Rio de Janeiro: Ed. 34. Ed. reviewed and enhanced by the author.

Virilio, P., 1996 [1977]. *Velocidade e política* [*Speed and Politics*]. Tranlated by C.M. Paciornik. São Paulo: Estação Liberdade.

Virilio, P., 2001. Conversación con Paul Virilio. *Revista Internacional de Arquitectura 2G*. N.18. Barcelona: Gustavo Gili.

Virilio, P. and Lotringer, S., 1984 [1983]. *Guerra Pura; a militarização do cotidiano* [*Pure War*]. Translated by E.Miné and L.G. dos Santos. São Paulo: Brasiliense.

Vivianne, C., 1998. *Le projet urbain, un ici et maintenant ou un nouvel ailleurs? Quelques reflexions sommaires*. In: Touissant, J. and Zimmerman, M., (eds.). *Projet urbain: ménager les gens, aménager la ville*. Paris: Pierre Mardaga Éditeur.

Wertheim, M., 2001. *Uma História do Espaço de Dante à Internet* [*The Pearly Gates of Cyberspace: a history of space from Dante to the Internet*]. Rio de Janeiro: Jorge Zahar.

WIENER, Norbert. *Cibernética: o uso humano de seres humanos* [*The Human Use Of Human Beings: Cybernetics And Society*]. 4ed. São Paulo: Cultrix, 1973.[1950]

Wikipedia, the free encyclopedia. *Rizoma* [*Rhizome*]. Available at <http://pt.wikipedia.org/wiki/Rizoma>. Accessed 28 June 2012.

Notes

1. *The city is me – The twenty-first century Urbanism* is a doctoral dissertation in urbanism, developed as part of the PROURB program of Rio de Janeiro Federal University (UFRJ), received the "CAPES Thesis Award for 2008" from the Brazilian Ministry of Education.

2. See the systemic thinking of Bertalanffy summarised in chapter 4. In a way it explored the generalized use of isomorphic procedures and, at the limit, made analogy evident as a heuristic instrument constitutive of any knowledge.

3. That is how Manuel Castells conceptualizes it when trying to define what is specific in the informational and knowledge society which we currently constitute. For Castells, "information" and "knowledge" are characteristics of human societies that vary according to space, time and cultures, without it being possible to distinguish, with the mentioned characteristics, what is new in our times. Hence the understanding that "what is actually new, both technologically and socially, is a society built around microelectronics-based information technologies. To which I add biological technologies based on genetic engineering, as they also refer to the decoding and recoding of information of living matter." (Castells (ed.), 2004: 7).

4. A small example of this situation is the news we read on September 28th, 2007: "New Zealand uses wiki so that citizens may create law" or "Police wiki lets you write the law" – where New Zealand's police department, in order to create a new Policing Act to replace the current one that dates back to 1958, is employing, as one of the means for the elaboration of this law, the tool called wiki, where citizens may edit parts of the suggested project or insert a totally new one. For the person in charge of creating the new law, the country's Police Superintendent Hamish McCardle, this might be extreme democracy. (This "wiki" tool is reminiscent of Wikipedia where, in theory, people can edit, through the Internet, several texts which are recorded and are added to or altered by someone else and the users can provide hyperlinks for the uploading of multimedia content, and the result is a

complete text about a given subject which, prior to going online, is checked and has its contents approved).

See original text on http://www.stuff.co.nz/4215797a10.html

5.   This understanding has already been described by several authors: In their book *Modernização Reflexiva* [*Reflexive Modernization*], Ulrich Beck, Anthony Giddens and Scott Lash jointly affirm that that which is "natural" is so intricately weaved with that which is "social" that human beings no longer know what is "nature" and "nothing else can be affirmed as such" (Beck, Giddens, & Lash, *Modernização Reflexiva* [*Reflexive Modernization.Politics, Tradition and Aesthetics in the Modern Social Order*]. São Paulo: UNESP Publisher, 1995, p. 8). According to Manuel Castells we are on a level where, after superseding nature to the point where we force ourselves to artificially preserve it as a cultural form, culture goes to referring, above all, to culture itself (Castells, Manuel. *A sociedade em rede* [*The network society: a cross-cultural perspective*], 2004, p. 505). The idea of "spontaneous artifice" and "industrial artifice" proposed by the theorist and psychoanalyst MD Magno is another testimony of the abandonment of the opposition between what is "natural" and what is "artificial" in favor of a topological and homogenizing view of the world's facts as *artifice*. On this topic see Araujo, Rosane. *O urbanismo em estado fluido* [*Urbanism in Fluid State*] in *A cidade pelo avesso* [*The City Inside Out*], 2006. Viana & Mosley. Org. Rachel C. M. da Silva.

6.   We employ a concept of the New Psychoanalysis which we will explain in chapter 5.

7.   Ascher, François. *Les noveaux principes de l'urbanisme: la fin des villes n'est pas à l'ordre du jour.* Paris: L'Aube, 2001.

8.   The definition of space suffers continuous change throughout history and, for a long time, under strong influence of our dualistic philosophies and religions which have always insisted on dividing reality into matter and spirit. The medieval image of the world may be understood through the explicitness of the physical space of the body and the immaterial space of the soul where "the architecture of the former was defined by the geocentric plan of planets and stars" (Wertheim, 2001: 28), and the latter's was "divided into three distinct regions or "kingdoms: Hell, Purgatory, and Heaven"(ibid: 28). From the end of the 17th century our physical view strengthens the materialist concept of reality and increasingly "over the past three centuries reality has come to be seen as just the *physical* world" (ibid: 113). Thus, at the end of the 18th century *monism* was installed and "for the first time in history, humanity had produced a purely physicalist world picture, one in which mind/spirit/soul had no place at all" (ibid: 114). In the last century we had the *relativistic* concept of space by Albert Einstein, where space and time "intertwine in a four-dimensional

multiple with time becoming, in fact, another dimension of space"(ibid: 29). Still in the second half of the 20th century, physicists invented the idea of eleven-dimension *hyperspace*. Within this concept of *hyperspace* there is, ultimately, nothing but space. The universe of eleven dimensions bears four great dimensions, being three of space and one of time, and "seven microscopic space dimension, all rolled up into some tiny complex geometric form"(ibid: 155). Currently we find ourselves facing digital space – *cyberspace*. When we interact in cyberspace our location can no longer be defined by coordinates of physical space.

9.   *La Ville Virtuelle III: espace public / espace privé.* Magazine Électronique n. 22: juin 2005. Magazine of the Montreal's Center of Contemporary Art. http://www.ciac.ca/magazine

10.   Released by Agencia Estado when the "2nd Conference of the United Nations Human Settlements Programme, HABITAT II" was held in Istambul, 1996.

11.   Stephen Grahan and Simon Mervin. *Towards the real time city* in *Telecommunications and the city: Electronic Spaces, Urban Spaces apud* http://www.eesc.sc.usp.br/nomads/tics_arq_urb/cidtempo.doc

12.   This topic will be developed in chapter 3.

13.   It is important to confirm that "unilateralism" in this case is understood from inclusion of different positions forming a single one, due to the dissolution of oppositions and undistinguished perception.

14.   See the several concepts of city where the authors no longer use, as main reference, the Euclidian Geometry or Geography. For instance: Informational City by Manuel Castells, Global City by Saskia Sassen, Videocity and Instant City by Paul Virilio, City of Control by Michael Hardt, Digital City by William Mitchell, Cybercity by Pierre Lévy, etc.

15.   This closely follows Bernard Lepetit (2001) and its quoting is practically literal. He says it in the context of his studies about the city in the Ancient Regime: "In order to qualify a city of the modern day, for a long time we settled for a simple vocabulary grading: the pre-industrial city preceded the industrial one. The implicit definition was very negative and excessively loaded with presuppositions. Therefore it seems necessary to replace it by a concept of 'Ancient Regime city' (…). For that it is necessary to integrate the ancient representations of city. In fact, the reality of the city of the Ancient Regime one tried to reach is – as for any other city – a practice of this reality, a practice of the city. This practice, in turn, integrates a certain number

of representations". The second sentence belongs to Marcel Roncayolo. Both quotations are from the article "Os espelhos da cidade: um debate sobre o discurso dos antigos geógrafos" ["Mirrors of the city: a debate about the discourse of ancient geographers"] (Lepetit, 2001: 266–7 and 268).

16.   That is the case of the study undertaken by Jean-Pierre Vernant of Greek religious and social space with the pairing the gods Hestia, protectress and symbol of the "house" and of the related meanings of fixity, immutability and permanence, and Hermes, also connected to the dwelling of men but in the sense of being a messenger and, for that reason and unlike Hestia, invoking movement, passage, mutation, transition (cf. Vernant, 1990: 151-191).

17.   We followed the arguments of Farouki (1996), especially the first chapter dedicated to the discussion of what is concept (its nature and typology) and knowledge with its constitutive demand for comprehension and explanation.

18.   This principle was formulated by Anaximander (*circa* end of 7th century – beginning of the second half of the 6th century B.C.), born in the city of Miletus, friend and disciple of Thales. Cf. Reali & Antiseri, 2004, v. 1: 19–21.

19.   It is the case, for instance, of systemic thinking and its developments and contiguities such as cybernetics, self-organization and complexity theories.

20.   We have taken the expression, as well as its underlying reasoning, from Godelier, 2004: 341-44.

21.   In the context it was stated, Castells reminded us that "in all societies humankind has existed in and acted through a symbolic environment". What was in question was a certain demystification of the alleged opposition between real and virtual. What was enlightening at the time he wrote was the fact that "reality, as experienced, has always been virtual because it is always perceived through symbols that frame practice with some meaning that escapes their strict semantic definition (…) All realities are communicated through symbols. And in human, interactive communication, regardless of the medium, all symbols are somewhat displaced in relation to their assigned semantic meaning. In a sense, *all reality is virtually perceived*." (Castells, 1999a: 395. Our italics.)

22.   Carbon is present in every living organism. The human body contains a large amount of carbon composites. That is why the carbon base is identified as constituent of the human body.

23.   This concept is more thoroughly developed in the item "The cognitive ecology of Pierre Lévy", chapter 4.

24.   With the digital revolution, wire, cable and microwave networks of analogical telecommunications give way to a vast structure of fiber optics networks. In this context of accelerated transformations – experimented with through new available forms for human interaction, based on the suppression of geographic distances and temporal limits – arises the term *Information Superhighways*, indicating the possibility of convergence of the different data networks that we know separately, responsible for operating radio, TV, telephones, etc., into one single great network. Therefore the term *infobahn* denotes, in Mitchell's book's context, the Information Superhighways and the Internet, which started to establish itself globally at the time the book was written.

25.   Agents are intermediate software programmed to perform tasks. Usually they take over typically human tasks, such as indicating a product from data related to a previous purchase history, writing an e-mail or even suggesting orthographical and grammatical corrections (cf. Mitchell, 1995: 13).

26.   Such difference is approached by Mitchell as in the science fiction movie "The Lawnmower Man" (1992), where the main character Jobe Smith has his body inserted in a spinning structure similar to that of Leonardo da Vinci's Vitruvian Man, while his avatar travels around the network.

27.   The term derives from the expression "cybernetic organism" and is used in the book's context to refer to artificial bodies, enhanced and animated by human intelligence.

28.   In this sense the author mentions a pioneer initiative taken by Blockbuster and IBM in 1993: transmitting videos stored in a central server to stores, where consumers would access such base and choose their videos which would be instantly recorded to CDs. Even bookstores could follow such a model, printing requested material in time, which would allow producers, sellers and consumers to save and access potentially more options. However, Mitchell had already foreseen that consumers, naturally, could do this at home: for the author, the download of books, magazines, newspapers, video and music could even be integrated with a recycling chain, especially of paper and printing cartridges (cf. Mitchell, 1995: 50 – 51).

29.   Mitchell even speculates on the possibility of a society without money where bank transactions would be performed online. Checks, credit and debit cards and even personal bank terminals associated to laptops or palmtops with wireless connections could become possible, acting as electronic wallets (cf. Mitchell, 1995: 82).

30.   Reference to the six chapters of the book.

31.   For François Ascher, western societies are starting to leave industrialism, entering a cognitive economy, whose foundations are production, appropriation of the sale and the use of knowledge, information, and procedures, in a process that privileges knowledge and technology – which demands qualified capital and personnel, not mattering whence they come – relegating material production to a second plan (cf. Ascher, 2001).

32.   The use of technologies propitiates the existence of a timeless time without chronological reference. The space of flows dissolves time, eliminating the sequence of events and making them simultaneous, thus creating a non-differentiated time that enables an everlasting present. Past, present and future and the written, oral and audiovisual modes of communication interact in multimediated information. Time is transformed by simultaneity and by timelessness (cf. Castells, 1999a: 457–92).

33.   According to Castells, responding to an essay by Barbara Adam about time and social theory, there is a tendency to adopt a contextual concept of human time: time is local (Castells, 1999a: 458).

34.   His studies with polyhedrons led him to demonstrate, through the so-called Euler number, that, despite the deformities a solid may suffer, the relation between faces, edges and vertexes remains constant and interdependent. The history of topology, or *analysis situs*, is directly connected to the investigation of the exceptions to Euler's enunciation (problem of curved surfaces, *n*-dimension spaces), connecting to the broader mathematical scenario of the 19th century, when investigations about the nature of the number and the structure of the numerical *continuum* resulted not only in strict definitions for negative, complex and irrational numbers, but also in the construction of a logical base for real numbers and in the foundation of the theory of the infinite numbers. All that decisively contributed to the development of non-Euclidian geometry of Riemannian base. (cf. Nagel & Newman, 2003).

35.   MD Magno's teaching has considered the topological issue since the 1970s, orienting itself by the routes once printed by his master Jacques Lacan. (Cf. Magno, 1986: 24–48).

36.   As, for instance, the work of the mathematician Auguste Ferdinand Möbius bears witness, and of artists like Escher and Magritte.

37.   Solà-Morales refers to the Vitruvian principles of *utilitas* (comfort/usefulness), *firmitas* (firmness) and *venustas* (beauty).

38. We use this resource for educational purposes, but we are aware that, in Euclidian geometry, we work, on the contrary, with the ideality of space and every concrete exemplification is always an imperfect copy of the mathematically-conceived ideal model.

39. Drawing taken from Magno, MD. *A Psicanálise Novamente* [*Psychoanalysis Novamente*]. Rio de Janeiro: Novamente, 2004. p. 60.

40. *Urbe* = city; *Orbe* = globe, world, universe.

41. Just as, etymologically, the term *architect* comes from the Greek *arche*, "first" or "origin", and *tekton*, "carpenter" or "constructor", replacing *arche* by *kyber*, "rudder", "helm", "government", "direction", the constructor element is maintained, but the new field of interactive navigation is added to the function of that which would no longer be the architect, but the *cybertect*.

42. Contemporarily there are several concepts used to translate the notion of man, which includes all sorts of technologies as its extension: post-organic man, bionic man, machine man, post-human man, cyborg, post-biological man.

43. The subject is a philosophic category that means the foundation – idea of place, center, reference center.

44. "Archimedes said that if he had one firm and immovable point he could lift the world 'with a long enough lever'; so I too can hope for great things if I manage to find just one little thing that is solid and certain". (Descartes, 1979: 91)

45. Substance is a broadly used concept in philosophy. It dates back to the first Greek philosophers, but has stayed as a fundamental concept for philosophy until current times. It expresses relations of attribution in the sense of establishing a predicate to something or someone. For Aristotle, substance is a "category of the being", in other words, it is predicate or a different class which defines essential aspects of the being.

46. "I am, I exist—that is certain. But for how long? For as long as I am thinking … Strictly speaking, then, I am simply a thing that thinks." (Descartes, 1979: 94).

47. It should be noted that this "I" is not by any means synonym or equivalent to a corporeal existence, because the principle of distinction between the substances, mental and corporeal, is sustained by Descartes until the end, for the case of *cogito*. (Descartes, 1979: 94).

48. For Beyssade, individualism is a demand for the Cartesian thinking system: "Descartes, herald of modern individualism, is philosopher of the ego, of egoity, if not of egoism. His first principle does not say *cogito*, but rather *ego sum, ego existo*, 'I am, I exist'. In a general demotion of all that is not I, the lonely and calm statement of I as first principle makes its modernity" (Beyssade, 1999: 47-48).

49. Kant offers a concise characterization of his century answering the question 'what is enlightenment?': "Enlightenment [Aufklärung] *is man's emergence from his self-imposed immaturity. Immaturity* is the inability to use one's understanding without guidance from another. *This immaturity is self-imposed* when its cause lies not in lack of understanding, but in lack of resolve and courage *to use it* without guidance from another. *Sapere Aude!* Have courage to use your *own* understanding [Aufklärung], that is the motto of enlightenment". (Kant, 1985: 100)

50. "It appears to me that the examples of mathematics and natural philosophy, which, as we have seen, were brought into their present condition by a sudden revolution, are sufficiently remarkable to fix our attention on the essential circumstances of the change which has proved so advantageous to them, and to induce us to make the experiment of imitating them, so far as the analogy which, as rational sciences, they bear to metaphysics may permit" (Kant, 1989: 19).

51. Philosophical position that states only the existence of subjective reason and what is considered as reality depends exclusively on subjective conditions.

52. For Aristotle, the concept of *substance* has central value in his philosophy, particularly in his Theory of Knowledge. His objective was to overcome the duality between the sensible and the intelligible, conjugating these two dimensions in the very concept of *substance*.

53. In this sense it is notorious how important the proof of God's existence is for Cartesian philosophy, as ultimate guarantee of knowledge. More generally, regarding the 17th century, Cassirer comments: "In the great metaphysical systems of that [17th] century – those of Descartes and Malebranche, of Spinoza and Leibniz – reason is the realm of the 'eternal verities', of those truths held in common by the human and the divine mind. What we know through reason, we therefore behold 'in God'" (Cassirer, 1992, vol.1: 32).

54. "For experience itself is a mode of cognition which requires understanding. Before objects, are given to me, that is, a priori, I must presuppose in myself laws of the understanding which are expressed in conceptions a priori. To these conceptions, then, all the objects of experience must necessarily conform" (Kant, 1989: 20).

55. "Its original significance was purely therapeutic: it aimed at creating a new and efficient method for treating neurotic illnesses. But connections which could not be foreseen in the beginning caused psycho-analysis to reach out far beyond its original aim. It ended by claiming to have set our whole view of mental life upon a new basis and therefore to be of importance for every field of knowledge that is founded on psychology" (Freud, 1976e, v. XIX: 266).

56. *Ich* in German. We will use the term Ego, according to the Standard Edition English translation.

57. "The philosophers' idea of what is mental was not that of psycho-analysis. The overwhelming majority of philosophers regard as mental only the phenomena of consciousness... What, then, can a philosopher say to a theory which, like psycho-analysis, asserts that on the contrary what is mental is in itself *unconscious* and that being conscious is only a *quality*, which may perhaps alter that act in no other respect?... they are scarcely aware that there are such things as obsession and delusions and they would find themselves in a most embarrassing situation if they were asked to explain them on the basis of their own philosophical premises. Analysts, too, refuse to say what the unconscious is, but they can indicate the domain of phenomena whose observation has obliged them to assume its existence. Philosophers, who know no kind of observation other than self-observation, cannot follow them into that domain" (Freud, 1976e, v. XIX: 268-269).

58. The statement that man's behavior is determined by historical and economic conditions that he does not even know is present in some thoughts. Darwin's theory of evolution positions man as organism determined by biological, environmental and evolutional conditions.

59. Contemporarily with the appearance of psychoanalysis, similar efforts took place in the field of physics. Notions such as identity, non-contradiction, determinism, locality, temporality, ontological unit, energy conservation were problematized by the theory of relativity. The technological development shares, by other means, the same presupposition.

60. "In some passages in a book which has since appeared by Dr. J. Breuer and myself (*Studies on Hysteria*) I have been able to elucidate, and to illustrate from clinical observations, the sense in which this psychical process of 'defence' or 'repression' is to be understood. There, too, some information is to be found about the laborious but completely reliable method of *psychoanalysis* used by me in making those investigations – investigations which also constitute a therapeutic procedure" (Freud, 1987a, v. III: 154).

61.   *"The Corner-Stones of Psycho-Analytic Theory.* – The assumption that there are unconscious mental processes, the recognition of the theory of resistance and repression, the appreciation of the importance of sexuality … these constitute the principal subject-matter of psycho-analysis and the foundations of its theory. No one who cannot accept them all should count himself a psycho-analyst" [Freud, 1976c, v. XVIII: 300].

62.   Term introduced by Freud in order to characterize the theoretical model proposed by psychoanalysis with its topographical, dynamic and economic references: "I propose that when we have succeeded in describing a psychical process in its dynamic, topographical and economic aspects, we should speak of it as a *metapsychological* presentation" (Freud, 1987b, v. XIV: 208) (italics in original).

63.   "If we cast our eyes once again over the various resistances to psycho-analysis that have been enumerated, it is evident that only a minority of them are of the kind which habitually arise against most scientific innovations of any considerable importance. The majority of them are due to the fact that powerful human feelings are hurt by the subject-matter of the theory. Darwin's theory of descent met with the same fate, since it tore down the barrier that had been arrogantly set up between men and beasts. I drew attention to this analogy in an earlier paper, in which I showed how the psycho-analytic view of the relation of the conscious ego to an overpowering unconscious was a severe blow to human self-love. I described this as the *psychological* blow to men's narcissism, and compared it with the *biological* blow delivered by the theory of descent and the earlier *cosmological* blow aimed at it by the discovery of Copernicus" (Freud, 1976e, v. XIX: 274).

64.   Nowadays, leading authors in the theoretical and technological field not only accept this statement, but already speak of a fourth narcissistic wound (Mazlish, 1993), this time operated by technology. About the role played by psychoanalysis in this contemporary mutation and how technology is expressive of the unconscious movements and its drive dynamics, see MD Magno (2004) and Medeiros (2003).

65.   "We cannot forget that Freud began by setting a radical determinism for the Unconscious, as is the case in *The Interpretation of Dreams*, chapter V, C, where he says that 'everything is unambiguously determined and nothing is left to arbitrary decision'. The belief in the possibility of unveiling the dreams demanded that he supposed a radical, absolute and unambiguous determination." (Magno, 1990: 10)

66.   His text *Beyond the Pleasure Principle* (from 1920) is the base and starting point of this turn.

67. About the philosophical use of the term "unconscious" see Abbagnano (2003: 550).

68. "Our right to assume the existence of something mental that is unconscious and to employ that assumption for the purposes of scientific work is disputed in many quarters. To this we can reply that our assumption of the unconscious is *necessary* and *legitimate*, and that we possess numerous proofs of its existence. It is necessary because the data of consciousness have a very large number of gaps in them; both in healthy and in sick people psychical acts often occur which can be explained only by presupposing other acts, of which, nevertheless, consciousness affords no evidence." (Freud, 1987b, v. XIV: 192) (italics in original).

69. First and second topographies are conceptual models conceived according to the hypothesis that psychism exercises different functions.

70. "We seek not merely to describe and to classify phenomena, but to understand them as signs of an interplay of forces in the mind as a manifestation of purposeful intentions working concurrently or in mutual opposition. We are concerned with a dynamic view of mental phenomena" (Freud, 1976a, v. XV: 86).

71. Psychoanalyst MD Magno extends to the limit the Freudian idea of topography without center when he uses reasoning that proceeds from music and architecture to exemplify the project of psychoanalysis as a non-tectonic thought. (Magno, 2004).

72. The mathematical approach is not free of charge. As we will see in the sequence, the General Systems Theory emphasized, ever since its first formulations in the 1940s, the formal characteristics of the systems, with their variables and parameters and, in this sense, their constituent concrete elements are a special application, according to the several domains, from the aspiration to the formal identity of the laws of the systems. Hence the usefulness of mathematical formalization in the construction of analysis models with the capacity to build transversalities between several science fields. Bertalanffy himself uses the mathematical law of exponentiality as an explanation for the growth of systems, giving as example the individual growth of certain bacteria and cells, the unrestricted growth of vegetable and animal populations and the unlimited growth of the population (Malthusian law) (cf. Bertalanffy, 1973: 90-93).

73. In the words of Bertalanffy, "the living organism was resolved to cells, its activities into physiological and ultimately physicochemical processes, behavior into unconditioned and conditioned reflexes, the substratum of heredity into particulate genes, and so forth" (1973: 53).

74.   This does not eliminate the concern of mathematician Norbert Wiener, 'father' of cybernetics, who affirmed that the price of metaphor – here indifferently taken as analogy – is eternal vigilance. In Lewontin, 2002: 10.

75.   Not to speak of the plain and simple repression of a theory due to the conceptual comfort of thinking with the resources of those which are already well established and the unwillingness to risk betting on the less known. An example of this is Heliocentrism, which waited almost two millennia to reenter the philosophical scene with Nicolaus Copernicus in the 16th century, from where it had been expelled, with the abandonment of the thesis by Aristarchus of Samos (4th century B.C.) of a universe centered on the sun. For more information regarding this detail of the history of astronomy, see Singh, 2006: 28-43.

76.   To name a few examples, see Dumouchel & Dupuy, 1983; Prigogine & Stengers, 1991; Johnson, 2003; Barabási, 2003; Magno, 2006 and 2007.

77.   Originally published in 1972, it was reviewed and published in 1980 with the title *Autopoiesis and cognition: the realization of the living*. Dordrecht: D. Reidel Publishing Company, 1980. Cf. also Dumouchel & Dupuy, 1983: 141–46.

78.   As the authors say, the organization of autopoietic systems is such that "their only product is themselves, with no separation between producer and product. The being and the doing of an autopoietic unity are inseparable, and this is their specific mode of organization" (Maturana & Varela, 2001: 57).

79.   It is like the litograph by Dutch artist M. C. Escher, where we see a young man who looks at a picture in which he [young man] appears, looking at a picture in which he appears, looking at a picture in which he appears …

80.   *Dicionário Eletrônico Houaiss da Língua Portuguesa* [*Houaiss Electronic Portuguese Dictionary*]

81.   Also see Lévy, 2003: 15.

82.   As the author reminds us, "some tendency to settle and rest, to go back to a favored spot that offers shelter or good feeding exists in many animal species", not excluding the human species. The author details the comparison: "Many creatures, even fish, come together in herds and schools for mating and for rearing their young. With birds, there is sometimes attachment to the same nest from season to season, and among the flocking species there is a habit of communal settlement at breeding time in protected areas like islands and marshes. Larger mating groups, drawing on

diverse strains, introduce possibilities of genetic variation that small inbred human groups lack. *These breeding and feeding grounds are plainly prototypes of the most primitive kind of permanent human settlement, the hamlet or village. One aspect of the early town, its sense of defensive isolation – along with its birdlike claim or 'territoriality' – has this long foreground in animal evolution"* (Mumford, 1991: 11-12, our italics).

83.   We follow the problematization proposed by Lévy, 1999: 111–21 and 247–50.

84.   The *iPhone*, released by Apple in January 2007. Cf. http://latam.apple.com.br/pr/articulo/?id=1361&r=br.

85.   In general, the term complexity refers to the margin from where it is no longer possible to arrange the elements of a system in relation to each other, making it impossible to explain its observable behavior as from its decomposition or its internal functioning rules. Regarding the insertion of such logic in scientific thinking, it is worth considering the proposition of French sociologist Edgar Morin, who associates complexity to a series of events and discoveries from the end of the 19th century which, highlighted in the 20th century, caused a true scientific revolution by shaking centuries of rationalism and determinism based on the certainty of scientific experiment in favor of a conception of world that considers unpredictability, indetermination, chaos and self-organization. (Morin, 2006).

86.   Albert-László Barabási & Eric Bonabeau (2003) 'Scale-free networks', *Scientific American*, 13: 64

87.   "In 1967 ... sent hundreds of letters to people in Nebraska asking them to forward the correspondence to acquaintances who might be able to shepherd it closer to a target recipient: a stockbrocker in Boston. To track each of the different paths, Milgram asked the participants to mail a postcard back to him when they passed the letter to someone else. Milgram found that the letters that eventually arrived at the final destination had passed through an average of six individuals – the basis of the popular notion of 'six degrees of separation' between everyone." (Barabasi, A & Bonabeau, Eric, 2003: 71)

88.   Contemporary with the appearance of psychoanalysis, similar efforts took place in the field of physics. Notions such as identity, non-contradiction, determinism, locality, temporality, ontological unit, energy conservation were problematized by the theory of relativity. The technological development by other means shares the same presupposition.

89.   Cf. Entries "individual", "substance" and "subject" by Nicola Abbagnano (2003),in *Dicionário de Filosofia* [*Dizionario di Filosofia*]. São Paulo: Martins Fontes, and José Mora (2001) in.*Dicionário de Filosofia* [*Diccionario de Filosofia*]. São Paulo: Edições Loyola,

90.   Theory created by psychoanalyst MD Magno in the lineage of Freud and Lacan, is a reconstruction of psychoanalysis based on the most important findings of these two masters, and has been shown compatible with the world's current situation and with contemporary scientific theories.

91.   MD Magno organized 22 seminars in Rio de Janeiro between 1976 and 1998, presented a total of eight "Introductory Conferences on the New Psychoanalysis", in 1999, and, since 2000, has been presenting lectures in the form of *Falatório* [*Chat*], where he deals with the elaboration of the field of the New Psychoanalysis. Besides these initiatives, MD Magno has been developing, for over 40 years, teaching activities, analytical work, clinical workshops, lectures, public interventions and videos. Most Seminars and *Falatórios* are published, as attests the bibliography of this book.

92.   It is important to go back to the first chapter of this work, where we affirm that "several concepts may be expressed by the same name". Thus we clarify that, despite the term "person" being loaded with an array of previous meanings, here it gains an original concept.

93.   This is a central concept of the NewMind psychoanalysis; we could also explain the term *Haver* in a James Joyceian way considering this like "thetobe", or in a French poetical way we could say that it is the same as "Il y a", whose scope and abstraction have a cosmological vocation, for being a neutral conceptual extension which exists [*há*, in Portuguese] studied by various routes and in diverse fields, which have been seeking to understand its basic structure and functioning, whether by an algorithmic, a quantum, an organic, a complex method, or other route. However, as a psychoanalytical concept, it remains connected to the Freudian postulation of drive as a traumatic experience of the impact of being (here and now) in the world and the concomitant acknowledgement – irreducible to any means of description – of the impossibility of evading it, even if this is desired.

94.   The term "formation(s)" in this theory is a specific concept which we will develop later, in this chapter.

95.   According to the *Dicionário Eletrônico Houaiss da Língua Portuguesa* [*Houaiss Electronic Dictionary of the Portuguese Language*] (2001) the etymology of the word *ecumenismo* [*ecumenism*] comes from the Greek *oikoumenikós, ê, ón,* which means

"from or open to the entire world", through Latin *oecumenicus, a, um,* which means "universal, of whole orbe". The "ecumenical" aspect of *I=Person* was developed by MD Magno in his 2004 *Falatório* [chat].

96. Hyperdetermination is a specific concept of New Psychoanalysis, which we will see farther ahead. In order to understand this part of the text we can say in advance that "for the New Psychoanalysis what counts, before anything else, is that our mind produces *articulation* and *prosthesis* as result of the drive thrust and of HyperDetermination … it is the HyperDetermination that enables the *creation* on any level it may appear" (Alonso, 2005: 143–59).

97. It concerns the concept of *Formations of Haver.* The name given to any emergence of *Haver*: any configuration, any coalescence, any thing or species, thought or resonance that shows up is called "formation". Examples of formations are the cosmos, a plant, a thought, an equation, a body, a computer, etc. *Formation* therefore names each and every conjuncture or composition that is noticeable, describable, or polarizable within *Haver.* The concept of *Haver* is presented further on in this chapter.

98. A synthetic exposition of what is the order of formations in its Primary, Secondary and Original levels is found in *A Psicanálise, Novamente* [*Psychoanalysis, NewMind*], conference 4: "O recalque" ["Repression"] (Magno, 1999)

99. The idea of 'spontaneous artifice' and 'industrial artifice', proposed by psychoanalyst Magno, indicates an abandonment of the opposition between what is 'natural' and 'artificial' in favor of a topological and homogenizing vision of the facts of the world as *artifice* – in this theory, the principle of artificiality becomes generic. It is interesting to stress the articulating aspect that constitutes any artifact of the world, whether it is physical, biological, cultural or technological data. We deal with formations which are articulations, that is, information systems (universe, life, society, ecosystems, etc.) which express themselves in their own language, but which can be transcribed into one another, as long as we have the adequate cognitive tools. Given the contingencies of the appearance of matter and life, we can consider spontaneous artifice as being the given formations we find, that constitute the universe around us, from galaxies to subatomic particles, from the evolution of life on our planet to their particular manifestations, systematically organized, to a greater or lesser degree of complexity, be they colonies of bacteria, beehives or organized groups of primates. Industrial artifice, in turn, corresponds to the creative and transforming plan of human activity, which creates society, artifact, knowledge and technology as information that couples, reads and transcribes the constituent information of spontaneous artifices.

100. From the Greek *soma, atos*, meaning body and, here in our case, indicating the basic constitution of the given or spontaneous formations as "own (=*auto*) body (=*soma*)".

101. It was biologist Konrad Lorenz who, in the 20th century, contributed to systemizing modern ethology, researching mechanisms underlying the selective behavioral triggers, allocating the understanding of this ethogram to its possibility of genetic inscription and its understanding in the phylogenetic perspective of the species, therefore of its evolution, as from the findings of the synthetic theory of evolution. Lorenz starts from an incipient base of investigation, which defined, in 1910, the concept of *imprinting*, that is, the idea of a behavioral model that will imprint itself in the species at some moment, for instance, in the experiments with birds that leave the nest right after hatching. The concept of imprinting tried to surround the empirical verification of a given clue of the newborn bird in its immediate relation to the surrounding figurations, mainly the maternal presence. The movement of this figure in the close surroundings would necessarily trigger, over a short period of time which was called the "critical period", a series of fundamental behaviors for its further survival and adult life, especially its sexual performance (Lorenz, 1995).

102. About the ideas of pole, focal zone and fringe zone applied to our theme, see item 5.4 in this chapter.

103. It is interesting to add that, for New Psychoanalysis, this functioning mode resulting from the Original Formation is not specific to our species. There is homology between the mental functioning of the species and the functioning of *Haver*. We could even affirm that the functioning mode is only one, in other words, there is replication of the functioning structure of the very *Haver* onto the *Person*'s mind. The concept of *Haver* will be developed further on.

104. Let us just think what it represented for mankind, just one century ago, the idea of the possibility of man visiting the Moon (!).

105. *Hei*, 1st person of the verb *Haver*, simple present tense. See "Haver" in this chapter.

106. We will return to this point, further on in the section on *Haver*.

107. It is important to clarify that, "indifference" in this theory is a very specific term, which does not mean lack of interest, carelessness. On the contrary, we are in the regime of hyperinterest, where "Indifference is eventual equal probability and moral equivalence" – events have the same probability and are morally equivalent. (MD Magno, 2007: 191).

108. We are using the verb "haver" in Portuguese – from *habere*, in Latin –, which is translated below as "there is" ["what *há*…"]. "Haver" encompasses and surpasses the meaning of "to exist", "to have" and "to be". It differs from other languages, even the closest neo-Latin ones, and is built from such a unique linguistic characteristic that the many aspects of its translation may be compromised (so, we will use below "Haver" and "há" in Portuguese). "Haver", used in new psychoanalys is as a verb and as a noun, concerns the very fact that *there is* everything (including our species) *before* any existence that can be described in a discursive way. We could also explain the term *Haver* in a James Joyce way considering it like "*thetobe*". In a french poetical way we could say that is the same of " l'il y a" , whose scope and abstraction have a cosmological vocation, for being a neutral conceptual extension of whatever exists [*há*, in Portuguese].

109. "This neutral place makes us feel at ease and I call it, using a term by Fernando Pessoa in his *Ode Marítima*, Absolute Wharf, because, sitting there, at the confines of this Total Polis which is Haver and on the edge of this ocean of Nothingness, which is não-Haver, we can indifferentiate what happens at the Polis of Haver. If we can place ourselves at this place beyond the enormous set of 'internal' determinations of Haver which, lending them their sustaining resistance, force the formations so that they may be constituted and sustained, we can invoke hyperdetermination – just to bear, with this term, the ambiguousness that the thing offers, for it seems that something, forcefully and forcedly determines even more than the 'internal' overdeterminations of the formations. This is the exact place whence everything is re-considered with indifference: the Absolute Wharf where the relation between Haver and não-Haver takes place, the relation of hyperdetermination. We cannot stay there, but we can invoke it as reference. And with this reference, in the indifferentiation of opposing 'internalities' of Haver, we have the condition to start conceiving, if not perceiving, what for us was not present for the understanding of our story – at least this" (Magno, 2004: 105).

110. Cf. Magno 2008: 30. According to the author: *Person* is a distinct pole with focus and fringe, with the possibility of being plural, and which appears within a network that is conjecturable as infinite. Node = intersection of lines (connections) on a network. Pole = detachment of a rallying point on one or several nodes of a network. Focus = visualization of the pole. Fringe = surrounding with all the connections that tend to the infinite. Polarizing a node is to establish it as pole, which we can consider focally or fringely.

On a plural pole, we can have a *person*, which is composed by several *persons* we can focalize.

A distinct pole, concerns a pole with ipseity – a unique character of a formation of *Haver*, which distinguishes it from all other formations; the Principle of Difference.

111. It should be noted that the notion of background is preponderantly conjectural, given that everything that shows up already presents itself in a polarized and fractal manner, which makes it impossible to prove this primordial homogeneity. A good metaphor for the comprehension of this concept is the notion of dark matter, in physics, which assumes a homogenous field where densifications that occurred in certain regions would cause the appearance of given formations. Therefore, background, focus and fringe are, substantially, the same thing. But even if we believe that, ultimately, this primordial homogeneity exists, we will not stop considering the differences that appear here and now. As example, Magno suggests that we think about a black cloth with luminescent drawings: we will only see the drawings, but the background is there and the drawings are constituted of this same background. Therefore, the focuses and fringes that emerge from the homogeneity of the background do not eliminate the presence of this primordial element. But for the reality of our observation, at the moment we distinguish the formations, we will see the drawings and the background, the stars and the sky, even if everything is constituted by the same thing. Thus, we consider that the network is established on differences and will never present itself as neutrality. Therefore, conceptually, if we say that focus and background are the same thing, it is correct, but if we say that focus and background have the same appearance, it is wrong. (Magno, 2007: 194–95).

112. In this sense the terms *persona*, mask in Latin and *personne*, which also means nobody in French, come in handy (Magno, 2007: 139).

113. In this perspective it is acknowledged that there are formations and they consider each other, in other words, there is orbiting between them. The word siderar (orbiting) has a Latin origin, so that cum-siderare means to orbit together. Sidus, in turn, is the orbiting of the stars, which are not impelled by any local force, but orbit by themselves, moved by powers of attraction and repulsion (Magno 2003: 64).

114. Recapturing the notion of singularity and the notion of limit in mathematics (which is asymptotic, though it concerns tending to and never effectively reaching), let us take the function $f(x)=1/x$. If x tends to the infinite, $f(x)$ tends to 0. In the other hand, if x tends to 0, $f(x)$ tends to the infinite. When the limit is increasingly taken closer to infinite, the division shown will result in a series of tiny fragments with extremely small value, which would support the notion of individual. In the case of the value of x approaching zero there is a resultant that tends to the infinitely large, where the Person can be situated as encompassment (Magno, 2007: 189).

115. Given that we have explained that, for the *Person*, the availability to Hyperdetemination, to *Revirão*, enables the inclusion of the reverse of that which

is assumed objectively given, the new, the creation: all this generates a process of expansion of the *Person*.

116. "*Utens, utentis*, in Latin; present participle of the verb *utor, uteri, uti, usus sum*: to use, to serve oneself from something." (Magno, 2007: 151).

117. I follow in this section 5.6 the arguments presented by MD Magno in his 2007 *Falatório* (Magno, 2009: 29–32).

118. "What, then, can a philosopher say to a theory which, like psychoanalysis, asserts that on the contrary what is mental is in itself unconscious and that being conscious is only a quality, which may or may not accrue to a particular mental act and the withholding of which may perhaps alter that act in no other aspect?" (Freud, 1976e, v. XIX: 268–69).

119. This uses the same reasoning of spontaneous and industrial artifice, as clarified in footnote 99.

120. "D'ailleurs, ce sont les autres qui meurent". Marcel Duchamp's epitaph.

121. We bear in mind what Lewis Mumford [1961] stated. For him, in the general domestication process that marks the Neolithic, "Perhaps the central event in this whole development was the domestication of man himself, itself an evidence of a growing interest in sexuality and reproduction". However, going beyond the limits of this domestication, from the point of view of reproduction and nutrition, the arrival of the city was structured on the same logics of kinship, (male) domination and the maintenance of social institutions that emerged in the Neolithic. In this process are articulated three characteristics of the human way of existing which are now deteriorating: sexual reproduction, kinship and the territory. In order to consider "the way of existence of the human species" as definition for *culture*, see three texts by MD Magno: [1999], especially *Conferência 5*: "Poder de cura e avatares do falicismo" [Conference 5: "Healing powers and avatars of phallicism"]; [1995], especially section "A extradição do incesto" ["The extradition of incest"]; [1994], especially sections 4 and 5, respectively "AMÃE…AMÉM and "Os cinco impérios" ["The five empires"].

122. This reasoning was developed by Magno, 2010: 211. Also see, in an exemplified form, Castells, 2003: 192, when this author refers to the "office on the run", presented in this work in item 3.2.

123. According to Magno, 2008:32. Ipseity is the unique character of a formation of *Haver* which distinguishes it from all other formations. That is, it is the Principle of

Difference. A pole is different when we acknowledge the difference. For instance, we know that a given person is not someone else.

124. The idea of focal zone and fringe zone as well as the graphic representation that we have reproduced is found in Magno, 2003: 420–23.

125. According to Houaiss & Villar (2001: 2254), *pole* means: (1) that which orients, guides; (2) area around which gravitates or where a given important activity takes place or an interest is centered; (3) center.

126. In this work the term *connection* is understood in a broad sense: informational, mental, cultural, political, symptomatic, situational, financial, intellectual, geographic, act or effect of connecting, social bond, professional bond, bond of interests, friendship bond, access, communication and telecommunication system, means of transportation, means of communication, vinculum, that which unites from one point to another the several sectors of an individual's life, etc.

127. According to the Houaiss dictionary, p. 1502, inhabiting = being present, populating, occupying.

Authors Index

Abbagnano, Nicola, 15, 145,165,168
Alonso, Aristides, 116, 145, 169
Anderson, Chris, 94, 145
Antiseri, Dario, 102, 153, 158
Araujo, Rosane, xiii, xv, xvii, 56, 60, 144,
    145, 156
Ascher, François, 5, 7, 28, 55, 76, 103, 145,
    156, 160

Bachelard, Gaston , 6 , 145
Barabási, Albert-László, 58, 95, 96, 97, 146,
    166, 167
Beck, Ulrich, 146, 156
Bertalanffy, Ludwig von, viii, 73, 74, 75, 76,
    77, 78, 146, 155, 165
Beyssade, Jean-Marie, 146, 162
Bonabeau, Eric, 146, 167
Bourbaki, Nicolas, 51, 52, 146
Bouzon, Emanuel, 15, 146

Calvino, Italo, 146
Cassirer, Ernst, 66, 146, 162
Castells, Manuel, 4, 5, 10, 20, 24, 25, 26, 27,
    28, 49, 55, 56, 57, 140, 141, 146, 147,
    155, 156, 157, 158, 160, 173
Cauquelin, Anne, 23, 147
Choay, Françoise, 147
Christelle, Robin, 5, 147
Coates, Nigel, 40, 41, 42, 43, 44, 147
Costa, Xavier, 32, 153

Da Matta, Roberto,15, 147,
Dantas, Isadora, 2, 14, 22, 48, 106, 128, 138
Dantas, Manoela, vi
Debord, Guy, 147
Deleuze, Gilles, viii, 58, 85, 86, 100, 147, 149
Descartes, René, viii, 58, 62, 63, 64, 65, 66,
    67, 90, 91, 98, 101, 146, 148, 161, 162
Dumouchel, Paul, 78, 79, 80, 148, 166,
Dupuy, Jean-Pierre, 78, 79, 80, 148, 166

Eliade, Mircea, 16, 148

Farouki, Nayla, 148, 158
Freud, Sigmund, viii, 58, 61, 68, 69, 70, 71,
    72, 73, 99, 102, 108, 118, 123, 148,
    163, 164, 165, 168, 173

Gibson, William, 92, 148
Giddens, Anthony, 146, 156
Godelier, Maurice, 149, 158
Guattari, Félix, viii, 85, 86, 100, 147, 149

Hardt, Michael, 44, 149, 157
Horan, 49
Houaiss, Antonio, 149, 166, 168, 174

Ianni, Octavio, 133, 149

Johnson, Steven, 149, 166
Jullien, François, 16, 149